THE INNER HISTORY OF THE KELLY GANG

J.J. KENNEALLY

ETT IMPRINT
Exile Bay

This 11th edition published by ETT Imprint, Exile Bay 2025

First published 1929. Reprinted 1929
New edition 1934. Revised edition 1945
Reprinted 1946, 1950, 1955, 1969, 1980
First Published by ETT Imprint 2021
First electronic edition by ETT Imprint 2025

ETT IMPRINT
PO Box R1906
Royal Exchange NSW 1225 Australia

ISBN 978-1-923205-65-9 (pbk)
ISBN 978-1-922698-04-9 (ebk)

Cover: Original Kelly Gang memorabilia, including cdvs, postcard, scrimshaw and Kate Kelly's initialled revolver

Cover and internal design by Tom Thompson

CONTENTS

Ellen Kelly (Thompson Collection); and George King, discharged from prison 3 January 1874.

1
THE KELLY COUNTRY

The "Kelly country" is that portion of north-eastern Victoria which extends from Mansfield in the south to Yarrawonga in the north, and from Euroa in the south-west of the Kelly country to Tallangatta in the north-east. Included in this area are the well-known centres of Benalla, Wangaratta, Yarrawonga, Euroa, Beechworth, Mansfield, Violet Town, Wodonga, Yackandandah, Greta, Lakerowan, Glenrowan, Moyhu, Edi, Whitfield, Myrtleford, Chiltern and Srathbogie.

In the days of the Kellys there was but one railway route in the north-east — from Melbourne to Albury — with a branch line from Wangaratta to Beechworth. Communication between railway townships and those beyond was by road or bush track, and sometimes through country exceedingly hilly and rough. The scattered settlers selected land for cultivation on the river flats and between the ranges and the plains and flat timbered country, while the hilly country provided grazing areas for their horses, sheep and cattle. From Strathbogie to Beechworth was a series of heavily timbered ranges intercepted by rivers and creeks. To-day, along these rivers — the Goulburn, Broken River, King, Ovens, Buckland, and Kiewa — the country is closely settled by a prosperous farming community.

ORIGINAL SETTLERS

The original settlers were hardy folk — the pick of their respective homelands — and were mainly immigrants from England and Ireland who sought the freedom of a country unhampered by oppressive land and industrial laws. Many of them were obsessed by a sense of the injustice of the laws and of the conditions applicable to rural workers in their homeland, and were determined that in this new home these conditions should not become established. It was not remarkable, therefore, that they regarded with suspicion any attempts to assert "authority," and were quick to resent any interference with what they considered their liberty in a free land. While the majority of these settlers were undoubtedly honourable and reliable, there was, nevertheless, a leaven of dishonest men who refused to live entirely within the law, and who, by their practices as horse, sheep and cattle thieves, became a source of continuous annoyance and loss to their neighbours, and anxiety to the administrators of the law. Many of them, indeed, acted with such remarkable cunning and discretion that they succeeded in convincing the authorities of their integrity. Their protestations of unswerving loyalty to the Crown and to the maintenance of law and order enabled many of them to attain positions of responsibility, and, as they prospered, they came actually to be regarded as dependable allies of the Administration, while the Kellys were blamed for their crimes.

THE BILLY-JIMMIES.

Billy and Jimmy were two very enterprising and ambitious young men whose parents had come from the well-known island "Great Britain." They worked together as horse, cattle and sheep thieves, and were very successful, not only in getting away with the stolen stock, but also in escaping from the slightest suspicion as to the actual nature of their calling.

They were expert horsemen and operated in the Mansfield, Benalla and King Valley districts. They were well acquainted with the various districts, and were first-class bushmen. At first they lived in the Mansfield district, but after becoming somewhat regenerated, and, in fact, quite respectable, they acquired interests in the Benalla district, where Jimmy also succeeded in securing the confidence of a section of the ratepayers. Although they had had a serious quarrel over the division of the proceeds of stolen stock, neither of them gave his accomplice away, until, in quite recent years, when Jimmy's health failed and his end was near. Billy happened to be on a periodical spree, and calling at his favourite hotel, was informed by the landlord that his old mate Jimmy was pretty bad. Billy replied: "I'll go and see the old ——." On arriving at Jimmy's home, Billy entered without knocking and walked into the sick-room, where he met Rev. A. C. McConan, a Presbyterian minister, and a prominent business man, Hugh Moodie. Billy nodded very respectfully to the sick visitors, and then turning to his former partner in crime said:—

"So it is here you are, you old b——, you had better make your peace with God while the parson is here. You remember that mob of bullocks WE stole from —— You remember that mob of sheep WE stole from ——? You remember that lot of cattle WE stole from —— You remember the time WE were sledging hides down the hill to get them out of the way of the police?"

Billy was just getting into his stride when the attendants in the sick-room said that Jimmy could not stand so much excitement, and Billy was rudely bustled out of the house.

The Billy-Jimmy confession spread like wildfire, and the few people who still believed all the accusations against the Kellys now freely admitted that they had wronged innocent people. And it is now generally admitted that the quickest way to get to the Wangaratta Hospital is to say something offensive about the Kellys in the Kelly Country, where stock-thieves are now called Billy-Jimmies.

The members of the police force originated from similar stock, and, as upholders of the law, their display of authority in the circumstances was sometimes a very regrettable one. They were regarded as tyrants and oppressors, and their often rough and ready methods did not tend to dispel the distrust of those whom they were destined to protect. This lack of harmony undoubtedly favoured the Kellys and their followers when driven to resistance in their later career. The Kellys had a multitude of friends, who, if they did not actually aid them, did much to hamper those who were charged with their apprehension.

THE KELLYS

JOHN (RED) KELLY

John (Red) Kelly, the father of Ned and Dan, was born in Co. Tipperary, Ireland. He was a fearless young man of some education and outstanding ability.

He was the type of young Irish patriot who was prepared to make, even, the supreme sacrifice for hit country's freedom. He was a man whom the landlords and their henchmen regarded as a menace to the continuation of the injustices so maliciously inflicted on the people of Ireland.

Like the other patriots, he was charged with an agrarian offence (but not assault or murder as falsely stated by the Royal Commission after Ned Kelly's execution). With jury packing reduced to a fine art, the ruling class in Tipperary had no difficulty in securing his conviction, and transportation to Van Diemen's Land. Among the Irish leaders who were treated in a similar fashion were: — John Mitchell, Smith-O'Brien, Maher, O'Doherty, and very many others.

After serving his sentence in Van Diemen's Land, John Kelly came to Melbourne, where he worked for some time as a bush carpenter. The gold fever attracted him to the diggings, where his labours were crowned with success. Returning from the diggings, he bought a farm at Beveridge and settled down to farm life. He married Ellen, third daughter of James Quinn, a neighbouring farmer.

Irish patriotism was such an unforgiveable crime in the eyes of British Government officials in the Colony of Victoria, that even the serving of a savage sentence would not wipe out the campaign of anti-Irish hatred so well organised in the Colonies.

John Kelly was continually hounded by the police, who, without the authority of a search warrant, frequently searched his home without success. The heads of the Police Department were very disappointed. The search continued until, at last, they found a cask with meat in it. John Kelly was arrested and charged with having meat in his possession for which the police said he had not given them a satisfactory account. The long distance from a butcher shop made it necessary to buy meat that would last for some weeks; hence the use of the cask. It is evident that the Bench at Kilmore regarded the charge against John Kelly as a "trumped up affair"; he was sentenced to only six months. Now, if John Kelly had been charged with cattle stealing as frequently stated by the enemies of Honor, Truth and Justice, he would have received a sentence of, at least, five years.

Although the sentence was for only six months, it proved to be a Death Sentence. Such was the treatment to which John Kelly was subjected in the Kilmore Jail that, notwithstanding his good health and perfect physique when sentenced, he died shortly after his release. Broken in health, he now sold his farm to conduct a hotel at Avenel. Shortly after his arrival at Avenel, John Kelly died.

MRS. KELLY

Shortly after her husband's death, Mrs. Kelly, with her eight orphans, left Avenel for Greta, where her brothers had already taken up land. Here on the Eleven-Mile Creek, five miles from Glenrowan, and eleven miles from Benalla, the Kelly family contrived to make a living, some by working for wages, and the others by improving their selection. It was apparently an uphill struggle, and their difficulties were considerably increased by the unwarranted attentions of the police in their determination to carry out the instructions of the Assistant Chief Commissioner of Police, Superintendent C. H. Nicolson, to "root the Kellys out of the district." At the time these instructions were given, there were no charges impending against any member of the Kelly family. It is very evident, therefore, that the police, metaphorically speaking, intended to use LOADED DICE to rob the Kelly family of their FREEDOM. It is only natural, therefore, that the Kellys developed a strong resentment to the attitude of the local police, and an equally strong dislike for the Police Force. Notwithstanding this systematic persecution the police failed to justly convict Ned and Dan Kelly of a felony.

A jury, consisting of the population of Greta, by their attitude, gave a most emphatic verdict that Ned Kelly's conviction, over the McCormack affair, was a most outrageous Miscarriage of justice. The same jury was equally emphatic in their verdict that the conviction of Ned Kelly in connection with the search for Wild Wright's horse, was also an outrageous Miscarriage of Justice. Therefore, the only honest conviction (even with loaded dice) was his resistance to four policemen and a bootmaker when trying to handcuff him at Benalla in 1877, seven years after the introduction of the infamous methods already referred to as "Loaded Dice." On this occasion Ned had to pay £3/1s., which covered the fine, costs and damage to police uniforms.

Added to their inherited resentment of oppression, the Kellys developed a bitter hatred of the law as it was then administered, and herein lay the origin of their subsequent career of resistance and defiance.

No other woman in Australia has ever been the victim of such libellous publications, slanderous statements, and savage persecutions as the loving mother of Ned Kelly had to suffer and endure at the hands of the Police, the Press, the judiciary, and the so-called ruling class. Her enemies openly asserted that she had kept a sly-grog shanty; yet, she was never charged with having done so, although Supt. Nicolson had given definite instructions to "bring the Kellys up on any charge, no matter how paltry." He explained, on oath before the Royal Commission, that the object of his persecution of the Kelly family was to take from them that outstanding "prestige" which they enjoyed where they were well known. Some of Mrs. Kelly's traducers alleged that her house was the meeting place of all the criminals in the North-eastern district of Victoria; yet, the worst person that had ever entered her home was Constable Alexander Fitzpatrick, whose superior officer at Lancefield declared that Fitzpatrick was not fit to be in the police force and could not be trusted out of sight; and on whose unsupported evidence three innocent persons, Mrs. Kelly, Wm. Williamson, and Wm. Skillion were convicted and savagely sentenced to long terms of imprisonment.

Some time after settling on the Eleven-Mile Creek, Mrs. Kelly married a neighbouring settler — George King — who came from California, North America. There were three children of the marriage, which was not a happy one. Ned Kelly thrashed King for ill-treating his mother. King left Greta never to return. King was not liked in Greta, and the local residents continued to refer to his wife as Mrs. Kelly. Therefore, for the purposes of this history, Ned Kelly's mother will be referred to as Mrs. Kelly, notwithstanding the fact that she was the lawful wife of George King.

Mrs. Kelly died at Greta on the 27th March, 1923. She had married King on the 19th February, 1874, at Benalla. She was then 36 years old. King's age was 25 years. Therefore, Mrs. Kelly was 85 years old when she died, not 95 years as was generally supposed. Mrs. Kelly and her family were very highly respected and loved by the people of Greta. This is very vividly demonstrated by the outstanding fact that although over sixty long years have passed away, no one can, with impunity, say one word against the Kellys in the district where they were best known.

As already stated, Mrs. Kelly died on the 27th of March, 1923, although the writer of a diabolical concoction, in book form, called "Dan Kelly," stated in his book that Dan Kelly's mother had died many years prior to 1911. But then, previous writers of Kelly Gang books seem to have taken great care to mislead their readers while they revelled in the suppression of Truth and the replacing of it with fiction.

Shortly before her death, Mrs. Kelly's name was entered at the Wangaratta Hospital as Mrs. King, with the result that the hospital staff were unaware that their patient was the mother of Ned Kelly.

Mrs. Kelly steadfastly refused to give any information about her family to the numerous newspaper reporters and travelling journalists who frequently visited her home, and she bluntly refused them any information about her sons. But to her intimate friends she talked freely, and displayed great pride in her sons. She always maintained that Danny was a better general than Ned, and would relate how Danny, though only 17 years old, put Heenan's hug on Constable Fitzpatrick and threw him on the broad of his back on the kitchen floor. Nevertheless she recognised Ned's general ability, and when speaking one day to a visiting journalist with whom she had been favourably impressed, she said: "My boy Ned would have been a great general in the big war — another Napoleon — whichever side he was on would have won."

Ned Kelly, aged 15.

NED KELLY

Edward (Ned) Kelly was born at Wallan Wallan, Victoria, in the year 1854, and was the eldest son. He was strongly influenced by the unjust treatment meted out to his father by the authorities at home and abroad. His father's death from prison treatment after serving a sentence of only six months on a "trumped-up charge" of having a cask with meat in it in his possession, intensified his distrust in the honesty of the police of that day. When Inspector Brook-Smith searched Kelly's home at Greta prior to the fight with the police at Stringybark Creek, he found meat in a cask and threw it out on the ground floor; but no one was arrested or charged "having meat in their possession for which the police said they had not been given a satisfactory account." Now, it were a felony for John (Red) Kelly to have meat in a cask at Wallan Wallan, why was it not also a felony to have meat in a cask at Greta?

In the early part of 1870, when Ned Kelly was 15 years old, he was arrested and charged with having held the bridle reins of Harry Power's horse, when Power, a bushranger, waylaid a Mr. Murray at Lauriston near Kyneton. As the police failed to produce any evidence of identification, Ned Kelly was discharged; but they (the police) were able to gloat over the fact that Mrs. Kelly, a widow with eight orphans, had to provide money for her son's defence.

During the latter part of 1870, there were record floods in the North-Eastern district of Victoria. Two hawkers were bogged in the vicinity of Kelly's homestead. One of the hawkers — Ben Gould — was bogged quite close to Kelly's house; the other, McCormack, with his wife, was bogged a mile away to the north. McCormack's horse got away from the camp and was making its way home to Benalla. Ned Kelly recognised the horse and caught it with the intention of returning it to its owner. Someone suggested that now, with an extra horse-power, Ben could be pulled out of the bog. This was done. Ned then took the stray horse back to its owner. McCormack not only did not thank him for his neighbourly act, but he accused him of having stolen his horse to pull his rival out. Ned replied: Your horse was making its way back to Benalla, and if I had not caught it you would have had to go twelve miles to Benalla for it. But, continued Ned, I did pull Ben Gould out of the bog, and brought him back to you.

Next day Ben Gould assisted the Kellys in branding and castrating calves, and decided to play a joke on McCormack.

Having no children Mrs. McCormack always accompanied her husband when hawking in the country. Gould made up a parcel of giblets taken from the bull calves and attached a note containing directions which, if followed, would increase the population, so much needed in a new country. Gould then handed the parcel to Ned Kelly, who, in turn, handed it to a younger boy, Tom Lloyd, saying: "Give this to Mrs. McCormack." The lad did as directed saying: "Ned Kelly gave me this parcel for you." McCormack and his wife were annoyed at the rude joke. A few days later Ned Kelly was passing McCormack's camp; the latter saw him coming and determined to give Ned a good thrashing, to teach him manners with a stick. McCormack appeared and blocked the track. Ned could neither escape to the right or to the left, and as McCormack advanced to waylay him, Ned jabbed his spurs into his horse, which made a sudden bound forward, knocking the aggressor down. Ned went on his way rejoicing at his escape. Bruised and defeated McCormack went to the Greta Police Station and laid two charges against Ned Kelly. He charged Ned with having sent his wife an obscene note, and with having committed a violent assault on himself. Ned was arrested, convicted and sentenced to three months on each charge.

This was the first win for the Assistant Chief Commissioner of Police, Supt. C. H. Nicolson, who played for the forfeiture of Ned Kelly's freedom with, metaphorically speaking, "Loaded Dice," as the following will prove even to the most sceptical. — Supt. Nicolson reported to Capt. Standish as follows:—

"I visited the notorious Mrs. Kelly's house on the road from hence to Benalla. She lived on a piece of cleared and partly cultivated land on the roadside, in an old wooden hut with a large bark roof. The dwelling was divided into five apartments by partitions of blanketing rugs, etc. There were no men in the house — only children and two girls about 14 years of age, said to be her daughters. They all appeared to be existing in poverty and squalor. She said her sons were out at work, but did not indicate where, and that their relatives seldom came near them. However, their communications with each other are known to the police.

"Until this gang (sic) referred to is rooted out of the neighbourhood, one of the most experienced and successful mounted constables in the district will be required in charge of Greta. I do not think the present arrangements are sufficient. Second-class Sergeant Steele of Wangaratta keeps the offenders (sic) referred to under as good surveillance as the distance and means at his command will permit. But I submit that Constable Thom would hardly be able to cope with these men. At the same time some of these offenders may commit themselves foolishly some day, and may be apprehended and convicted in a very ordinary manner."

When the above was written there was no charge, of any kind, pending against any member of the Kelly family. Yet they were referred to as offenders.

The above report was brought forward in evidence before the Royal Commission in June, 1881, and was further added to by the following evidence given on oath by the Assistant Chief Commissioner of Police, Supt. C. H. Nicolson, as his brazen confession of having used, metaphorically speaking, "Loaded Dice."

"This (the foregoing report) was the cause of my instructions to the police generally, and I had expressed my opinion since to the officer in charge of that district, that without oppressing the people or worrying them in any way, he should endeavour, whenever they committed any paltry crime, to bring them to justice and send them to Pentridge even on a paltry sentence, the object being to take their prestige away from them, which was as good an effect as being sent to prison with very heavy sentences, because the prestige those men get up there from what is termed their flashness helped to keep them together, and that is a very good way of taking the flashness out of them."

Although Supt. Nicolson, as Assistant Chief Commissioner of Police of Victoria, used the above quoted Loaded Dice in playing to forfeit the freedom of members of the Kelly family, he was doomed to failure. The Royal Commission caused his removal from the Police Force in the Police Purge of 1881.

After doing six months by a most outrageous Miscarriage of Justice in the McCormack affair, Ned Kelly was released from gaol in May, 1871, but his troubles were by no means over. The Loaded Dice was still on active service.

A young man named Wild Wright had been working in the Mansfield district, and decided on a visit to his relatives at Greta. He considered the distance too far to walk, and he had no other means of transport. He, however, preferred to ride, and without asking permission, took the mare belonging to the local schoolmaster. On arrival at Greta he turned the animal into a paddock pending his return journey. His holiday over, he discovered that the horse had got out of the paddock and wandered away. Wright now enlisted the help of Ned Kelly in the search. Ned believed the mare belonged to Wright. In the meantime the schoolmaster had reported the disappearance to the police,

Ned Kelly
August 8/1874

and a description of the animal had already been published in the "Police Gazette." It was unfortunate for Ned that he had succeeded in the search, for, when leading the horse back through Greta, to return it to Wright, whom he believed to be the rightful owner, he was intercepted by the local constable in front of the police station. Constable Hall, who was in charge of Greta, was struck by the resemblance, the mare Ned was leading, bore to the one reported as having been stolen from the schoolmaster near Mansfield.

Without inquiring how or why Ned Kelly became in possession of the stolen horse, Constable Hall attempted to be somewhat diplomatic, and invited Ned to come into the police station to sign a paper in reference to Ned Kelly's recent discharge from the Beechworth gaol. Ned replied: "I have done my time, and I will sign nothing."

The constable thereupon attempted to drag Ned Kelly from his horse, apparently for Ned's refusal to sign the fictitious paper. Ned jumped off his horse on the off-side. He was promptly seized by the burly constable and thrown to the ground. Ned fought like a wild cat. As the constable was holding this sixteen years old lad down, the latter thrust his long spurs with considerable force into the policeman's buttocks. Hall, answering promptly to the spurs, made a flying leap forward, covering several yards.

Ned Kelly, regaining his feet, made a run for his horse. There were 14 brickmakers working close by, and some of them were attracted to the scene. One of the brickmakers seized the sixteen years old lad by the legs and brought him down. The policeman was so angered by the injury inflicted on his dignity by Ned Kelly's spurs that he threw himself on the prostrate lad and savagely belaboured him on the head with his revolver. Ned was badly cut about the head and bled freely. He carried the scars to the end of his life. So freely did Ned bleed that his clothes were thoroughly saturated with blood, and when dried, his clothes were stiff enough to stand up.

He presented a dreadful sight when brought before the Wangaratta Court next day, and the spectators commented severely on the brutality of the police when arresting a mere boy.

Wild Wright was also arrested and charged with "horse stealing"; Ned Kelly was charged with "receiving," knowing the horse to have been stolen. They were tried and convicted. No one can beat Loaded Dice, particularly when used departmentally.

Ned Kelly was sentenced to, three years for "receiving" under the above circumstances.

Wild Wright was sentenced to 18 months for deliberately stealing the horse. The Loaded Dice was not used against him.

It is alleged that one James Murdoch, who was afterwards hanged for murder at Wagga Wagga, N.S.W., received £20 from Hall to give evidence against Ned Kelly.

The police always admitted that Ned Kelly was no fool. Therefore, he would not lead Wright's mare in front of the Police Station if he knew she had been stolen. This second most outrageous miscarriage of justice created intense anger in the Greta district, and developed, in those who knew the facts, supreme contempt for the police, who described the settlers of Greta as a lawless people.

The attitude of the police and the judiciary as stated above destroyed the last ray of hope which the Kellys, their relatives, friends and sympathisers may have had of obtaining a fair deal from the police and the judiciary while the dice were still loaded and on active service against them.

Ned Kelly was discharged from goal in 1874 after serving his second sentence, the result of fiendish persecution by the police.

Constable Thomas Kirkham, who in after years was one of his pursuers, stated that Ned Kelly was a fine manly man, and possessed a high moral character; that his conduct in gaol was exemplary in every way.

Notwithstanding the pressing anxiety of the police to bring the Kellys up on any charge, no matter how paltry, it was not until 1877 that that Ned Kelly experienced further police hostility.

During a visit to Benalla in that year, he was arrested on charges of being drunk and with having ridden his horse across a footpath. He asserted that on this occasion his liquor had been drugged, and vehemently protested against being charged with drunkenness. When he was being brought next morning from the lockup to the Court House, he escaped from the constable in charge of him, and took refuge in the shop of King the bootmaker. He was pursued by the Sergeant and three constables, who, with the assistance of the bootmaker, tried to handcuff him. A fierce fight ensued, the odds being five to one — four policemen and the bootmaker against Ned Kelly. In the fight Ned Kelly's trousers were literally torn off him. Constable Lonigan, taking advantage of the torn garment, seized him by the privates and inflicted terrible torture on his victim.

While suffering the pangs of this terrible torture, Ned Kelly cried out: "If ever I shoot a man, Lonigan, you will be the first" — an exclamation prophetically true, as later events will show. Although there were four policemen and the bootmaker against him, Ned successfully resisted them, and the fight was terminated only by the arrival of Mr. Wm. McInnes, J.P., a local flour-miller, who rebuked the police in strong terms for their brutality and cowardly violence. Satisfied now that he had beaten the four policemen and the bootmaker, Ned held out his hands to Mr. McInnes, and invited him to put the handcuffs on him.

In order to make sure that the police would not inflict any further violence on their prisoner, the J.P. accompanied him to the Court where the sum of £3 1s. paid for the fines, damages to uniforms and costs. (It was Supt. Hare who, in later years, described Ned Kelly as the greatest man in the world.)

This fine was the only genuine conviction ever recorded against Ned Kelly prior to his being driven to the bush to become a bushranger.

To the everlasting discredit of a large section of Australia's bitterly anti-Kelly Press and equally bitter anti-Kelly authors of so-called Kelly Gang books, the Australian and overseas publics were led to believe that Ned Kelly must have had at least from 20 to 30 prior convictions against him before being outlawed. Whereas the foregoing four charges are the only charges ever made against Ned Kelly before being outlawed. These four charges are as follow:—

(1) The first, holding bridle reins of Harry Power's horse, was dismissed.

(2) The second, the McCormack affair, a conviction — an outrageous miscarriage of justice.

(3) The third, a schoolmaster's horse, a conviction — also an outrageous miscarriage of justice.

(4) The fourth, drunk and riding across a footpath and resisting the police, the only genuine conviction, which £3 1s. settled.

Now, if the situation were reversed, and four Kellys and a bootmaker attacked one policeman, and with this terrible odds, one of the Kellys grabbed the policeman, as Lonigan grabbed Ned Kelly, what would the anti-Kelly Press and the depravity of anti-Kelly authors have published?

Although Ned Kelly suffered severely from the injury inflicted on him by Lonigan, he thought no more about the prophecy in reference to the shooting of him.

That prophecy, however, preyed on Lonigan's mind and when he was ordered to join Sergeant Kennedy's party, he expected something unusual to happen.

He had a premonition that Ned Kelly's prophecy would come

true. Ned Kelly had not recognized Lonigan when he fired the fatal shot; he thought he was shooting at either Flood or Straughan. That prophecy!

KATE KELLY.

It was the police who made a heroine of Kate Kelly, when deceived by the exhibitions of expert horsewomanship freely given, for their benefit, by Steve Hart, when, dressed as a woman he rode about in side-saddle. Therefore, whenever they saw an equally expert exhibition of horsewomanship by Mrs. Skillion (nee Margaret Kelly) with whom they were not acquainted, they jumped to the conclusion that it was Kate Kelly who was also a first-class horsewoman.

It was Mrs. Skillion (seen below), some years older than Kate, who possessed the unlimited confidence of her brothers and their mates. It was Mrs. Skillion who was always in close touch with her outlawed brothers and supplied them with the necessaries of life. Kate did not, at any time, play an important part in her brothers' affairs. It was Mrs. Skillion who frequently led the police, who were on foot, on many a wild goose chase over rough and extremely difficult country. Although mounted on a good horse, she allowed the footsore police to keep her in sight. They were sure that the bulky bundle she carried on the saddle was supplies for the outlaws. When satisfied that the exhausted police could not be on active service for some days, she spurred her horse, and, lost in the timber, returned home well pleased at the success of her strategy.

Kate Kelly, though thoroughly loyal, was too young to possess that mature judgment and discretion with which her elder sister, Mrs. Skillion, was so gifted. It was this lack of discretion and judgment that caused Kate to be led into appearing on the stage of a Melbourne theatre the night after her brother was executed.

It was Mrs. Skillion who, with Tom Lloyd, went to Melbourne for ammunition and successfully fooled Rosier and the police. And it was Mrs. Skillion who knelt between the charred remains of Dan Kelly and Steve Hart and delivered the most scathing invective on the savagery and cowardice of the police at the siege of Glenrowan.

DAN KELLY

Dan was the youngest of "Red" Kelly's three sons. All accounts of him show he was of a quieter and less forceful nature than his brother Ned, although the general public have been led, through the vicious misrepresentation by the police, to regard him as a treacherous and blood thirsty scoundrel. This misrepresentation was encouraged to some extent by the remarks of his brother Ned when addressing the men imprisoned in the storeroom at Faithful's Creek station near Euroa. In order to prevent anyone from attempting to escape Ned Kelly said: "If any of you try to escape, Dan Kelly and Steve Hart will shoot you down like rabbits just for the fun of it." This was taken literally, and Dan Kelly was regarded by those who were not personally acquainted with him as a bloodthirsty ruffian. Although he was regarded as an outlaw from the time he was 17 years of age till he was 19 years at his death at Glenrowan, he killed no one, he shot no one, offered violence to no neighbour and insult to no woman.

CONSTABLE FLOOD

In his anxiety to carry out Supt. Nicolson's instructions to root the Kellys out of the district, Constable Ernest Flood, in 1871, arrested Jim Kelly and his little brother Dan. Jim was about 13 years old and Dan was only 10. Jim was employed by a local farmer, with whose consent he rode one of his employer's horses for the purpose of going home to see his mother. He met Dan on the way and took him on the horse behind the saddle. Before going much further they were intercepted by Constable Ernest Flood, who arrested the two children on the charge of illegally using a horse.

Senior-Constable Flood gave evidence on oath before the Royal Commission on the 29th June, 1881, as follows:—

Question by Commission: Did you prosecute the members of the Kelly family continuously while you were in that district?

Constable Flood: "I did, a good number of them. I could give the names." (Looking at his notebook.)

Question. — Try and do that and give about the dates. — I arrested James and Dan Kelly when they were mere lads for illegally using horses in 1871. They were discharged on account of their youth and their intimacy with the owner of the horses, one of the brothers having been a servant of the person who owned the horses.

Answering another question, Senior-Constable Flood said: "I think Mr. (Superintendent) Barkly had a great deal to do with the removal of men. I know he had me removed, and I was much aggrieved at the way he got me removed."

Question. — What reason did he give you? — There was a charge preferred against me by a man named Brown, a squatter at Laceby, and an investigation was held by Mr. Barkly over it. I was treated most unfairly in the matter.

Question. — He (Brown, the squatter) charged you with going amongst his horses and disturbing them? — Yes.

Seeing that the Kellys were blamed for all the horses stolen in that district, it would not do to charge Constable Flood with being a suspected horse thief. Supt. Barkly, therefore, removed him from Greta to Yandoit, near Castlemaine, where there were only a few working horses, and consequently no temptation to disturb or interfere with them.

The inference behind the charge against Flood was that he either stole or planted horses and then blamed the Kellys or their relatives for the offence.

For the next five years no charge of any kind was made against Dan Kelly, but at the age of 15 years he was charged with having stolen a saddle, and notwithstanding the anxiety of the police to convict, the evidence they adduced failed to impress the bench, and the little boy was again discharged. But perseverance brings its reward, and on the following year Dan Kelly was charged with doing wilful damage to property.

The bench accepted the evidence of the owner of the property, D. Goodwin (who was afterwards sentenced to four years' imprisonment for perjury in connection with the same property), and Dan Kelly was at last convicted and sentenced to three months in gaol. This was the only conviction against Dan Kelly before being outlawed.

On the following year someone at Chiltern lost a horse, and the police took out a warrant for Dan Kelly, and this was the unfortunate warrant which brought about the Fitzpatrick episode. One of Dan Kelly's cousins was joined with him in this case of alleged horse stealing.

The cousin was arrested, and as there was no evidence to commit, he was discharged. This discharge also cleared Dan Kelly.

Because he was the elder, and because, perhaps, he was possessed of more initiative and determination, Ned Kelly assumed the leadership, and in several instances asserted himself and evinced his mastery. On one occasion the two brothers quarrelled, and Dan, determined to clear out, went over to his cousin's homestead for a couple of days. Ned followed him and became reconciled, reminding Dan that their only hope of maintaining their freedom was by sticking together. He also reminded Dan of the past injuries they had experienced at the hands of the authorities, and prevailed upon Dan to return home. There were three occasions on which Dan differed from Ned in the carrying out of their plan of campaign, and subsequent events proved that in each case Dan was right. The first difference occurred at the battle of Stringybark Creek, when Dan wanted to handcuff McIntyre. The second was Dan's objection to the Glenrowan program, and the third was when Dan suggested that Constable Bracken should be handcuffed to the sofa in Mrs. Jones' Hotel. While their mother had great pride in Ned's ability to lead, she always maintained that Danny was a better general than Ned.

STEVE HART

Steve Hart was born at Wangaratta in the year 1860, and, after leaving school at an early age, worked on his parents' farm on the Three-mile Creek. He became an expert bushman and an accomplished horseman. He fell in with the suggestion to join the Kelly youths when they were seeking alluvial gold on the Stringybark and Kelly's Creeks. He, too, had experienced a period of police persecution, and doubtless found in the Kellys friends in need. He appears to have been possessed of considerable courage and resource, and during the period of his outlawry frequently rode about in feminine attire. So successful was this disguise that he was taken to be one of the Kelly sisters, and the police attributed many of his daring exploits to Kate Kelly. Steve Hart was never prominent as the Kelly brothers were, but he was at all times a faithful follower and courageous ally.

JOE BYRNE

Joe Byrne was a native of Beechworth, and of the members of the gang appears to have had the least provocation for defiance of the law. While still in his 'teens he was intimately associated with Aaron Sherritt, with whom he was convicted of having meat in his possession suspected to have been stolen. Joe Byrne's voluntary association with the Kellys appears to have been the result of that hero worship which creates so strong an impression upon some natures.

Like Ned Kelly, he was an expert marksman, a good horseman, and a first-class bushman. He had a good knowledge of alluvial digging, and readily accepted Ned Kelly's invitation to join the two Kellys and Steve Hart in their mining venture on the Stringybark and Kelly's Creeks, where they worked with some success from the end of April to the 26th October, 1878, when their mining activities were suddenly terminated by the fatal fight with the police. Byrne was described as a handsome youth, who possessed no mean educational ability. He was Ned Kelly's right-hand man, and was always consulted by the leader on all questions of strategy. During the period of his outlawry he frequently visited his mother's home, which was continuously watched by the police.

The fact that the police never intercepted him was due either to the cleverness of Joe Byrne or to the incompetence and insincerity of the police. With his revolver he rarely, if ever, missed a two-shilling piece thrown in the air.

Such were the youths who comprised the famous Kelly Gang, and such was their fame in police circles that almost every crime committed in the North-Eastern district of Victoria was attributed to their activities. There can be very little doubt that the contemptuous disrespect which the Kellys and their friends held for the authorities was considerably increased by the many crimes and misdemeanours that were thus wrongfully attributed to them. Undoubtedly, also, such groundless charges tended to increase the sympathy and practical assistance of their friends and neighbours for those who, they considered, were denied what they termed "equal justice."

THE ADMISSION

After the capture of Ned Kelly at the "Siege of Glenrowan" some of the truth leaked out. Inspector Wm. B. Montfort, who succeeded Superintendent Sadleir at Benalla, gave evidence before the Royal Commission on 9th June, 1881, as follows:—

Question by Commissioner: If there was frequent crime in the district undetected, and the offender not made amenable to justice, would you not know that the man (policeman) stationed there was more than likely inefficient?
Inspector Montfort: Not necessarily.
Question: Would the book show the action the constable took on that information?
Inspector Montfort: It would only show that he made inquiries in a general way; it would not give the details. For instance, two men might come over from New South Wales and go to Moyhu and steal horses there, and successfully pilot them across into New South Wales, and it would be a difficult thing to make the police officer responsible for that. It does not necessarily follow that the thieves live in the district.

In answering another question, Inspector Montfort said: "When I went to Wangaratta in 1862 the great trouble the police had then was with the Omeo mob of horse stealers. They used to come across to Wangaratta, steal horses, go to Omeo, and plant them in the range and alter the brands, and sell them in Melbourne or in New South Wales. I could mention the names of the parties. There is still the same complaint (June 9, 1881). That is why I consider the doing away with the Healesville station was a great mistake at the time." This clearly proves that the police knew that the horse stealing in the Kelly Country was not done by the Kellys.

In order that Inspector Montfort might now speak with even greater freedom, the Royal Commission took the following evidence from him, on oath, behind closed doors:—

Question: How was it that, on the prosecution of McElroy and Quinn there, they were not made amenable to some sort of justice to keep them quiet?
Inspector Montfort: The case against McElroy was not proved. The charge was that he snapped a loaded gun at Quinn with intent to do him grievous bodily harm, and that was not proved to the satisfaction of the justices. It was sworn to right enough by Quinn, but the justices did not believe him. There was subsequently a cross-summons taken out by McElroy against Quinn for some alleged insulting language made use of by Quinn at Mrs. Dobson's public-house (at Swanpool). It is usual in the bush to have cross-charges made. I suggested to the bench that they should postpone the hearing of the case against Quinn for a week, but they decided they would hear it to-morrow (June 10, 1881). I did that because I considered that Quinn was taken by surprise; that he, in ignorance, trusted me to defend him, when I had no status in the court to do anything of the kind, and I considered that it would be treating him with injustice not to let him have the option and opportunity of employing a solicitor.
Question: You were prosecuting McElroy?
Inspector Montfort: Yes. I might say, in connection with this, that a great deal of the difficulty with these men (Kellys and their friends) would be got over if they felt they were treated with equal justice — that there was no "down" on them. They are much more tractable if they feel they are treated with equal justice.

This admits police persecution in the form of Loaded Dice, and could be admitted only behind closed doors.

Constable Fitzpatrick.

2
THE FITZPATRICK EPISODE, APRIL 15, 1878

Early in 1878 a resident of Chiltern reported to the police that his horse had been stolen by some persons unknown. The police made inquiries, and ascertained that two youths were seen in the vicinity who were about the size of Dan Kelly and one of his cousins. Without any further ado warrants were taken out for the arrest of Dan Kelly and his cousin. The latter was arrested and brought before the court, and had no difficulty in proving his innocence, and was, therefore, discharged. This discharge also cleared Dan Kelly.

Constable Strahan was in charge of Greta, but was away on a week's leave, whilst his wife and family remained at the Greta police station. Sergeant Whelan, of Benalla, intended to send Constable Alex. Fitzpatrick to Greta to relieve Strahan, who went on leave on Saturday, 13th. But as Fitzpatrick had not yet returned from a visit to Cashel police station the Sergeant sent Constable Healey out on patrol to Greta on Sunday, April 14, with instructions to return to Benalla on Monday, 15th.

Fitzpatrick returned from Cashel on Monday forenoon, and Healey returned from Greta at 1 o'clock in the afternoon. Sergeant Whelan then despatched Fitzpatrick at 2 p.m. on Monday, April 15, with definite instructions to take charge of Greta during the absence of Constable Strahan. Sergeant Whelan, on oath before the Royal Commission, stated:—

"At 1 o'clock on April 15 Healey returned from Greta, and I despatched Constable Fitzpatrick at 2 p.m. He received the direction to remain and take charge of the station. At 2 a.m. the next morning he returned to Benalla and rapped at my quarters, and told me that he had been shot by Ned Kelly and wounded in the arm. That was on the morning of the 16th. I examined his arm and saw a mark like a bullet wound. I sent for Dr. Nicholson, and had him attended to. I took his statement at the time."

Fitzpatrick left Benalla at 2 p.m. on Monday, April 15, and called at Lindsay's public-house at Winton, which is five miles from Benalla. He had several drinks there. He drank spirits. He arrived at Mrs. Kelly's house at 5 p.m. well under the influence of liquor.

Fitzpatrick asked Mrs. Kelly if her son Dan was about. In replying, Mrs. Kelly, who received him courteously, said: "He's not in, but I don't think he's far away; he might be up at the stockyard." Fitzpatrick did not indicate the reason for which he wanted Dan. He rode up to the stockyard, which was about 150 yards from the house, and met Dan there. He told Dan that someone at Chiltern had taken out a warrant for him and one of his cousins for stealing a horse. Dan replied that he had nothing to do with the horse stolen from Chiltern, and added: "All right, I'll go with you, but I suppose I can have something to eat and change my clothes."

Fitzpatrick agreed, and they both returned to the house. They went into the kitchen, and Fitzpatrick took a seat in front of the fire, while Dan explained to his mother that he had to go to Greta with Fitzpatrick. Dan's sister, Kate, in the exercise of her domestic duties, was passing by Fitzpatrick, when the latter seized her and pulled her on to his knee. Kate resented this, and Dan, in defence of his sister, sprang at the constable, and a fierce struggle ensued. Dan Kelly, though only a youth of 17 years, had some knowledge of wrestling, and threw the inebriated constable to the floor. Fitzpatrick, on regaining his feet, drew his revolver just as Ned Kelly appeared at the door. The constable levelled his revolver at Ned Kelly, but Dan Kelly struck him a violent blow as he fired, and the bullet lodged in the roof. The two brothers then seized the constable, and disarmed him. Fitzpatrick, during the struggle, struck his left wrist against the projecting part of the door lock. Finding himself overpowered and disarmed, the constable made the best of his position. He expressed his regret for what had happened, and promised that he would not make any report of the occurrence. The whole party then appears to have become quite friendly, and had tea together. After the meal they were joined by two neighbours, Skillion and Ryan, and at 11 o'clock that night Fitzpatrick left Kelly's house and set out to return to Benalla instead of going to Greta.

He again called at Lindsay's public-house, at Winton, and had several drinks of brandy and arrived at the Benalla police station at 2 o'clock next morning, April 16. Dr. John Nicholson, of Benalla, dressed the wound on his wrist, which was only skin deep. Fitzpatrick then reported that the wound on his wrist was inflicted by a revolver bullet which had been fired at him by Ned Kelly. He also asserted that Mrs. Kelly had struck him on the helmet with a fire shovel, and that a splitter named Williamson and Skillion, Mrs. Kelly's son-in-law, were present at the time and were armed with revolvers. No time was lost in issuing warrants for the arrest of Ned and Dan Kelly, Williamson (a selector), Skillion and Mrs. Kelly.

Although Ned Kelly expected that Fitzpatrick would not report the occurrence, as he had promised, he soon learned that there was a warrant out for the arrest of his brother. He decided that Dan should be kept out of the way of the police, and accordingly made arrangements with Joe Byrne, who knew something about mining, and Steve Hart to accompany Dan and himself to Stringybark Creek to work an abandoned alluvial claim. They collected some mining tools and sufficient rations for two weeks, and set out forthwith on this venture.

Sergeant Steele, of Wangaratta, duly received a report of the "Fitzpatrick episode," and on Tuesday, April 16, went to Greta with Constable Brown to execute the warrants for the arrest of Ned, Dan and Mrs. Kelly, Skillion and Williamson. When giving evidence before the Royal Commission on May 31, 1881, Sergeant Steele thus described the arrest of the three latter:—

"I started with Constable Brown for the Eleven Mile Creek. We watched Mrs. Kelly's place for some considerable time from the hill opposite the house. At 9 o'clock in the evening we arrested Williamson. I went to Skillion's place, but could not find him, so I took Williamson to Greta and returned again at about 1 o'clock in the morning in company with Senior Constables Strahan and Brown, and arrested Skillion. We also arrested Mrs. Kelly. She had not been in her bed at all during that night. I was there on three occasions and she had not been to bed. Jim Quinn, her brother, was in the house."

By the Commission. — "What was the charge on which they were arrested?" — "For aiding and abetting Ned Kelly with shooting with intent to murder Constable Fitzpatrick."

By the Commission. — "Had Mrs. Kelly an infant with her when you arrested her?"

Sergeant Steele. — "I do not think so; I think not at the time. I think she had a child in gaol if I recollect rightly."

Mrs. Kelly was arrested by Steele at 1 o'clock in the morning of April 17, 1878, although he could have arrested her early in the afternoon of April 16 and taken her with her very young baby in her arms to Benalla. He took her in a dray a journey of 15 miles before daylight on a bitterly cold morning. In his evidence, Sergeant Steele said:— "We took Williamson, Skillion and Mrs. Kelly to Greta (four miles), and then brought them on to Benalla (15 miles) in a dray. They were remanded from time to time, and committed for the offence with which they were charged."

Mr. Frank Harty, a prosperous and well-known farmer, proffered bail for Mrs. Kelly, but immediately bail was refused.

This occurred in the British Colony of Victoria, and not in a foreign country controlled by savages.

Mr. Wm. Williamson, who is still alive and lives at Coolamon, N.S.W., on hearing that Mr. J. J. Kenneally had undertaken to see that, at last, justice should be done to him and others concerned, wrote the following letter, which speaks for itself:—

Millwood-road,
Coolamon,
25/5/28.

Mr. J. J. Kenneally.
Dear Sir, — I am sending you under separate cover a photo of myself. I would like it returned as soon as possible; it is the only photo of myself.

I would like to give you an account of my arrest. In the police evidence they said they arrested me at Kelly's (house). I was arrested at my own selection, after coming in from a hard day's splitting, fully half a mile from Kelly's (house). They (the police) only came for information and I refused to give them any. When they could get nothing out of me, Sergeant Steele said, "Put a pair of handcuffs on him." One of them went inside and turned the hut over looking for firearms. The milking cow was lying down near the hut; they were listening to her chewing her cud. They (the police, Sergeant Steele and Constable Brown) thought it was one of the Kellys. One of them covered me with a revolver, although I was already handcuffed. He told me afterwards that he nearly shot me, as he intended to have one. They arrested us one at a time, although they could have taken us all together.

After we were sentenced, Fitzpatrick was escorting us to the gaol. He had a handkerchief to his eyes, and said, "Well, Billy, I never thought you would get anything like that." I was released after the Royal Commission; whether Fitzpatrick had anything to do with that, I don't know.

I had sent a written statement of facts to the Commission. Some time after I was told that I was granted a pardon; that was worse than the sentence. I was granted a pardon for a thing I did not do. You cannot be surprised at anything the police would do, as they were only the offsprings of old "lags." The judge never read the evidence; he got it all out of the papers before the trial. The papers had us already convicted. When he (Judge Barry) was summing up to the jury, he said, "Well, gentlemen, you all know what this man Kelly is." But they (the jury) were a long while before they came in with their verdict.

Ned (Kelly) sent word to us to hang something out of the window of the cells we were in, and he would come and stick up the gaol and rescue us. But I did not like the idea of it, and persuaded Skillion not to have anything to do with it. I felt sorry for poor Skillion, as he did not even know what he was arrested for. But I blame myself for Skillion being arrested, as he was mistaken for Burns. I pulled Burns back in the dark, when he was going into Fitzpatrick's presence at Kelly's Homestead after the brawl. Had I let Burns go forward, Skillion would not have been in trouble. When arrested, the police gave me a horse to ride which they could not ride themselves. They (the police) put me on it handcuffed. It gave a couple of bucks and then bolted. I was getting away from them (the police), and they threatened me with a revolver if I did not pull the horse up. It was pitch dark. I don't know if they fired or not; anyhow, they never hit me. They got me to Greta, and I believe they would have let me go then had I given them any evidence. The next one they brought in was Skillion, who said, "They cannot do anything to me, I am innocent." But they did, all the same. Then they brought two more in — Ned Kelly's mother and Alice King, the baby — the only one they didn't lay a charge against. It was then some time near the morning. You may use this as you like, and publish any part you like. — Yours faithfully,

(Signed) WILLIAM WILLIAMSON.

On June 6, about seven weeks after her arrest, the following paragraph appeared in the Beechworth paper:—

Mrs. Kelly.

A day or two since Mr. W. H. Foster (police magistrate) attended at the Beechworth Gaol and admitted to bail this woman who had been committed for trial for aiding and abetting in an attempt to murder Constable Fitzpatrick at Greta. It was an act of charity, as the poor woman, though not of the most reputable of characters, had a babe in her arms, and in the cold gaol, without a fire, it is a wonder the poor little child lived so long during this bitter wintry weather.

The fear that the baby would die in gaol was apparently the motive for now granting bail.

Constable Fitzpatrick, before the Royal Commission on July 6, 1881, said:—

"When I first went to the place (Mrs. Kelly's) Dan was not there — only Mrs. Kelly and some of the younger children of the place, and I entered into conversation for a while to see if there was any chance of Dan putting in an appearance. Mrs. Kelly knew who I was, and I drew her attention to the sound of someone cutting wood behind the hut on the creek where they lived, and I said: 'I'll go up and see who they are.' I went up there and found Williamson, a man that used to live with them, splitting rails, and asked him had he a licence, and he said, 'No, he did not require one splitting wood on selected land'; so after I had spent a few moments with him I was heading for Greta. I was going straight there — the station I was en route for; I was on horseback. I had occasion to pass by Kelly's new hut at the time — the one they were living in at the time. As I was passing I noticed two horsemen entering the slip panels in front of the old hut. I rode round to where they were, and by the time I got round one of the men disappeared, and Skillion was holding one horse by the mane and had the other horse — the one he had been riding with the saddle and bridle on — he was holding that, and third horse he had caught in the panel just after coming in. The horse that had been ridden had the bridle off. I asked Skillion who was riding the horse. He told me he did not know. I examined the mare and saw it was the one Dan Kelly was riding two or three days previous to that, when I had seen him. I said, 'That is Dan Kelly's mare,' and he said, 'Yes.' I said, 'Where is he?' and he said, 'Up at the house, I suppose.' That is the new hut. So I rode up to the place again and called out, 'Dan.' He came out, and as soon as I saw him I walked up to him. He had his hat and coat off, and a knife and fork in his hand. I said, 'I am going to arrest you on a charge of horse stealing, Dan.' 'Very well, you will let me have something to eat before you take me?' I said, 'All right.' He said, 'I have been out riding all day.' So he went back into the hut, and I followed him in. As soon as I went inside Mrs. Kelly accosted me, calling me 'a deceitful little — — —.' She said she always thought I was. She said, 'You will not take him out of this to-night.' I said it was no use talking that way, that I had to do my duty, and Dan said, 'Shut up, mother! that is all right.' I was scarcely in the place three minutes when Ned Kelly rushed in and fired a shot at me and said, 'Out of this, you — — —.' Dan was sitting down to have something to eat. I was standing up alongside of him with my right side to him. Ned fired a second shot and it lodged in my wrist. With that I turned to draw my revolver, and just as I slewed to the right Dan Kelly had my revolver pointed at me. He had snatched it while my attention was drawn to his mother and Ned."

Question. — Where was Williamson?

Fitzpatrick. — He had come to the door of the bedroom and Skillion was with him; they both had revolvers in their hands. They were not in the hut when I came in.

Question. — Were they in the hut when you were fired at?

Fitzpatrick. — Yes; just as the third shot went off.

Question. — Was Skillion in the hut?

Fitzpatrick. — He came to the hut as soon as Ned Kelly found out it was me. Williamson came out of the bedroom door and had a revolver in his hand, and Skillion just came to the door while he was forcing himself in where Ned Kelly was standing.

Question. — Then you had three men to fight besides Mrs. Kelly?

Fitzpatrick. — Yes, and Ned Kelly said, "That will do, boys." If he had known it was Fitzpatrick he would not have fired a — — shot.

Question. — When you left Benalla that morning were you under instructions to do any certain duty?

Fitzpatrick. — Yes.

Question. — Who gave the instructions?

Fitzpatrick. — Sergeant Whelan.

Question. — What were the instructions?

Fitzpatrick. — The instructions came from headquarters.

Question. — What were they?

Fitzpatrick. — To take charge of the Greta station temporarily in the absence of Senior Constable Strahan.

Question. — Was Strahan away from his station?

Fitzpatrick. — He was.

(12824). Question by Commission. — How far (away) was Ned Kelly when he fired?

Fitzpatrick. — About a yard and a half from me; he had just come from the side of the hut door. As soon as he had fired the first shot Mrs. Kelly seized an old shovel that was at the fireplace and rushed at me with it.

(12825). By the Commission. — He missed you the first shot?

Fitzpatrick. — Yes; she rushed at me with this shovel and made a blow at me, and smashed my helmet completely in over my eyes, and as I raised my hand to ward off the shovel Nod Kelly fired a second shot and it lodged in my wrist. With that I turned to draw my revolver, and just as I slewed to the right Dan Kelly had my revolver pointed at me. He had snatched it while my attention was drawn to his mother and Ned Kelly.

Question. — When you left Benalla it was for the purpose of taking Strahan's duty?

Fitzpatrick. — Yes.

Question. — Did you ever do that duty? Was it your first time of being ordered to do duty of that character — sole charge of a station?

Fitzpatrick. — Yes.

Question. — Would it not have been your duty to have gone direct to take charge of the station where the man was not in charge?

Fitzpatrick. — The sergeant agreed with my suggestion by telling me the complaint against Dan Kelly and telling me to be careful with him.

Question. — Did the officer at Benalla, Sergeant Whelan, know when you left that morning that you were to arrest Dan Kelly if you got the chance?

Fitzpatrick. — Yes, he was aware of it.

Question. — How was he?

Fitzpatrick. — Because I told him if I saw him on my way I would take him to Greta, bring him in to Benalla, and remand him to Chiltern the following day. I suggested that to him.

Question. — Have you read Sergeant Whelan's evidence on that point?

Fitzpatrick. — No.

Question. — Then you say you had told the official who gave you the instructions that you would arrest Dan Kelly if you got the chance?

Fitzpatrick. — Yes.

Question. — Was it he who told you of the warrant being out, or did you yourself see it in the "Gazette" notice?

Fitzpatrick. — I fancy I saw it.

Question. — Did you go direct from Winton to Greta upon the Greta road that morning?

Fitzpatrick. — Yes.

Question. — Were you at Lindsay's public house on that occasion on the morning of your being shot?

Fitzpatrick. — No, not in the morning; it was in the afternoon.

Question. — When you left there (Lindsay's) what road did you go to Greta?

Fitzpatrick. — I turned off to the right by the Eleven Mile Creek.

Question. — When you were fired at that time what occurred?

Fitzpatrick. — Ned Kelly prevented them from doing any more, and I fell down on the floor insensible.

Question. — What really did occur afterwards?

Fitzpatrick. — After I got up Ned Kelly examined my hand, found a bullet in my wrist, and said, "You must have it out of that," and I asked him to let me go into Benalla to let the doctor take it out and he refused; and I saw he was determined to take out the bullet. He wanted to take it out with a razor, and I took out my penknife and he held my hand and I took it out. It was not very deep in; it was a small-sized ball.

Question. — What did you do after that? Did you leave the house immediately?

Fitzpatrick. — No; I could not leave for some time. They kept me till 11 o'clock, after I came round, and would not let me go.

Question. — Where did you go from there (Greta)?

Fitzpatrick. — To Winton — through Winton to Benalla.

Question. — You said that Williamson and Skillion had revolvers. How do you know they were revolvers?

Fitzpatrick. — I could swear it.

Question. — What position were they in?

Fitzpatrick. — Just coming in. Skillion alongside with Ned Kelly with a revolver in his hand, and Williamson came in out of the bedroom with a revolver.

Question. — How long before that had you seen Williamson chopping wood?

Fitzpatrick. — Fifteen minutes.

Question. — Had he a revolver then?

Fitzpatrick. — No, I did not see one.

Question. — How did he get into the house before you?

Fitzpatrick. — I do not know.

Question. — Were there two doors to the bedroom?

Fitzpatrick. — There was only the one entrance.

Question. — How did he get in before you and Dan Kelly?

Fitzpatrick. — He may have removed a sheet of bark at the back and come in. I did not see him come in.

Question. — You said if Williamson got into the house he might have got through by removing a sheet of bark. Was the house bark or slabs?

Fitzpatrick. — Bark and slabs.

Question. — Where was the bark — on the sides or on the roof?

Fitzpatrick. — I cannot say whether the outside walls were of bark.

Question. — Then they had no particular reason for firing at you?

Fitzpatrick. — Any constable would have been in the same position.

Such was the evidence of Constable Fitzpatrick before the Commission which sat in 1881 to inquire into the cause of the Kelly outbreak and the management of the police during the pursuit. It is noticeable that Fitzpatrick swore to the following:—

(1) Ned Kelly, at a distance of less than five feet, failed to strike Fitzpatrick at the first shot, although Ned Kelly was acknowledged to be an expert marksman.

(2) Ned Kelly, at such close range, failed again to strike Fitzpatrick's body with his second shot, and struck his wrist, which Fitzpatrick had at the moment raised above his head to shield himself from a threatened blow, which blow was not delivered seeing that the defending left hand was in no way injured by the fire shovel.

(3) Ned Kelly, a clever marksman, missed Fitzpatrick altogether with the third shot at a similar range.

Now although, according to Fitzpatrick, Kelly fired on him at a range of less than five feet, the alleged bullet wound in Fitzpatrick's wrist was only skin deep! A bullet wound from a revolver used in those days would have smashed right through Fitzpatrick's wrist at the exceptionally close range of a yard and a half. It appears perfectly clear, therefore, that Fitzpatrick's statement in evidence was ridiculously false, although it was deemed sufficiently satisfactory to lead to the prompt conviction of Mrs. Kelly, Skillion and Williamson. Fitzpatrick's injured wrist was attended to by Dr. John Nicholson, who, giving evidence during the trial at the Beechworth Assizes on October 9, 1878, said:—

"On April 16 I was called to the police barracks, Benalla, to see Constable Fitzpatrick. Examined his left wrist, found two wounds, one a ragged one and the other a clean incision. They might have been produced by a bullet — that is, the outside wound. There could not have been much loss of blood." (In the doctor's opinion the other wound could not have been caused by a bullet, although Fitzpatrick had sworn that it had been caused by a bullet.)

To Mr. Bowman (for the defence). — "I didn't probe the wound, so do not know if the two wounds were connected. There was a smell of brandy on him. A constable present said Fitzpatrick had had some drink. It was merely a skin wound."

Dr. Nicholson met Fitzpatrick afterwards, in the street, and told him frankly that the wound in his wrist could not have been caused by a bullet.

Two farmers — Joseph Ryan, of Lakerowan, and Frank Harty, of Winton — swore that Skillion had been in their company since 2 p.m. on April 15, and that they both had tea at Harty's at about 5.30 p.m., and that they did not return to Kelly's house till 7 p.m. The row with Fitzpatrick took place at about 5 p.m. Peace was restored, and the Kelly family and Fitzpatrick had had tea before Joe Ryan and Skillion returned from Frank

Harty's. It was impossible, therefore, for Skillion to have been present when Fitzpatrick was manhandled by Ned Kelly and his brother Dan.Victoria, and also flowing, in its upper reaches, through a jumble of hills.

Also it was impossible for Williamson to have been present. He was splitting rails half a mile up the creek when Fitzpatrick entered the Kelly's house. Williamson would not have had time to cover the distance and reach the house before the third alleged shot was fired.

Furthermore, Fitzpatrick swore that Williamson did not enter the house before him (Fitzpatrick), nor did he see Williamson enter the house after him (Fitzpatrick). When closely questioned by the Commission as to how Williamson, not having entered the house, could come out of the bedroom, Fitzpatrick affirmed that Williamson may have obtained entrance by the removal of a sheet of bark at the rear of the house.

As the house was built of wooden slab sides and a bark roof, it was obviously impossible for Williamson to remove a sheet of bark from the roof in time to be present before the fracas was over.

Therefore it seems clear that Williamson was not present at all, and that Mrs. Kelly, Skillion and Williamson were innocent of the charge on which they were so promptly convicted and severely sentenced.

Ned Kelly strongly objected to his sister's name being brought into his mother's defence, although her counsel (Mr. Bowman) considered the attack on Kate Kelly proved ample justification for what had really happened. Ned contended that the evidence of Joe Ryan and Frank Harty would prove that Skillion was not present, and that consequently Fitzpatrick's evidence was palpably false. Their evidence, Ned contended, was sufficient to secure the acquittal of his mother, Skillion and Williamson, without bringing Kate's name into the case at all. In deference to Ned's objection, Kate's name was not mentioned at Mrs. Kelly's trial.

Ned Kelly naturally thought that his mother would be tried in a Court of Justice, notwithstanding the fact that he himself, had twice been previously tried in a court of loaded dice.

He did not think it possible that a mother with a very young baby in arms would be denied her inalienable right to be tried in a Court of Justice. Ned was, however, bitterly disappointed. The only evidence produced against his mother was that given by a constable who was well known to be a flash, drunken, immoral blackguard, who was

was shortly afterwards dismissed in disgrace from the Force on the following charges: "That he (Fitzpatrick) was not fit to be in the Police Force; that he associated with the lowest persons in Lancefield; that he could not be trusted out of sight, and that he never did his duty."

It would be almost unbelievable, if it were not already an established fact that, at the Supreme Court at Beechworth on 9th October, 1878, the evidence given by two highly respectable farmers was rejected with scorn, and the perjured evidence of a constable who "could not be trusted out of sight" accepted as sufficient excuse to send this mother with a baby in her arms to gaol for three years' hard labor.

But then the Kellys had to be "brought up on any charge no matter how paltry, the object being to take their prestige away from them."

It was this unique outrageous miscarriage of justice that caused Ned Kelly to offer armed resistance to an administration correctly described as "Loaded Dice."

(Australian prisoners of war in Germany, in 1944, were granted a holiday to celebrate the birthday of Ned Kelly, King of Australia.)

Judge Redmond Barry

3
TRIAL AT BEECHWORTH

When Wm. Skillion, William Williamson, and Ellen King were called, many looked surprised. It was not known outside Greta that Mrs. Kelly had been married to George King some time after she settled on the Eleven-Mile Creek. The jury consisted of several ex-policemen and others who were prejudiced against the Kellys, and on Fitzpatrick's unsupported evidence a verdict of guilty was brought in.

JUDGE BARRY'S SENTENCE

Although Mrs. Kelly, Skillion and Williamson were arrested and brought to Benalla on April 17, 1878, their trial did not take place until October 9, when they were all convicted and duly sentenced by Judge Barry to long terms of imprisonment.

In imposing on Mrs. Kelly a sentence of three years' hard labour, Judge Barry laid emphasis on the atrocious crime of aiding and abetting in the shooting of a police constable, and added: "If your son Ned were here I would make an example of him for the whole of Australia — I would give him 15 years."

Ned Kelly was not charged before that court. He was neither charged nor tried; yet was he thus prejudged and condemned.

It has always been an axiom in British communities that the Court must always consider an accused person to be innocent until he has been fairly tried and justly convicted, but the law and the axiom was not only violated, but also strangled by those charged with its administration. This judicial outburst was tantamount to an open declaration of war on the part of authority against the elder of the Kelly youths, and when Ned Kelly, working on the alluvial diggings at Kelly's Creek, was told of the threatened sentence he understood its significance, and said: "Well, they will have to catch me first, and now that they have put my mother in gaol I will make the name of Ned Kelly ring for generations."

The hand of the law was against him and his. Sooner or later the **authorities would** seek him out and crush him. Well, it would be a battle henceforth. He would forsake the peaceful ways of a miner on the Stringybark and Kelly's Creeks, and live in defiance of the law. The perjured evidence of Fitzpatrick, the terrible sentence passed upon his mother, and the voluntary condemnation of himself by the judge awakened in him all the combative instincts of his race. He abandoned his quiet work, and, with his trusted companions, decided to maintain their liberty at all costs.

Skillion and Williamson strove in vain to prove that they were not present during the scene at the Kelly hut; and so, after being six months in gaol awaiting trial, they were each sentenced to six years' hard labour.

The sentence on Mrs. Kelly was considered a very savage one by most people in the district, where she was so well known. Even Mr. Alfred Wyatt, police magistrate, whose headquarters were at that time at Benalla, when giving evidence before the Commission, said:— "I thought the sentence upon that old woman, Mrs. Kelly, a very severe one." Yet he was not even suspected of being a Kelly sympathizer. In fact, he was on the Bench at Beechworth when the Kelly sympathisers were presented, and when the officials applied for one of the numerous remands. In addressing "Wild" Wright, who stated in court that "they would never catch the Kellys until they let their innocent mother out of gaol, put the scoundrel, Fitzpatrick, in," Mr. Wyatt said:— "I would like to give you fair play if I could."

Strange words, indeed, from a police magistrate who had sworn to do justice without fear or favour!

Later, in giving evidence before the Royal Commission, the same magistrate said:—

"My view was that the arrest of the Kelly sympathisers was a mistake — all those arrests — and it prolonged itself as a mistake. It caused bad feeling, alienated a number of persons . . . who I had reason to believe might have been relied upon for help before the murders (of Kennedy, Scanlan and Lonigan) and up to the time of the murders. My reason is that an informal offer was made to me to bring the Kellys in if the Government would liberate Kelly's mother. That was before the murders of Lonigan, Scanlan and Kennedy."

Question. — Did you make that known to the police authorities?

Witness. — I did.

MR. ENOCH DOWNES

Mr. Enoch Downes, truant officer, residing at Beechworth, when giving evidence before the Commission on July 20, 1881, said that he called at Mrs. Byrne's house in reference to a truancy case, and in speaking about the outlaws to Mrs. Byrne, mother of Joe Byrne, said:— "Well, your son had no reason to join the outlaws — the Kellys. There is some excuse for them."

"In fact, I spoke a little freely about the action of the judge in passing sentence on the Kellys' mother at the time; I spoke feelingly on the action (of the judge). I did not believe in the sentence, and I told her so freely. I thought if policy had been used or consideration for the mother shown that two or three months would have been ample."

In August, 1878, Superintendent Sadleir, of Benalla, made some arrangements for a party of picked policemen to go in pursuit of Ned and Dan Kelly. The police believed that the Kellys already had sufficient provocation to show fight if they were attacked. Thus, on August 10, Superintendent Sadleir wrote to Sergeant Kennedy, of Mansfield, as follows:—

"It seems to be certain that Ned Kelly is in the neighbourhood of Greta, or from thence to Connelly's and the bogs near Wombat. I am very anxious to make some special efforts to have the matter set at rest and his apprehension effected, if possible. I have consulted with the senior constable in charge at Greta, and it appears that there is not much likelihood of him and the constable with him there doing much towards arresting Kelly or even disturbing him for the neighbourhood. It has been proposed to collect, for the purpose of a thorough search, what constables are in the district who know Kelly personally, sending, say, two of them to Mansfield to act with Sergeant Kennedy from that end and the others to act with the Greta police, and to search simultaneously up and down the King River and neighbouring places. I shall be glad to receive any suggestions that Sergeant Kennedy may have to offer on the subject, and whether he is of the opinion that anything might be gained by his coming here for a day or so to consult with the sub-officer taking charge of the party starting from Greta end — that is, supposing the expedition should be determined on."

On August 16 Sergeant Kennedy answered as follows:—

"I beg to report for the Superintendent's information that I am of opinion that the offender Kelly could be routed from his hiding place if the arrangements proposed by the Superintendent were properly carried out.

"The distance from Mansfield to the King River is so great and the country so impenetrable that a party of men from here would, in my opinion, require to establish a kind of depot at some distance beyond the Wombat — say, Stringybark Creek, seven miles beyond Monk's. By forming a camp there it would enable the party to keep up a continuous search between there and the flat country towards the King River, Fifteen Mile Creek and Holland's Creek. While the Mansfield men would be doing the ranges and creeks in the neighbourhood, the men forming the

Greta party would be operating on the flat country along the rivers and creeks abovementioned. I feel sure that by efficiently carrying cut this plan Kelly would soon be disturbed, if not captured. I believe Kelly has secreted himself in some isolated part of that country lying between Wombat and King River, and in a similar way to which Power (the bushranger) did; and seeing that he was a mate of Power I think it is reasonable to conclude he would imitate his example in this respect, seeing it was the means of keeping Power in comparative safety so long. I am not aware if Mounted Constable Michael Scanlan 2118, of Mooroopna, is personally acquainted with Kelly, but I am sure there is no man who could render more service in the proposed expedition than he could, as he knows every part of that country lying between here and the King River. I am of opinion Constable Scanlan, Constable McIntyre and myself would be quite sufficient to undertake the working of that country without any more assistance. I should like to have a personal interview with the sub-officer taking charge of the party starting from Greta."

The place where Sergeant Kennedy proposed to establish a depot was where he subsequently met the Kellys in armed encounter.

Superintendent Sadleir was not quite agreeable to send the party of only three suggested by Sergeant Kennedy, as none of them could definitely recognise the wanted men. Hence he selected Constable Lonigan to accompany the party.

The expedition was delayed through several causes, but on October 18 Superintendent Sadleir wrote to Sub-Inspector Pewtress, the officer in charge of Mansfield, as follows:—

"It has been decided to carry out the plan proposed by me on August 10 last, but which has unavoidably been delayed. I wish the party to start work early on Tuesday next (22/10/78) from each end, i.e., from Mansfield and Greta. As I have already informed Sergeant Kennedy by telegraph, he will be required here to consult with the other sub-officers engaged in this matter. Let him come by to-morrow's coach, bringing a plain saddle with him, as I wish to take back a horse specially fitted for this expedition. Constable McIntyre and Constable Scanlan will also form two of the party from Mansfield end."

"P.S. — This matter must be dealt with by everyone concerned as strictly confidential."

On October 21 (Monday) Superintendent Sadleir gave final instructions:—

"A party which will consist of Sergeant Kennedy, Constables McIntyre, Scanlan and Lonigan will start from Mansfield on Friday next, commencing the search for offenders Kelly from the Wombat end.

"Constable Lonigan is ordered to report at Mansfield on Wednesday next (23/10/78), but should he not arrive in time the party must start without him. Both Constables Scanlan and Lonigan can recognise Kelly should they be so successful as to come upon him. The other party start from this end on Friday morning. The men forming it are:— Senior Constables Strahan and Shoobridge and Constables Thom and Ryan."

On Thursday, October 24, a gold escort from Woods' Point arrived at Mansfield in charge of Senior-Constable John Kelly, and with Benalla as its destination. Senior-Constable Kelly was met at the coach by Sergeant Kennedy. The latter, in confidence, informed Senior-Constable Kelly that he was going out in search of the Kellys. Kennedy asked Kelly to let him have a Spencer rifle, which Constable Horwood of the escort party had with him. Senior-Constable Kelly replied that as they only had one rifle between them it would be very injudicious to part with it, but after some consideration he said: "Get a second revolver and give it to Horwood and you can have the rifle." This was the long-range weapon that Constable Scanlan carried and used in the fatal expedition.

The police left Mansfield before daylight as a party of diggers on Friday morning, October 25. The party comprised Sergeant Michael Kennedy and Constables Scanlon, Lonigan and McIntyre, the latter being the cook or rouseabout of the party. They arrived at the spot where Sergeant Kennedy had intended to establish a depot as a base from which to explore that part of the country. They arrived early in the day, and made their camp. The police were attired in civilian clothes, and resembled a party of prospectors, and under ordinary circumstances would doubtless have succeeded in their mission to Stringybark Creek. But the men they sought considered that a state of war existed between them and the police, and knowing that the police were in every way better prepared and better armed they were ever watchful. It is doubtful whether any disguise would have succeeded in passing their scrutiny.

4
THE BATTLE OF STRINGYBARK CREEK

Ned and Dan Kelly, with their mates, Joe Byrne and Steve Hart, worked constantly mining for gold from April till October 1878. They lived in a log hut built years before by some previous prospectors on Kelly's Creek. In those days, when gold was frequently discovered in large quantities and very rich patches, the pioneer miners were not satisfied with the yields at Stringybark and Kelly's Creeks, and left for other fields. The Kellys did not get a great quantity of gold from these creeks, but they secured enough to keep the kettle boiling at home and at their mining camp. They had a regular system of communication with their home at Greta, and were regularly supplied with food and clothing. They were informed of the latest developments at their mother's trial, and of any police movements. At first Ned had left home to keep Dan out of the reach of the warrant which brought Fitzpatrick to their home. But Ned himself was "wanted" now for his participation in the Fitzpatrick episode.

From their camp on Kelly's Creek, Joe Byrne on some occasions went to Mansfield for provisions, but as he was a stranger there, his visits attracted no attention.

The spring came in early that year, and there was good grass on the banks of the creeks, and more care had to be taken in controlling the roving habits of their horses. Thus it happened that when, on one occasion, Dan Kelly went down to head them back towards their camp, he noticed the track of a strange horse. He followed this track, and, before he had gone far, noticed that the trees along the trail had been blazed. Still following the trail, he found a series of "baits" at intervals through the timber. To the experienced bushman the interpretation was simple. Strange horse, blazed trail, baits. Solution: Tolmie's boundary rider had been there, laying baits to poison dingoes, which were plentiful in the neighbourhood. Tolmie was the local squatter, who had a large run in the district.

The Kellys had been informed by their relatives and friends that the Mansfield police were preparing to go in pursuit of them. They were also informed that the Mansfield police had boasted that they were seeking them and that they would bring the Kellys back with them, dead or alive. The police preparations started in August, as already stated, but the actual pursuit was delayed until the end of October.

The boundary rider who came across the horses of the Kellys informed his employer (Mr. Tolmie) that he believed the Kellys were camped in the vicinity of Stringybark Creek. Mr. Tolmie, in turn, passed this information to Sergeant Kennedy, whom he took out to Wombat Ranges and showed him the shingled hut on Stringybark Creek, near which the police party afterwards pitched their tent.

Later, on a Friday afternoon, Ned Kelly, while reconnoitering, heard a report of a shotgun, which Constable McIntyre discharged at some kangaroos, and came across the tracks of the police horses on their way to this hut, and on the following morning he discovered the tracks of horses going in another direction. He reported each of these discoveries to his brother Dan and their companions. The mining party ceased work, and considered the situation. The Kellys had only two firearms — a rifle and a shotgun.

Dan was deputed to find out exactly where the police were camped. After a careful reconnaissance he returned and reported that the police were at the shingled hut on Stringybark Creek, and that their tent was pitched in the open space nearby. He mentioned also that the police had long guns — a disquieting piece of news. On Saturday the Kellys observed that some of the police had gone out riding, and decided that their only hope of retaining their liberty would be to capture the party of police remaining at the camp before the return of their comrades.

Shortly after noon they heard the report of a shotgun, which Constable McIntyre had discharged at some parrots. There was now no time to wait. After hasty preparation, they stealthily approached the police camp, which was about a mile distant, and, coming to the edge of the cleared patch on which the police had pitched their tent, they took observations. They decided to demand the surrender of the police at the tent and take their guns. If this plan succeeded the Kellys were fairly confident of success in ensuring the surrender and disarming the other party of police on their return to camp.

The Kellys saw two men sitting on a log near the camp fire. One of them (McIntyre) got up and took up a shotgun; the other (Lonigan) drove the horses down a little distance and put the hobbles on them. They then returned to the fire and stood the gun against a stump. The one who had shotgun stood by the fire and the other man sat on a log. The Kellys thought there were other men asleep in the tent. Ned took Constable Lonigan to be Constable Strahan, who had been described by Captain Standish as "a blathering fellow," and who had said that he would not ask him (Ned) to stand before firing on him — that he would fire first, and then call surrender. McIntyre he mistook for Constable Flood, against whom the Kellys had very bitter feelings. After a hasty consultation with his companions, Ned advanced, while Dan kept McIntyre covered. Suddenly Ned Kelly cried out, "Bail up! Throw up your arms." The police were taken completely by surprise. Lonigan drew his revolver and made a run for a bigger log, about six or seven yards away, instead of dropping down behind the log on which he had been sitting. He had reached the log and raised his revolver to take aim when Ned Kelly fired. His gun had been loaded with a charge of swandrops, and Lonigan, jumping up, staggered some little distance from the log, as he cried, "I'm shot!" and fell dead. — That prophecy!!

McIntyre instinctively threw up his hands. He could do nothing else, as he had left his revolver in the tent, and he could not reach the shotgun, which he had placed against a stump, a little distance away.

Ned Kelly then called out, asking McIntyre who was in the hut. The latter replied, "No one," and Kelly advanced and took possession of Lonigan's and McIntyre's revolvers and the shotgun and shot cartridges, from which he extracted the shot and reloaded with swandrops, in place of small shot. He asked McIntyre where his other companions were, and McIntyre said that they had gone down the creek, and that he did not expect them back that night. McIntyre inquired of Kelly if he was going to shoot him (McIntyre) and his mates when they returned, and Kelly replied that he would shoot no man if he gave up his arms and promised to leave the police force. Conversation followed between the Kellys, and their prisoner, in the course of which, it is stated, McIntyre said the police all knew that Fitzpatrick had wronged the Kellys, and that he (McIntyre) intended to leave the force, as he was in bad health, and proposed going home to Belfast, in the north of Ireland. McIntyre admitted that Sergeant Kennedy and Scanlan had gone out to look for Kelly's camp, and told also about the police party, under Senior-Constable Shoobridge, which had set out from Greta to look for the Kellys.

Having assumed control of the police quarters, Ned Kelly despatched Joe Byrne and Steve Hart to their own camp to see if there were any signs of Kennedy and Scanlan. They returned and reported that there was no sign of the mounted constables. Further conversation between Ned Kelly and McIntyre ensued, and the former inquired why the police carried Spencer rifles, breech-loading shotguns, and so much ammunition. The police, he said, were supposed to carry only one revolver and six cartridges in the revolver, whereas this party had 18 rounds of revolver cartridges each, three dozen cartridges for the shotgun, and 21 Spencer rifle cartridges, besides all the ammunition the others had away with them. It appeared, he said, as if the police not only intended to shoot him, but also to riddle him. However, he remarked, he was unacquainted with McIntyre, Kennedy or Scanlan, and desired only that they surrender and leave the district. McIntyre said he would get Kennedy and Scanlan to surrender if Kelly would not shoot them, pleading that they could not be blamed for doing their honest duty.

"So they knew that Fitzpatrick had wronged us," mused Ned; "then why don't they make it public and convict him? The police will rue the day that Fitzpatrick got among them!"

Dan Kelly had come back from the spring, and the other two had returned from their hasty visit to the miners' hut on Kelly's Creek, when Ned Kelly heard sounds of horses coming up the creek. He immediately told McIntyre to advise Kennedy and Scanlan to give up their arms and they would not be harmed. As the mounted police came in sight Kennedy was about twelve yards in front of Scanlan. McIntyre approached Kennedy and told him that the Kellys had surprised them in their camp; that Lonigan, who showed fight, had been shot dead by Ned Kelly, and that he advised his companions to surrender.

Kennedy, however, drew his revolver, and, jumping off his horse, got behind a tree, leaving his horse between himself and Ned Kelly.

Then came the command from Kelly: "Bail up! Throw up you arms!" Constable Scanlan, who carried the Spencer rifle, slewed his horse around to gallop away, in order to be out of range of revolvers and shotguns, while he himself could then easily fire with the rifle at long range. In the excitement, however, his horse became confused and refused to answer the bit, and Scanlan fired at Ned Kelly without levelling the rifle, the bullet going through Ned Kelly's beard. He was in the act of firing again when Ned Kelly fired, and Scanlan fell from his horse and died almost immediately.

Both Kennedy and Scanlan were well within range when they came into the clearing. Scanlan was only thirty yards from Kelly, and Kennedy about twenty yards, and both could have been shot without being challenged, or without being given the opportunity to surrender.

Thus, although Ned Kelly claimed that he was at war with the authorities, on this occasion at least he upheld his vow that he would shoot to kill only in a fair fight.

McIntyre lost no time in scrambling on Sergeant Kennedy's horse. The horse was roused by the shots and got away about 20 yards before McIntyre succeeded in getting into the saddle. Ned Kelly could have shot him then, but did not appear to concern himself with McIntyre, who had given up his arms; he was concerned with Kennedy, who was armed, and who apparently intended to fight to a finish. Attention diverted to McIntyre meant neglecting Kennedy, who was armed and firing, as opportunity presented, at the Kellys.

Kennedy opened fire from behind a tree. Dan Kelly advanced, and Kennedy fired at him, the bullet passing just over his shoulder. Kennedy then ran and got behind another tree. At this moment Ned fired and wounded Kennedy in the armpit. Ned picked up Scanlan's rifle, but, not understanding the mechanism, promptly dropped it and again seized his own shotgun. By this time Kennedy, having crossed the creek, had contrived to place some distance between himself and Kelly, but in running he dropped his revolver and was turning to surrender when Kelly, unaware of his intention, fired again. The charge entered Kennedy's chest, and he fell mortally wounded.

When McIntyre galloped away on Kennedy's horse he stooped on to the horse's neck and the scarf he was wearing was flying about him. Dan Kelly followed him some distance, but McIntyre quickly got out of range. The Kellys were under the impression that McIntyre had been shot. Ned came up to Kennedy where he had fallen. He was satisfied that Kennedy could not live. Kennedy begged that his life be spared, so that he might again see his wife and children. He was in great pain, but his appeal to be spared was refused. Ned Kelly's subsequent explanation was that Kennedy was hopelessly wounded, and could not live long. He was suffering great agony, and, as McIntyre had escaped to give the alarm, they could not remain to look after him. If left alive Kennedy would, Kelly said, be left to a slow, torturing death at the mercy of ants, flies, and the packs of dingoes, which were fairly numerous in those parts. Therefore he decided to put an end to the sufferings of the wounded sergeant, and, as the latter momentarily turned his head, Kelly fired and shot him through the heart.

Thus perished three of the bravest men of the Victorian police force. It is little wonder that the story of the dreadful tragedy awakened everywhere feelings of horror and indignation and led to a renewal of the determination of the authorities to stamp out the Kellys.

Constable McIntyre galloped away for some distance through the scrub. His horse fell, but he mounted again and pushed on. Again the horse went down, and this time McIntyre assumed that the animal had been wounded by the Kellys. He therefore took off the saddle and bridle and pushed on for about a mile on foot.

He discovered a large wombat hole, and, fearing that he was being pursued, crawled into it and wrote in his notebook:— "Ned Kelly and others stuck us up to-day, when we were disarmed. Lonigan and Scanlan shot. I am hiding in a wombat hole till dark. The Lord have mercy on me. Scanlan tried to get his gun out." Later on, after leaving his narrow shelter, he wrote in his book again:— "I have been travelling all night, and am very weary. 9 a.m., Sunday. I am now lying on the edge of a creek named Bridges." (This was Blue Range Creek.)

McIntyre reached McColl's farm about midday on Sunday. He related the story of events on the Wombat Ranges, and was given a horse to ride into Mansfield, a distance of about three miles. Here he excitedly repeated his story, and it was some time before he was able to give a really coherent account of what had happened. At the subsequent inquest he stated that Lonigan was shot dead just as he reached the shelter of a big log, that Scanlan was shot without being able to use his rifle, and that Sergeant Kennedy had surrendered before McIntyre snatched the reins of Kennedy's horse, and, scrambling into the saddle, galloped away.

Had Sergeant Kennedy surrendered as McIntyre described, then his body would have been discovered quite close to that of Scanlan. But Kennedy's body was not discovered until the following Thursday morning, five days after the tragedy, about a quarter of a mile, and across the creek from where Scanlan had fallen. The discovery of Kennedy's body a quarter of a mile away bears out Ned Kelly's statement that the sergeant had kept up a running fire, that he retreated from tree to tree, until he fell mortally wounded.

McIntyre evidently considered that it would not look well for him if he admitted that he had taken Kennedy's horse while the latter, during a gallant fight, was using it as a barrage against the bushrangers' fire. McIntyre varied this evidence at Beechworth in August, 1880, at Ned Kelly's trial, in order to square it with established facts. Allowance appears to have been made for his hysterical condition when giving evidence at the inquest at Mansfield.

5
THE SEARCH FOR THE BODIES

There was great excitement in the peaceful town of Mansfield when the news of the tragedy was made public. A search party was organised, and Inspector Pewtress, Constables Allwood and McIntyre, Dr. Reynolds, and five civilians started off late on Sunday afternoon to recover the bodies of the brave police officers. The party called at Monk's sawmills, and there secured a reliable guide, who led them through dense scrub and thick undergrowth to the scene of the tragedy. There they arrived about midnight, and had no difficulty in finding the bodies of Lonigan and Scanlan. Rain fell in torrents, and the search for the body of Kennedy was delayed until the following day. It was expected that, in accordance with the report of McIntyre, the body would be found quite close to the spot where that of Scanlan lay.

After searching for some time on Monday is was evident that the morale of the party was becoming seriously affected. It was feared apparently that the Kellys would return and annihilate the whole search party. Finally, it was decided to tie the bodies of Lonigan and Scanlan together and "pack" them on horseback through the dense scrub and timber to Monk's sawmill. There a buggy was obtained, in which the bodies were taken to Mansfield and placed in the mortuary room of the Mansfield Hospital, where the subsequent inquest was held.

Two members of the Wright family were in Mansfield when the bodies of Lonigan and Scanlan were brought in. The local police authorities showed signs of nervous strain, and they arrested "Wild" Wright on a charge of using threatening language. They also arrested his totally deaf and dumb brother, "Dummy" Wright, on the same charge. This was considered the limit of police hysteria. The charge, of course, could not be sustained, and "Dummy" was discharged and the police ridiculed.

Police now began to filter into Mansfield from the surrounding districts. Another attempt was made to discover Kennedy's body. A party was organised and arrived on the scene of the tragedy on Tuesday afternoon. A search was made until evening, but no inducement could persuade the members of the search party to remain there until the following morning.

The fear that the Kellys might attack them was so demoralising that the volunteer searchers, when night fell, went back to Mansfield.

It was now thought that Kennedy had been taken away alive by the Kellys, and Superintendent Sadleir, who arrived from police headquarters at Benalla, interviewed "Wild" Wright, in the Mansfield gaol, and offered him £30 if he would find Kennedy, alive or dead. A special proviso was put into the "conditions" with regard to the protection of Kennedy from injury or death should Wright discover him alive. It was arranged that Wright should go at once to Greta and interview Mrs. Skillion, from whom Wright asserted he would obtain the full facts. While these arrangements were being made a larger search party was organised and set out on Wednesday for the scene of the conflict.

The searchers hitherto had been misled by McIntyre's statement that Kennedy had surrendered before he (McIntyre) snatched the bridle reins and galloped away on Kennedy's horse.

The search commenced on Wednesday, and on Thursday morning the search party widened out considerably, and at 8 o'clock a farmer named Tomkins, crossing the Stringybark Creek, came across Kennedy' body a quarter of a mile from where McIntyre had sworn he had surrendered.

The wounds on his right breast and armpit were recognisable, and the last and fatal wound was clearly seen on his left breast. The clothing was blackened by powder, showing that the shot had been fired, as Ned Kelly subsequently stated, at very close range.

The police and press, thinking the Kellys shot Sergeant Kennedy, and Constables Lonigan and Scanlan with single bullets, jumped to the conclusion that the several wounds, caused by each charge of swandrops, had been inflicted after death.

These assertions of police and press were not, however, supported by the evidence of Dr. Reynolds, of Mansfield, who made the post-mortem examination of the bodies of Scanlan, Lonigan and Kennedy.

Kennedy's body was brought to Mansfield. By this time the confidence of many of the search party was shaken in McIntyre's evidence as to whether Kennedy had surrendered. The searchers' view to a great extent coincided with the statement delivered for publication by Ned Kelly at Jerilderie to one of the prisoners in the hotel when the bank was robbed by the Kellys in February, 1879. Dr. Reynolds, who examined Kennedy's body, said that an ear was missing. From appearances he concluded that it had been gnawed off by native cats.

Before despatching the first search party to Wombat Ranges, Inspector Pewtress wrote his comments on McIntyre's somewhat rambling report, and despatched Constable Thomas Meehan to deliver this to Superintendent Sadleir at Benalla.

Meehan left Mansfield unarmed, but in uniform, at 5 p.m. on Sunday, October 27, 1878, and was instructed to get a change of horses at Dawes station, half way between Mansfield and Benalla. The distance from Mansfield to Benalla by the main coach road is forty miles. The following is Constable Meehans evidence on oath:

"I went as far as Barjarg — a station — and saw two suspicious-looking men on the road, and I could not get past them, because I had no arms (fire arms) at all, and I was in uniform. I said to myself these men have euchred everything — they have shot the police — and what am I to do? I have no firearms, and I have been despatched on this message. Then I returned to Joe Allen's (a farmer, who lives about a mile back from Barjarg), going back towards Mansfield again. I went back with the object of getting firearms. Allen was not at home. Then I asked Mrs. Allen how far was it back to Hickson's. I went to Hickson's and he was out, and there was nobody there at all. Hickson's place was about 100 yards off the road, and I said to myself I must do something. I must use my head, as I have no firearms, and I took the mare I was riding back and took the saddle and bridle off her, and took the boots off that pinched me. I took them off in the excitement of the moment, and made the best of my way to Broken River, my station (Dawes). I travelled all night, and got there the next day. I did not know the country at the time; I was a stranger. I let the horse go. Then I came on to Benalla, and gave information to Mr. Sadleir after that. Mr. Nicolson was in Benalla at the time, and there were five of us despatched to catch the Kellys. Sub-Inspector Pewtress interviewed me and said, Meehan, I will never forget you as long as you are in my district for making such a fool of yourself as you did that night when you went out!"

After the fight on Stringybark Creek the morale of the Victorian police seems to have been somewhat shaken. In fact, it was considered very unwise of Supt. C. H. Nicolson to have bragged of "taking the flashness out of the Kellys.

FLIGHT

After the death of Kennedy, Ned Kelly covered the body with the victim's cloak and rejoined his companions. Dan Kelly reported that McIntyre had got clear away, and felt somewhat annoyed at Ned for refusing his suggestion to handcuff him. Ned agreed that McIntyre's escape had been unfortunate. If they had held McIntyre they could have given attention to the burying of the three dead policemen, but now that McIntyre had escaped there would surely be an immediate hue and cry. The Kellys had to get away from the scene as soon as possible. They collected from the police camp everything that was of immediate use to them, and then set the camp on fire and destroyed what they did not want. The Kellys secured four police horses, viz., Kennedy's pack horse and the mounts of Scanlan, Lonigan and McIntyre, and the three weeks' rations which the police had brought with them. They then went back to their camp, and after throwing their tools down a shaft and covering them with stones and clay, they set out for the meeting place where they had previously arranged to meet their providore Tom Lloyd that (Saturday) night.

That (Saturday) night (26/10/1878) the providore arrived with a supply of rations, and the proceeds of the sale of some gold — about £12 in cash. On his arrival the providore suspected that something had happened. He noticed a strange horse — a police horse. Then he saw the Spencer rifle, and, picking it up, said, "It's heavy." Ned replied, "Yes, and very deadly." He noticed that the food they were eating was not their usual diet, and he remarked, "You are living high." Ned replied that they had had an engagement with the police that day (Saturday), and that three of the police were dead.

Ned then explained how they had discovered the police camp, and the manner of the attack, with fatal results to the three policemen who showed fight; how McIntyre had surrendered, and afterwards escaped on Kennedy's horse.

Discussion regarding their future plans was renewed. It was decided to return at once to their home at Greta, and then make their way to hold up the bank at Howlong. As they were at war with the Government, and the police employed by the Government, it was absolutely necessary to raise enough money to conduct successfully their plan of campaign. There was, Ned Kelly told them, no middle course for them. They would have to "go on" or "go under."

Rain fell in torrents, and long before they had covered half the journey they were all drenched to the skin. When, however, they were within a few miles of their own homestead, the providore was sent on ahead to see if the coast was clear at the house, and prepare the family for the return of the party. It was pitch dark when the providore rapped at the door and was invited to "Come in."

He got a change of clothes and put on a white shirt with a stiff front. While he was changing his clothes he hastily recounted the outline of the fight with the police on the Wombat Ranges.

The providore now hastened back to meet the Kellys, and report "Line clear." He had ridden back for some distance, when suddenly he was startled with, "Bail up! Throw up your arms!" But as he recognised it was Ned Kelly's voice, he quickly regained his composure, and said, "Surely you're not going to turn on your mate?" "Oh!" said Ned, "it's you? I didn't know you with that white shirt on. When you left us you looked different, and I thought you were one of the police." Continuing, Ned said, "You know, we can't take any risks now." The providore had met and passed Dan Kelly, Joe Byrne, and Steve Hart without seeing them, and neither of them saw the providore. Ned, who rode behind the others, was quick to detect the person with the changed appearance.

The other three pulled up when they heard Ned give the challenge, and came back to see their faithful friend — the providore — pulled up. They went home, and after changing their clothes and partaking of a good meal, they related in detail what happened on Saturday at Stringybark Creek. After a few hours' rest both men and horses were refreshed.

ON THE RUN

The rain having ceased, the sky cleared, and shortly after midnight the Kellys left home, and made for the Greta Ranges. Here they camped during the next day, Monday (28/10/78).

They started at dusk for the Beechworth Ranges, crossing the King River, and keeping as much as possible off the main roads. They camped on the Beechworth Ranges, and were observed by some people while in this neighbourhood. These people reported to the police what they had seen. On this report the police organised that notorious failure afterwards known as the "Charge of Sebastopol," or the raid on "Rats' Castle." The Kellys pushed on from Beechworth Ranges to Barnawartha, and in due course arrived on the banks of the Murray River. They knew there was a punt there, and expected to cross the Murray in it to reach Howlong on the other side.

They found the river in flood as a result of recent very heavy rains. They met one of the Baumgartens, who told them there was no hope of getting across the Murray while the flats on both sides were flooded, and that the police were about there in droves. Baumgarten also gave them the views the police held on the Kellys and their alleged plans. The Kellys camped in the vicinity of Baumgarten's till dusk; they then set out for the Warby Ranges.

They travelled all night and passed through North Wangaratta and crossed the Ovens River, and pushed on for the Warby Ranges.

They had run out of meat, and shot a sheep to replenish their meat supply. At the foot of Warby Ranges Kennedy's pack-horse knocked up and was left behind.

The Kellys peacefully camped on the top of the Warby Ranges, resting themselves and their horses for some days. While reconnoitering it happened one day that they saw a party of policemen led by a local blackfellow following their tracks. As soon as they came to the discarded pack-horse the Kellys fired a rifle shot to attract the attention of the police. The police distinctly heard the shot, and immediately turned back, and made for Wangaratta at top speed. When they reported on this expedition, the police laid all the blame on the blacktracker. The tracker, they said, was too cowardly to proceed. He actually ordered the police to go first and "catchem Kelly." The police resented such orders and the refusal of the blacktracker to go on to capture the Kellys. The police, anyhow, considered the present was not the proper time to take the "flashness" out of the Kellys. The Kellys started from Warby Ranges and went back to their home at Greta. Their horses had had a very bad spin up to the present, and they themselves were worn out for want of sleep, and, not knowing that the demoralised state of the police affected the officers more than the men, they decided to take no unnecessary risks. They accordingly decided to discard their horses and move about at night on foot, and rest and sleep in the standing crops by day. The police had received information that the Kellys would be likely to come to Frank Harty's farm, near Winton.

The Kellys also had information that the Police intended to interfere with Harty, who had offered to bail Mrs. Kelly out. The Kellys took up their position in Harty's crop to defend this farmer from the vindictiveness of the police.

The police took up their position on the hill near Harty's house.

Harty knew the Kellys would protect him, and could afford to display his independence; but he did not know they were in his crop. And the police did not know that the Kellys were watching them. They (the police) were not afraid of Harty. The scene resembled the cats in the crop watching the mice on the hill. After a few days the police retired from Harty's, and went back to Benalla to recuperate, after their strenuous efforts to capture the outlaws. When some one of the Kelly relatives asked Ned Kelly why he didn't pop over the police who were watching Harty's house he replied: "So long as the police keep within the laws of truth and decency, he would not shoot at them, but if the police start shooting, or refuse to obey orders when called upon by him to surrender, then he was prepared to shoot, and shoot to kill. As long as the police behave themselves, and keep out of their way, they (the Kellys) would not hurt them." The night following the withdrawal of the police from Harty's, the Kellys moved towards Benalla, to the crop of another farmer. The weather was pleasant and the crops were on the turn. The four outlaws were very comfortable, watching train loads of police passing up and down the railway line. Next day the owner of the crop happened along, and suddenly came on the Kellys in his crop. He was taken aback, but quickly recovering his presence of mind, said: "Oh! So its here ye are, boys," and hurriedly added, "I was just having a look to see when the bit of crop would be ripe enough to cut; but," he continued, "I won't touch it while you boys are here."

Ned Kelly, as spokesman for the outlaws, thanked the farmer for his interest in their safety. "We're shifting from here to-night," said Ned, "so that you may go ahead with the harvest when the crop is fit to cut."

No. 1. Wombat Ranges, where Troopers were shot.

6
A DECLARATION OF WAR

THE report of the encounter in the Wombat Ranges and the deaths of valuable members of the police force soon travelled throughout Australia, and created considerable sensation. It caused the immediate passing by the Berry Government of an Outlawry Act, under which it became lawful for any individual to shoot and destroy the four bushrangers. This Act also provided penalties for any person who harboured the outlaws or withheld information concerning them from the authorities. This was a declaration of war.

Having now been definitely made outlaws, the Kellys arranged a programme, the first item on which was to be a "hold up" of the National Bank at Euroa. Mounted on four splendid horses, they set forth, and arrived en route at Younghusband's Faithful Creek station, some four miles from Euroa. The manager, Mr. McCauley, was not present on their arrival, but they made themselves known to housekeeper, Mrs. Fitzgerald, to whom they gave assurances of safety for herself and any others who allowed them to proceed unmolested. They then commenced to intern all the station hands in the storeroom, repeating their assurances, and Byrne was posted as a "prisoners' guard." Addressing their captives, Ned Kelly informed them if anyone attempted to escape, "Steve Hart and Dan will shoot you down like rabbits." This intimidating threat was an unfortunate one, as later events showed. Actually neither Dan Kelly nor Steve Hart was of a "bloodthirsty" disposition, and there is no record to substantiate these words of their leader, but these words were seized upon by the police, and, on their subsequent publication, created an impression in the public mind which was untrue, unfair and unjust.

During the afternoon, a local farmer, who had been to Euroa for men to bind his crop, was passing the homestead. He was stopped and introduced to Ned Kelly by Mr. Fitzgerald. Ned Kelly explained to the farmer that he would have to join the other prisoners. "Oh, I don't mind, but my boy, a lad of 14 years and Paddy Burke are down at the hut, and they'll be expecting me home." "We'll soon settle that," said Ned Kelly, "we'll go and bring them up here where they'll be safe." "Very good", replied the farmer, and he went away with Ned Kelly and Steve Hart to the hut, which was but a short distance away. They found Paddy Burke at the hut, but the boy was away. Burke said he thought the boy had gone down to the creek for a swim. They all went to the creek, where they found the lad, and his father told him to accompany them up to the station. The lad eyed the two strangers, Ned Kelly and Steve Hart, whom he believed to be two men his father had brought from Euroa to assist in binding the crop. He did not like the look of these two for "binders." That boy, to-day a man in the sere and yellow leaf, says he enjoyed the novelty of the whole affair. No one was afraid, but all were under some restraint excepting the womenfolk, who were allowed the free range of the premises.

Late in the afternoon Mr. McCauley returned, and was formally introduced by the station foreman, Mr. Fitzgerald, to Ned Kelly and his associates. He, too, was placed under surveillance, although he was allowed more freedom about the house than the other captives.

Later still, a hawker named Gloster and his assistant, Beecroft, came on the scene. The former was ordered to join the party in the store. He refused, and made a run for his waggon, in which he had left his revolver. The Kellys did not want a disturbance; it would interfere with their plans regarding the Euroa Bank. Ned Kelly followed the hawker and caught him as he was climbing into his waggon for his revolver, and dragged him down. He and his assistant, Beecroft, a youth of about 18 years, were immediately compelled to join the prisoners in the storeroom.

The Kellys selected new suits from the hawker's stock, as they desired to be very respectably dressed when they set out for the bank of Euroa. They offered Gloster money for these outfits, but he refused to take it.

Ned Kelly conversed freely with the prisoners, and related incident of cruelty and persecution his family had been subjected to by the police, and he seems to have convinced the majority that he and his brother had been goaded to take to the bush in order to prevent the extinction of their family. After sunset the prisoners were allowed out for a spell in the fresh air, prior to retiring for the night. The outlaws took it in turns to keep watch over the prisoners, and against any attempt to poison them — there was a reward of £4000 on their heads — and carefully avoided tasting any food until some of their prisoners had first partaken of it.

During an allusion to their fight with the police on the Wombat Ranges, Ned Kelly emphasised the fact that they had met the police in a fight for life. The police had sought them to take them back to Mansfield dead or alive. They had killed three of the four policemen in a fair fight. The one who had surrendered and was disarmed, they permitted to escape.

Next morning, Dec. 10, 1878, the Kellys were about early. They temporarily released the captives from the storeroom, and all hands had breakfast together, except the outlaws, who observed their usual caution and went to breakfast two at a time. After breakfast a party of sportsmen approached the station in a spring cart driven by a local resident named Casement. The sportsmen were Messrs. Dudley and McDougal. Mr. Tennant, another member of the party, was on horseback. Seeing them approach, Ned Kelly mounted his horse and rode to meet them, and told them to turn back, as the station was "held up." As the party descended from the cart, Ned Kelly accused Casement of being "Ned Kelly," and of having stolen the horse and spring cart. This evoked an outburst of indignation from Mr. Casement and his companions. Mr. Casement believed Ned to be a constable, and Mr. Dudley asked on what authority they were thus accused. "We have not stolen the cart, we are all honest men. I'll report you to your officer"! In giving evidence at Beechworth in 1880, Mr. Dudley said that Tennant, who was a Scotchman, came up on horseback and asked: "What is the matter, Harry?" Dudley replied, "The Kellys are about." Tennant said, "Aye, mon, get up and load your guns." When Kelly showed the handcuffs, however, his visitors, although wrathful, submitted and were put into the storeroom, Mr. Dudley, before internment, again loudly announcing that he would report Ned Kelly to his superior officer for his conduct as an officious constable. When they reached the storeroom Ned Kelly said to Stevens, the groom, "Tell the gentlemen who I am." Stevens thereupon introduced "Mr. Ned Kelly and his party."

THE ROBBERY AT THE EUROA BANK

The plan of the outlaws was to obtain a cheque for a minor sum from Mr. McCauley, and arrive at the bank at 3 p.m., just about closing time. This they secured, and, leaving a guard over the station prisoners, they proceeded to Euroa. Ned Kelly drove the shooting party's cart, Steve Hart, and Beecroft, drove the hawker's wagon, and Dan Kelly rode on horseback.

They reached the bank a few minutes before three o'clock. Hart drove the hawker's waggon into the yard of the bank. This was not noticed by passers, because the hawker himself used frequently to drive in there. Leaving the waggon, Hart entered the bank from the back. As he was coming in he met the housemaid, Miss Maggie Shaw, with whom he had been at school in Wangaratta. She said, "Hello Steve!" He replied, "Mum's the word." This meeting was subsequently cited and established Hart's complicity in the adventure. Ned Kelly left the spring cart on the street outside the bank. He entered the bank just on the stroke of three o'clock, and, holding Mr. McCauley's cheque in his hand, carefully closed the bank door. Dan Kelly kept guard outside. Ned Kelly observed the entry of Steve Hart into the bank, and he then withdrew the cheque he was presenting, and presented his revolver at the astonished official. The bank officials were commanded to throw up their hands, and, being completely taken by surprise, promptly complied.

The bank revolvers having been secured, Ned Kelly asked Mr. Scott, the manager, if there were any women on the premises. Mr. Scott informed him that there were only Mrs. Scott and the housemaid. Ned Kelly inquired if Mrs. Scott was in a delicate state of health — he did not want to give her a fright if she was — and, receiving a negative reply, he then requested that Mrs. Scott be asked to come in. Mrs. Scott was called in, and introduced to Ned Kelly, who assured her solemnly that her husband's life was in her hands. If she gave an alarm her husband would be shot, but otherwise no harm would befall him. The manager and the clerks were then required to hand over all the cash in the bank, and Ned Kelly put the money into a sugar bag. Subsequently Mr. Scott produced some whisky, and they drank to the success of their daring venture. Ned Kelly then requested Mr. Scott that, as he now had no money in the bank, and as it was after banking hours, he and his family should come out to Faithful's Creek, and have tea with them, the Kellys. He told Mr. Scott to put his horse in the buggy and accompany him and his mates to Faithful's Creek. It was quite a procession which then set out from Euroa to the station, Dan Kelly, with Beecroft, driving the hawker's waggon, then Mrs. Scott and family in the manager's buggy, Ned Kelly with Mr. Scott and Miss Shaw in the spring cart, and Steve Hart on horseback following in the rear.

As Steve Hart was about to mount upon the horse the local policeman passed him. Steve said, "Good day," but the constable only grunted, and Steve felt somewhat annoyed.

Arrived safely at Faithful Creek Station, tea was served. The prisoners appeared to regard the Kellys with amazement and admiration on account of their success in robbing the bank and bringing the manager and staff with them to join the party. So impressed was Mrs. Scott with the quiet and manly bearing of Ned Kelly that she remarked during the meal: "Surely, Mr. Kelly, you don't say that you are the man who has been outlawed?" To this Ned Kelly replied that he was outlawed on account of the perjured evidence of Constable Fitzpatrick, who was responsible for his mother being awarded three years in gaol on a charge of which she was entirely innocent, adding, for the information of his listeners, an outline of the persecution to which, he said, he and his family had been subjected by the authorities. It is worthy of note that wherever Ned Kelly explained to the public how his people had been persecuted by the police he made very many friends.

Before bidding farewell, the outlaws gave an exhibition of horsemanship, which entertained and surprised their prisoners, and, after a strict injunction not to leave the station for three hours, the Kellys, with the £2000 they had secured, left Faithful Creek, and making their way across the hilly country, arrived in Greta Ranges long before daylight next morning, December 11, 1878. They came to their "Post Office," a marked tree stump, and placing upon it a projecting stick, thus indicated to their friends that they had returned from Euroa, and were camped a couple of hundred yards away in the direction towards which the stick pointed. Early on the same morning Mrs. Skillion arrived at the "Post Office," and taking the direction thus indicated, found the outlaws once more "at home". The prisoners, at Faithful's Creek, were so favourably impressed with Ned Kelly and his companions that they remained five hours before attempting to leave the station.

From his temporary sanctuary Ned Kelly, three days later, issued the following letter to a member of the Legislative Assembly (Mr. Cameron):—

December 14.

Dear Sir, — Take no offence if I take the opportunity of writing a few lines to you wherein I wish to state a few remarks concerning the case of Trooper Fitzpatrick against Mrs. Kelly, W. Skillion and W. Williamson, and to state the facts of the case to you. It seems to me impossible to get any justice without I make a statement to someone that will take notice of it, as it is no use me complaining about anything that the police may choose to say or swear against me, and the public, in their ignorance and blindness, will undoubtedly back them up to their utmost. No doubt, I am now placed in very peculiar circumstances, and you might blame me for it, but if you know how I have been wronged and persecuted you would say I cannot be blamed. In April last an information was (which must have come under your notice) sworn against me for shooting Trooper Fitzpatrick, which was false, and my mother, with an infant baby, and brother-in-law and another neighbour, were taken for aiding and abetting and attempting to murder him, a charge of which they are as truly innocent as the child unborn. During my stay in the King River I run in a wild bull, which I gave to Lydicher, who afterwards sold him to Carr and he killed him for beef. Some time afterwards I was told I was blamed for stealing this bull from Whitty. I asked Whitty on Moyhu racecourse why he blamed me for stealing his bull, and he said he had found the bull and he never blamed me for stealing him. He said it was — — — (the policeman) who told him that I stole the bull. Some time afterward I heard that I was blamed for stealing a mob of calves from Whitty and Farrell, which I never had anything to do with, and along with this and the other talk, I began to think that they wanted something to talk about. Whitty and Burns not being satisfied with all the picked land on King River and Bobby Creek, and the run of their stock on the Certificate ground free, and no one interfering with them, paid heavy rent for all the open ground, so as a poor man could not keep his stock, and impounded every beast they could catch, even off Government roads. If a poor man happened to leave his horse or a bit of poddy calf outside his paddock, it would be impounded. I have known over sixty head of horses to be in one day impounded by Whitty and Burns, all belonging to poor men of the district. They would have to leave their harvest or ploughing and go to Oxley, and then perhaps not have money enough to release them, and have to give a bill of sale or borrow the money, which is no easy matter, and along with all this sort of work, — — —, the policeman, stole a horse from George King (my step-father) and had him in Whitty and Jeffrey's paddock until he left the force, and this was the cause of me and my step-father, George King, stealing Whitty's horses and selling them to Baumgarten and those other men. The pick of them was sold at Howlong, and the rest was sold to Baumgarten, who was a perfect stranger to me, and, I believe, an honest man. No man had anything to do with the horses but me and George King. William Cooke, who was convicted for Whitty's horses, had nothing to do with them, nor was he ever in my company at Peterson's, the German's, at Howlong. The brand was altered by me and George King, and the horses were sold as straight. Any man requiring horses would have bought them the same as those men, and would have been potted the same, and I consider Whitty ought to do something towards the release of those innocent men, otherwise there will be a collision between me and him, as I can to his satisfaction prove I took J. Welshe's black mare and the rest of the horses, which I will prove to him in next issue, and after those had been found and the row being over them, I wrote a letter to Mr. S., of Lake Rowan, to advertise my horses for sale, as I was intent to sell out.

I sold them afterwards at Benalla and the rest in New South Wales, and left Victoria, as I wished to see certain parts of the country, and very shortly afterwards there was a warrant for me, and as I since hear, the police sergeants Steele, Straughan and Fitzpatrick, and others, searched the Eleven Mile and every other place in the district for me and a man named Newman, who had escaped from the Wangaratta police for months before April 15, 1878 . . . I heard how the police used to be blowing that they would shoot me first and then cry surrender. How they used to come to the house when there was no one there but women, and Superintendent (Brook) Smith used to say, "See all the men I have out to-day. I will have as many more to-morrow, and blow him into pieces as small as paper that is in our guns," and they used to repeatedly rush into the house, revolver in hand, and upset milk dishes and empty the flour out on the ground, and break tins of eggs, and throw the meat out of the cask on to the floor, and dirty and destroy all the provisions, which can be proved, and shove the girls in front of them into the rooms like dogs, and abuse and insult them. Detective Ward and Constable Hayes took out their revolvers and threatened to shoot the girls and children whilst Mrs. Skillion was absent, the eldest being with her.

The greatest murderers and ruffians would not be guilty of such an action. This sort of cruelty and disgraceful conduct to my brothers and sisters, who had no protection, coupled with the conviction of my mother and those innocent men, certainly make my blood boil, as I don't think there is a man living could have the patience to suffer what I did. They were not satisfied with frightening and insulting my sisters night and day, and destroying their provisions, and lagging my mother with an infant baby and those innocent men, but should follow me and my brother, who was innocent of having anything to do with any stolen horses into the wilds, where he had been quietly digging and doing well, neither molesting nor interfering with anyone, and I was not there long, and on October 25 I came on the track of police horses between Table Top and the bogs, and crossed them and went to Emu Swamp, and returning home I came on more police tracks making for our camp. I told my mates, and me and my brother went out next morning and found police camped at the shingle hut, with long firearms, and we came to the conclusion our doom was sealed unless we could take their firearms. As we had nothing but a gun and a rifle if they came on us at our work or camp, we had no chance only to die like dogs. As we thought our country was woven with police, and we might have a chance of fighting them, if we had firearms, as it generally takes forty to one. We approached the spring as close as we could get to the camp, the intervening space being clear. We saw two men at the log. They got up, and one took a double-barrel fowling piece and one drove the horses down and hobbled them against the tent, and we thought there was more men in the tent, those being on sentry. We could have shot these two men without without speaking, but not wishing to take life, we waited. McIntyre laid the gun against the stump, and Lonigan sat on the log. I advanced, my brother Dan keeping McIntyre covered.

I called on them to throw up their hands. McIntyre obeyed and never attempted to reach for his gun or revolver. Lonigan ran to a battery of logs and put his head up to take aim at me, when I shot him, or he would have shot me, as I knew well. I asked who was in the tent. McIntyre replied, "No one." I approached the camp and took possession of their revolvers and fowling piece, which I loaded with bullets (swandrops) instead of shot. I told McIntyre I did not want to shoot him or any other man that would surrender. I explained Fitzpatrick's falsehood, which no policeman can be ignorant of. He said he knew Fitzpatrick had wronged us, but he could not help it. He said he intended to leave the police force on account of his bad health. His life was insured. The other two men (Joe Byrne and Steve Hart), who had no firearms, came up when they heard the shot fired, and went back to our camp for fear the police might call there in our absence and surprise us on our arrival. My brother went back to the spring, and I stopped at the log with McIntyre. Kennedy and Scanlan came up. McIntyre said he would get them to surrender if I spared their lives as well as his. I said I did not know either him, Scanlan or Kennedy, and had nothing against them, and would not shoot any of them if they gave up their firearms and promised to leave the force, as it was the meanest billet in the world.

They are worse than cold-blooded murderers and hangmen. He said he was sure they would never follow me any more. I gave him my word that I would give them a chance. McIntyre went up to Kennedy, Scanlan being behind with a rifle and revolver. I called on them to throw up their hands. Scanlan slewed his horse round to gallop away, but turned again, and, as quick as thought, fired at me with the rifle, and was in the act of firing again when I shot him. Kennedy alighted on the off side of his horse and got behind a tree and opened hot fire. McIntyre got on Kennedy's horse and galloped away. I could have shot him if I chose, as he was right against me, but rather than break my word I let him go. My brother advanced from the spring. Kennedy fired at him and ran, and he found neither of us was dead. I followed him. He got behind another tree and fired at me again. I shot him in the armpit as he was behind the tree. He dropped his revolver and ran again, and slewed round, and I fired with the gun again and shot him through the right chest, as I did not know that he had dropped his revolver and was turning to surrender. He could not live, or I would have let him go. Had they been my own brothers I could not help shooting them or else lie down and let them shoot me, which they would have done had their bullets been directed as they intended them. But as for handcuffing Kennedy to a tree, or cutting his car off, or brutally treating any of them, it is a cruel falsehood. If Kennedy's ear was cut off, it has been done since. I put his cloak over him and left as honourable as I could, and if they were my own brothers I could not be more sorry for them. With the exception of Lonigan, I did not begrudge him what bit of lead he got, as he was the flashest, meanest man that I had any account against, for him, Fitzpatrick, Sergeant Whelan, Constable Day, and King, the bootmaker, once tried to handcuff me at Benalla, and when they could not Fitzpatrick tried to choke me.

Lonigan caught me by the . . . and would have killed me, but was not able. Mr. McInnes came up, and I allowed him to put the handcuffs on when the police were bested. This cannot be called wilful murder, for I was compelled to shoot them in my own defence, or lie down like a cur and die. Certainly their wives and children are to be pitied, but those men came into the bush with the intention of shooting me down like a dog, and yet they know and acknowledge I have been wronged. And is my mother and her infant baby and my poor little brothers and sisters not to be pitied? More so, who has got no alternative, only to put up with brutal and unmanly conduct of the police, who have never had any relations or a mother, or must have forgot them. I was never convicted of horse-stealing.

I was once arrested by Constable Hall and 14 more men in Greta, and there was a subscription raised for Hall by persons who had too much money about Greta in honour of Hall arresting "Wild" Wright and Gunn. Wright and Gunn were potted, and Hall could not pot me for horse stealing, but with the subscription money he gave £20 to James Murdock, who has recently been hung in Wagga Wagga, and on Murdock's evidence I was found guilty of receiving, knowing to be stolen, which J. Wright, W. Ambrose, J. Ambrose, T. H. Hatcher, and W. Williamson and others can prove. I was innocent of knowing the mare to be stolen, and I was once accused of taking a hawker by the name of McCormack's horse to pull another hawker named Ben Gould out of a bog . . . At the time I was taken by Hall and his 14 assistants, therefore I dare not strike any of them, as Hall was a great cur, and as for Dan, he never was tried for assaulting a woman. Mr. Butler (P.M.) sentenced him (Dan) to three months without the option of a fine for wilfully destroying property, a sentence which there is no law to uphold, and yet they had to do their sentence, and their prosecutor, Mr. D. Goodman, since got four years for perjury concerning the same property. The Minister of Justice should inquire into this respecting their sentence, and he will find a wrong jurisdiction given by Butler, P.M., on October 19, 1877, at Benalla, and these are the only charges was ever proved against either of us, therefore we are falsely represented. The reports of bullets having been fired into the bodies of the troopers after death is false, and the coroner should he consulted. I have no intention of asking mercy for myself of any mortal man, or apologising, but wish to give timely warning that if my people do not get justice, and those innocents released from prison, and the police wear their uniform, I shall be forced to seek revenge of everything of the human race for the future. I will not take innocent life, if justice is given, but as the police are afraid or ashamed to wear their uniform, therefore every man's life is in danger, as I was outlawed without cause, and cannot be no worse, and have but once to die, and if the public do not see justice done I will seek revenge for the name and character which has been given to me and my relations, while God gives me strength to pull a trigger.

The witness which can prove Fitzpatrick's falsehood can be found by advertising, and if this is not done immediately, horrible disasters shall follow. Fitzpatrick shall be the cause of greater slaughter to the rising generation than St. Patrick was to the snakes and toads of Ireland, for had I robbed, plundered, ravished and murdered everything I met, my character could not be painted blacker than it is at present but, thank God, my conscience is as clear as the snow in Peru, and as I hear a picked (packed) jury, amongst which was a discharged sergeant of police, was empanelled on the trial (of Mrs. Kelly), and David Lindsay, who gave evidence for the Crown, is a shanty keeper, having no licence, and is liable to a heavy fine, and keeps a book of information for the police, and his character needs no comment, for he is capable of rendering Fitzpatrick any assistance he required for conviction, as he could be broke any time Fitzpatrick chose to inform on him, I am really astonished to see Members of the Legislative Assembly led astray by such articles as the police, for while an outlaw reigns their pocket swells: "'Tis double pay and country girls"; by concluding, as I have no more paper unless I rob for it, if I get justice, I will cry a go. For I need no lead or powder to revenge my cause, and if words be louder, I will oppose your laws. With no offence (remember your railroads), and a sweet good-bye from

EDWARD KELLY, a forced outlaw.

This letter was addressed to Mr. Cameron, M.L.A., on December 14, 1878, and its most striking feature is the appeal the outlaws make for a fair deal. He asks nothing for himself, and frankly admits how he got even with Whitty and others by stealing and selling their horses. Another feature of the letter is the charitable outlook of the outlaw in pleading the cause of the "poor man.

In Ned Kelly's letter to Mr. Cameron, as reproduced in this chapter, a policeman is referred to in two places, although his name is omitted.
1) "He said it was ——— (the policeman) who told him that I stole the bull."
2) "along with all this sort of work, ———, the policeman, stole a horse from George King" In both instances the name missing is "Farrell".

7
THE POLICE IN PURSUIT

SUPT. C. H. Nicolson was instructed by Captain Standish on Monday, October 28, to proceed to Benalla, as news had come through of the shooting of Sergeant Kennedy and Constables Lonigan and Scanlan. He said he found the people at Benalla, and, in fact, all along the line, in a state of great excitement. Next day, Tuesday, 29th October 1878, he despatched Supt. Sadleir to Mansfield, the scene of the tragedy.

As they had no idea that Joe Byrne and Steve Hart had joined the Kellys, the police concluded that the two men reported by McIntyre as being with Ned and Dan Kelly were William King and Charles Brown.

On 2nd November the police received a report that the Kellys had been seen three days before (31/10/78) between Barnawartha and the Murray River. Detective Kennedy, with a part of police, searched this locality, and were afterwards joined by Supt. C. H. Nicolson, who remained searching that district until the 5th November. On this date the Kellys were "at home" on Eleven-Mile Creek.

On the 4th November the police received a report that the Kellys had passed under the bridge at Wangaratta, and a party of police, under Inspector Brooks Smith, went in pursuit. He secured the services of a local blackfellow to track the Kellys. This tracker followed the outlaws' tracks towards the Warby Ranges, and when nearing the foot of the ranges the party came upon a horse that had evidently knocked up — it was Sergeant Kennedy's pack-horse. As the police crowded around this horse a report of a rifle or gun was heard as coming from the top of the ranges. The blacktracker said the Kellys were "up thar; you go catchen Kelly." But Inspector Brooks Smith decided to return to Wangaratta with the pack-horse, and when reporting this incident the inspector stated that, as the blacktracker was too frightened to proceed, they (the police) had no option but to retreat with the "prize" pack-horse, and report at Wangaratta. The police were very angry with this blacktracker for the cowardice he displayed in refusing to go forward and capture the Kellys. If he would go on, they felt sure of capturing the outlaws, although further tracking was unnecessary, as the Kellys already made their presence known by discharging a rifle. By the time this report was sent to headquarters the outlaws were resting in Frank Harty's crop.

On November 6th a report came to the police headquarters that the Kellys had been seen near Sheep Station Creek, near Sebastopol. Next day Captain Standish, Chief Commissioner of Police; Supt. C. H. Nicolson, assistant C.C. of police; and Supt. J. Sadleir went to Beechworth, and with a party of police and civilians, all mounted, and numbering about fifty, intended to sneak noiselessly upon the outlaws, and take them asleep in one of the houses in the vicinity.

In giving his evidence on oath in reference to this incident, Supt. C. H. Nicolson said: "Capt. Standish and Mr. Sadleir were very much engaged in talking. I could not hear what they said, there was a confounded noise. I saw the men riding together, and I devoted myself to knocking the men into some order. I went to the various sub-officers and asked, 'Where are your men?' and I said, 'Keep them together.' That is how I occupied myself."

Question: "You desire us to understand that you were interfered with, and men brought there without your knowledge who should not have been?"

Supt. Nicolson: "No, I merely mention that as an instance. I am coming to something more important. I have been attacked about this, and I intend to tell you what I saw. We then came to a hut called 'Sherritt's,' and, as related by Captain Standish, the hut was empty. I would not mention such a thing as I am going to mention except that insinuations had been made that I had almost avoided meeting the Kellys — it was insinuated yesterday. I knew nothing about what was going. I was riding by myself with two or three men near me, when Mr. Sadleir came up and said to me: 'Now, Mr. Nicolson, this is the house of the Sherritts. You will do this and you will do that, and the outlaws are said to be here.' I turned to Mr. Sadleir and said: 'You send some men into that paddock, and see the men do not escape by the back', and said to two or three men about me (mentioning their names), 'Come along with me'. And I galloped with those men to the hut at full speed. I found the cavalcade was very noisy — we were expecting to get these men asleep — and called to the men to come with me, and I galloped to the front."

Question: "Were you under his (Captain Standish) control, or were you not?"

Supt. Nicolson: "I received no instructions from Captain Standish."

Question: "Who was in charge — you, Captain Standish, or Mr. Sadleir on that morning?"

Supt. Nicolson: "I never thought of taking charge. I left the matter with Captain Standish and Mr. Sadlier."

Question: "Was Mr. Sadlier in charge up to that point?"

Supt. Nicolson: "Yes. I did not interfere with him, as this was his information that we were out upon."

Question: "At what distance could a man have heard the noise of the police you spoke of?"

Supt. Nicolson: "One man told me afterwards that he heard us a mile away."

Question: "Did this whole body of men remain after you searched the hut?"

Supt. Nicolson: "After searching three huts the men dispersed."

This ended the fiasco which was known afterwards as "Rat's Castle" or "The Charge of Sebastopol."

The Kellys were to be taken while asleep in a hut, yet the morale of the police was so seriously affected that nothing less than a cavalcade of 50 horsemen was considered necessary to make sure of their capture. If the Kellys had been in any of the huts visited, the thundering noise of 50 horsemen travelling over stony country would have been sufficient to give the outlaws a most effective alarm. This expedition was the laughing-stock of the whole countryside. Captain Standish, who was over all as Chief Commissioner of Police, was in doubt as to his position in this big failure, because Supt. C. H. Nicolson was in charge of the pursuit of the Kellys. Then, again, Supt. C. H. Nicolson, who was in charge of the Kelly hunt, was in doubt, because Mr. John Sadleir was superintendent in charge of that particular district. Each of the three heads said he left the leadership of this fiasco to the other two.

The next move by Standish, Sadleir and Nicolson was to try and catch the outlaws by persuading the friends of the latter to betray them. Supt. Sadleir was informed who Aaron Sherritt was, and that he (Aaron Sherritt) was likely to know all about the Kellys.

Superintendent Sadleir on oath said: "I spoke to him (Aaron Sherritt), and asked him just to do what he could to assist us, and make certain promises which I forgot. I was a stranger to him, and he was not satisfied with my authority. I then called, I think, first to Mr. Nicolson and asked him to come and speak with him, and I think he was still uncertain about whether we had any authority. I then told him of Captain Standish, and I asked Captain Standish to speak to him. I think we were out of hearing of the police standing around us, but they could see all that we were doing. He seemed to promise. I expected that he would do something; in fact, there was a promise to that effect from him. We came to an understanding. I do not know what the terms were. I think I was the first to speak to Aaron Sherritt. I am pretty sure of it."

Question: "Did Aaron Sherritt accompany you from the time you met him at Byrne's house?"

Supt. Sadleir: "We had searched Byrne's house when he turned up. We searched to see if any of the property of the murdered men was there; and when the whole thing was over, a light-looking, high-shouldered man walked in, and Strachan said, 'Here is the man that knows the Kellys well, and will be of use to you; he knows all that is going on.' And then I went and spoke to Sherritt; and as I have explained the matter went on to the end."

On November 11th the Kellys were reported as having been seen on that date crossing the railway at Glenrowan, going from Greta to Warby Ranges. Supt. Nicolson met Supt. Sadleir next day, the 12th, at Glenrowan. They had two black-trackers with them, in addition to a party of policemen.

This search is described by Supt. Sadleir on oath as follows:—

"We had one or two trackers with us. The tracks were perfectly plain, and the tracks took us to the foot of the ranges without any trouble. It will be a mile or two, altogether, where the tracks are still visible. Those trackers took us clean away from them; they left the tracks. . . . They took us off the tracks, and took us to a swampy ground, where there were thousands of tracks, where all the cattle of the neighborhood came to water, and we could not get the trackers back again to take up the tracks where they left them. I am perfectly satisfied that they were simply misleading us."

Question: "Were they (the trackers) actuated by a spirit of fear or sympathy?"

Supt. Sadleir: "They (the trackers) were actuated by the spirit of self-preservation, because they knew they would be the first to be shot. In fact, it was too much to ask them to lead you into a place where an ambush might be, and ask them to go first. Our police could not go first, because they would interfere with the tracks and obliterate everything, but these men would not show us — would not follow the tracks any further. We then had to strike out for ourselves independently of the blacks, and while waiting for luncheon a small party under Sergeant Steele, through some mistake of orders, got out of sight, and we could not pick them up again."

It would have been very unwise for the police to venture forward when nearing the outlaws, because they (the police) would interfere with the tracks. Apparently the "heads" thought it safer to retire from the search than run the risk of obliterating the tracks made by the Kellys. If the Kellys were close at hand the tracks were not wanted, so that the search ended, like others, in the police returning home safely.

On December 6 the Kellys were reported as having been seen at

Gaffney's Creek. The local Gaffney's Creek police, however, made inquiries, and could not find a trace.

By the time the police reached Euroa after the bank robbery the Kellys were at home at Eleven-Mile Creek, visiting again their friends and relatives about Greta. Shortly afterwards Supt. Nicolson gave up the Kelly hunt on account of ill-health, and was superseded by Supt. F. A. Hare.

The Kelly home at Eleven-Mile Creek, Kate Kelly (left) Ellen Kelly sitting down with her children. Supt. Hare (below).

4
THE SPY INDUSTRY

ON 12th December, 1878, Supt. Hare arrived at Benalla to succeed Supt. C. H. Nicolson, whose health broke down under the heavy strain which the pursuit of the Kellys entailed. Supt. Hare spent the first three or four weeks in going over the correspondence that had gone through the office, so as to make himself thoroughly conversant with what had been done by Mr. C. H. Nicolson.

Towards the end of December he had a good grip of the situation. The Kellys were as elusive as the rainbow as far as the police pursuit was concerned. Captain Standish, Supt. Hare, and Supt. Sadleir, after consultation, came to the conclusion that the best way to capture the outlaws was to arrest all those who had either favoured the Kellys or who had adversely commented on the actions and attitude of the police and the Government. And although no charge could be laid against these people, who were known to be active Kelly sympathisers, the Government, on the advice of Captain Standish, Supt. Hare and Supt. Sadleir, illegally and unlawfully deprived more than twenty freeman of their liberty, and in order to do so the Government, at the suggestion of the heads of the Police Department, violated one of the most cherished principles of civilised nations — the liberty of the subject. In giving evidence on oath Supt. Francis Augustus Hare is reported by the Government shorthand writers verbatim as follows:—

"The first month or so I did not go out with the search party. I remained at Benalla, and my time was fully taken up going about the district making inquiries and getting things in order. About this time all the sympathisers were arrested by the order of Captain Standish. We all acted together, Captain Standish, myself, and Mr. Sadleir. Captain Standish was there. He was in supreme command at the time. Those sympathisers gave us a great deal of trouble. I had to go some five or six or seven times to Beechworth every Friday afternoon, and remain there all day Saturday — sometimes all Sunday, because I could not get away on Sunday — applying for a remand, and fighting for it."

Question: "What was the nature of the annoyance the sympathisers gave which led to their arrest?"

Supt. Hare: "I will state first what we did with reference to the arrest of those men, and upon what information. All the responsible men in charge of different stations who had been a long time in Benalla — the detectives and officers — were all collected at Benalla by Captain Standish's orders. They (the different constables and officers and detectives) all went into a room, and were asked the names of the persons in the district whom they considered to be sympathisers. I had nothing to do with it, merely listening and taking down names that fell from the mouths of the men."

Question: "Who asked the questions?"

Supt. Hare: "The whole party, Captain Standish and Mr. Sadleir, and I myself asked some."

Question: "Did Captain Standish ask each constable: 'Whom do you consider a sympathiser in your district, and so on?'"

Supt. Hare: "Captain Standish, Mr. Sadleir, and myself asked that. I knew nothing about the sympathisers, but one man came forward and said, 'There is so and so Smith.' 'What did he do?' 'Well I know he is a useful friend of the Kellys. On one occasion I saw him follow us about.' Then we said, 'Put his name down.' Then the detectives knew a great many men, and they went through the same process of inquiry, and so we selected a certain number of names."
Question: "How many?"

Supt. Hare: "I should think about twenty. The Government were aware of the action we were taking, and it was with their consent we did all this. It was necessary for us to arrange to capture all the sympathisers in one day, because if we had not done so it would have been just as much difficulty in catching them as the Kellys; so it was done confidentially, and on a certain day all the men were arrested with but two or three exceptions. There was one case of a man, of the name of Ryan, of Lake Glenrowan. There were two brothers very much alike. We picked out one brother as being a great friend of the Kellys, and the two constables who went out to arrest this man saw what they thought to be the man, but it was really his brother, and when they found their mistake they let him go, he not knowing what was up; but, thinking there was something wrong, took a short cut, and they saw him galloping up to his brother, but the constables caught him before he got there. As to the cause of the arrest, it was found these sympathisers were annoying us in every possible way, watching every move we made. One or two men, I heard before I came up, were watching the police at all times. A man named Isaiah ('Wild') Wright was one."

Question: "Were there any remarks about either of them besides watching?"

Supt. Hare: "I was not there; I know this was the substance of the complaint."

When arresting the Ryan referred to at Lake Rowan Hotel, the police at first arrested Mr. John Ryan, who had only one leg and an artificial cork leg. The police discovered that their prisoner was not the man they wanted; he was the man with the cork leg. Constable Gibson took the one-legged prisoner's horse and rode three miles out to Joe Ryan's farm. He came upon Joe Ryan where the latter was burning off, and said to him, "Your brother John has met with a nasty accident; his horse fell with him and he is at the Lake Rowan Hotel." Mr. Joe Ryan hastily put the bridle on his horse, jumped on him, and, without changing his clothes, raced to the Lake Rowan Hotel. Constable Gibson kept up with him. When approaching the hotel Joe Ryan asked, "Where is my brother?" "In the bar parlour," replied Gibson, and Joe Ryan hastily tied his horse to the fence and rushed into the bar parlour. He saw a number of policemen there. His brother was amongst them. As soon as he entered the room one of the constables laid his hand on Joe Ryan's shoulder and said, "I arrest you as a sympathiser of the Kellys!" and Joe Ryan was handcuffed and put on a coach to be taken to Benalla. Just as the coach was about to start, one of the young men at the hotel mounted the step of the coach and wished Joe Ryan good luck. Constable Gibson cautioned the young man to come down, or he would kick his ——. Joe Ryan replied if he had the handcuffs off the police would not dare put a hand on his young friend, Mr. D. Wall.

Supt. Hare, continuing, said:—

"About five or six days before the Jerilderie robbery, Aaron Sherritt came to Benalla (that was the first time I had ever seen Aaron Sherritt), and asked to see Captain Standish. He was away from Benalla. I explained to Aaron who I was, and asked him what he wanted Captain Standish for. He said, 'I have some important information to give him and I wish to speak to him privately.' I told him Captain Standish would not be back that night. I led Aaron to believe I did not care to hear his news, but kept him engaged in conversation; I heard his name and knew who he was. Captain Standish informed me when he returned that he had never seen him either from the day that he spoke to him at the Sebastopol affair at Mrs. Byrne's, which Mr. Nicolson referred to. Some time after — about an hour — Sherritt said, 'I think I can trust you with my information'; and then he told me that on the previous afternoon, about two o'clock, Joe Byrne and Dan Kelly came to his selection. This is not Mrs. Sherritt's house; Aaron was not at that time living with his mother, he was living on his own selection; it was midway between Mrs. Sherritt's and Mrs. Byrne's. He said Joe Byrne came to him whilst he was working on his selection. He told me Joe Byrne jumped off his horse, and that he had always been his most intimate acquaintance; he said he came and sat down beside him; he had been his school fellow and with him in crime nearly all their lives; he said Dan Kelly was very suspicious, and would not get off his horse, and did not get near him, and he said they sat talking for a long time, and then asked him to join them, as they were going across the Murray, and intended going to Goulburn, in New South Wales, where the Kellys had a cousin. He said they urged him to go for a long time as a

scout. Sherritt never told me at that time that they were going to stick up a bank. He told me he refused to go with them, and after some pressing Joe Byrne said, 'Well, Aaron, you are perfectly right; why should you get yourself into this trouble and mix yourself up with us.' He said they were talking to him for about half an hour, but kept looking round and watching every move that was made. I do not remember any further conversation then. I told him not to go into the town. He was a remarkable looking man. If he walked down Collins-street everybody would have stared at him — his walk, his appearance and everything else was remarkable. I said, 'Be careful, now you are in Benalla, that you are not seen here; do not go into the town, but get some hotel near the railway station.' I gave him £2 for coming down to give this information."

Question: "Did he advise you to take any steps to prevent the Kellys going to New South Wales?"

Supt. Hare: "No; he merely came down to give the information to Captain Standish. He led me to believe they were going to leave the colony, and he gave me the brands of the two horses that the outlaws were riding — Joe Byrne was riding a magnificent grey horse, and the other a bay."

The Kellys had suspected that Aaron Sherritt was a police spy, and Joe Byrne and Dan Kelly called on him and gave him the story of a visit to Goulburn, New South Wales, after they had completed their plans to go to Jerilderie, which was in a very different direction. They pressed Aaron Sherritt to join them to test how deeply he was involved with the police. The Kellys were right, and their plans were well laid. The police spy put the police on the wrong trail. While the police were making all arrangements to intercept the Kellys from going to Goulburn, they went to Jerilderie without meeting any opposition.

Supt. Hare had established a party of police in a cave to watch Mrs. Byrne's house. The party was supposed to be unknown to anyone except to the police themselves. However, Mrs. Byrne had discovered them. She came across the police asleep in their camp, and Aaron Sherritt with them. She watched for more definite information, and was attacked by the police.

CHIVALRY OF THE POLICE

Of course, Supt. Hare and his men were not afraid of an unarmed old woman, and apparently they were sufficiently demoralised to attack her. The age of chivalry, as far as this police party was concerned, had gone.

Let Superintendent Hare tell what he and his men did. In giving evidence on oath Superintendent F. A. Hare said: "The sentry saw the old woman (Mrs. Byrne) again, and I called the sergeant, and said, 'We had better give her a fright.' The sentry saw her going right over us, up the range, to peer over a rock to look down upon us. I said to Senior-Constable Mills, who was with me, 'Go up and give the old woman a fright,' and he went up in the direction she was going, and hid behind a rock, where he could see her. She used to go crawling along like a rabbit, and only show her head over the rocks. At last she passed the rock where the constable was hidden, but he was on one side and she on the other. He followed her, and directly she got about a yard or two he gave a tremendous yell and jumped on her. The old woman lost her presence of mind, and almost fainted, and said, 'What? What? I am only looking for cattle,' and then she soon recovered her assurance and got impertinent, and said, 'I will get my son to shoot the whole lot of you'." (If the old lady had been armed, it is certain that Senior-Constable Mills would not have dared to jump on her. It was no wonder, therefore, that the police were severely censured for their failure to get in touch with the Kellys, and the success achieved by Supt. Hare and his party in avoiding the Kelly Gang was severely commented on by some of the Melbourne papers.)

Continuing his evidence on oath, Supt. Hare said: "The duty was arduous and great responsibility was thrown upon the leader. There was a great deal of work to be done by day and night. Some of the Melbourne papers used to describe our life as a pleasant picnic. I never asked the men to do anything that I did not share the work with them myself."

After describing the strenuousness of the police party's life, especially in packing up, Superintendent Hare continued on oath: "Once or twice we were very near them (the Kellys), but they managed to escape us in the mountains. In sending parties out in search of the gang my idea was that we should compel them to be continually on the watch; and I did not like to give them undisputed possession of the country in which they lived by keeping my men out of it. (This evidence admits a state of war.) The outlaws knew all our movements, although some of their sympathisers were in gaol, and our party could be tracked by themselves or friends for any distance. Ned Kelly knew all our camps in the Warby Ranges; and when going to Beechworth with one of the constables of my party, he (Ned Kelly) told him of all our movements, and described the men who used to go and look for the horses at daylight. He said there were two young men who used to go out and get the horses. Each man had his own work to do in the search party, and directly I called them in the morning the two used to go and catch the horses. One man was told off to light the fire and boil the billy of tea; the others had to pack up the swags — the hardest work we had. It took a long time to pack up everything we were carrying. Ned Kelly described the men and everything we did."

Supt. Hare's evidence gives the impression that the police parties were as cumbersome as a travelling circus, with all the packing up that had to be done.

Sometimes the police search parties or picnic parties used to put a great deal of energy into the tracking of another police party, and persuade themselves that they were right on the Kellys.

Here is an example given in evidence by Supt. Hare:— "I said to the men with me: 'To-morrow, instead of going down that river (the Ovens), there to where the tracks lead, let us work back to see where they come from.' They all agreed it was a very good idea (they knew they would be much safer, even on double pay, to see where the tracks came from), because we could tell whether they were the police, the outlaws, or the time they were made if we knew where they came from. Moses (Queensland tracker) picked up the tracks next morning, and went back again and worked them back, and when he got to a certain place, where there were two big stones, he said, 'Take off saddle here,' and I said, 'Where?' and he said, 'Here, one fellow saddle here, and one fellow there.' And we all jumped off our horses, and we found first an empty tin, such as we used to have preserved meat in — it was of the same description as we had — and then I found another one, and found a police strap, a Government strap, and the men came to the conclusion that it was Senior-Constable Kelly's party, because when I had removed him from the house where he had charge of I told him to go and form a camp in the mountains so that he could watch the house, and we gave them some of our provisions — he had none at the time. He came from Wangaratta without any provisions; and we recognised that these were the tins we had given him before. I subsequently made inquiries, and I found this was the very camp, and that he had gone down the tracks towards the Ovens, and had gone up that way to Wangaratta."

9
SYMPATHISERS

AFTER returning from the Euroa bank robbery, the first thing was to pay out some of the proceeds of the Euroa trip. The farmer who found the four young men in his crop, and who was willing to sacrifice his crop rather than expose the Kellys to the risk of being discovered, was not forgotten. He received a very practical mark of the outlaws' appreciation of his friendship. They moved about freely in the hills, and frequently visited their home. While in the ranges they indulged in rifle and revolver practice to such an extent that all of the four mates were first-class marksmen with any kind of firearm.

They saw, however, that twenty of their friends had been arrested and unlawfully kept in gaol without even a shadow of a *prima facie* case against them. But under war conditions ordinary laws were usually scrapped. The Kellys declared that the authorities were outlaws, and the latter returned the compliment.

Some of the men arrested as sympathisers were not known to the Kellys, but evidently they had been watching the police. These men had been deprived of the rights of an ordinary cat. It is said that a cat may look at a king, but evidently that privilege was not to be enjoyed by free men in a so-called free country. The friends of the Kellys may not look at the police.

When the twenty-odd men were arrested and imprisoned in Beechworth Gaol, the methods pursued by the police fell in for more and more public condemnation. Even those who had no time for the Kellys expressed themselves as being thoroughly disgusted with the methods of the police. Of these sympathisers some were not on friendly terms with others who were arrested, and the police canvassed the prisoners every day for news of the whereabouts of the Kellys. After being in prison for six weeks the police visited one of the most active and open of the sympathisers, and requested him to tell them (the police) where the Kellys were then hiding.

The prisoner replied: "I've been in this cell for the past six weeks, and I can give you my positive assurance that the Kellys are not here, and have not been here during the past six weeks."

The police were convinced. They knew by the prisoner's manner and earnestness that he has telling the truth; they therefore ceased to make further inquiries from the prisoners, and shortly afterwards the sympathisers were liberated.

The sympathisers were not a happy family. On one occasion "Wild" Wright and John McIlroy had a fight. Wright was leading on points, although his opponent was putting up a great fight, and when the former was about to deliver a deadly uppercut his hand was seized by one of the other sympathisers, who, while holding the "Wild" man's hand, struck him a very heavy blow on the jaw and laid him out, and the result was declared a draw.

It was the rule of the prison authorities to let the prisoners out in the big yard to wash and exercise. There was only one washing basin provided for all the sympathisers. The prisoners were let out in turn. Frank Harty was first out, then followed Ben Gould, with "Wild" Wright close on the latter's heels. Harty had just started to wash, while Ben Gould was getting ready. "Wild" Wright was a young man, 6ft. 1in. in height and weighing 13 ½ stone without any spare flesh, and possessed a thorough knowledge of the "noble art." Wright made it a practice to walk up to the washing basin, and, laying one hand on Harty's shoulder and the other on Ben Gould's, pushed them aside, saying, "Men first, dogs come last." This offensive treatment rankled, and both Harty and Gould decided to resent this insult in a practical fashion. They interviewed some of the leaders of the sympathisers with the request that they should not interfere when the two outraged prisoners turned on "Wild" Wright.

It was all arranged, and next day as Harty came out, followed by Ben Gould, they both got ready, stripping ostensibly to wash, but in reality to fight. "Wild" Wright, as before, pushed them aside with the usual remark, "Men first, dogs last." The other two flew at him. The suddenness of the attacked surprised Wright, who first made a hit at one and found the other attacking him from behind. He would then turn to the one behind him, then the other would deal Wright a blow from the rear. At last Wright got a heavy blow home on Harty and laid him out for a few seconds. He then caught Ben Gould by the right shoulder with his left hand, and dealt the latter a heavy blow on the ribs, knocking him yards away. In yielding to the force of "Wild" Wright's terrific blow Ben Gould left his shirt in the "wild" fellows hand. Ben sustained a fracture of three ribs and was therefore out of action. Wright then turned to Harty, who, nothing dismayed, was making a vigorous rear attack. The situation looked ugly for Harty, but the others then interfered and called time, just as the warders rushed on the scene. "Wild" Wright was afterwards placed in a separate division from the rest of the sympathisers.

As public opinion was getting more and more pronounced at the illegal and unlawful treatment that law-abiding citizens had been subjected to by the police, on April 22, 1879, all the remaining sympathisers were released from Beechworth Gaol without money, and without any compensation, or means of returning home except to walk and beg their way. Some of these men had to go 25, 30, and even 50 miles. Their prison experience made them extremely bitter against the police and very determined to help the Kellys more than ever.

They were held in gaol and treated as convicted criminals from January 2 to April 22, 1879, without any evidence being submitted against them.

BEECHWORTH COURT PROCEEDINGS, JANUARY 18, 1879. KELLY SYMPATHISERS.

Twenty Kelly sympathisers were presented at Beechworth Court on the following charge:—

"That they did cause to be given to Edward Kelly (adjudged and declared to be an outlaw) and his accomplices information tending to facilitate the commission by them of further crimes, contrary to the provisions of the Felons Apprehension Act 1878."

Mr. Bowman (for the Crown) said he did not ask for a committal, but merely for a remand, and the Crown had a right to this up to two terms (remands).

Mr. Albert Read (for some of the accused): "The whole affair," he said, "was making a laughing-stock of justice."

Mr. Bowman said he would withdraw the charges against Henry Perkins, Daniel Delaney, Wm. Woods, Robert Miller, Walter Stewart, and John Stewart, and these six men were accordingly discharged.

Mr. Zincke (for the other accused) was asked to agree to the remand of the accused, but notwithstanding that he emphatically refused they were remanded for eight days.

KELLY SYMPATHISERS BEFORE THE BEECHWORTH COURT

Report in *Ovens and Murray Advertiser*, February 11, 1879:—

On Isaiah ("Wild") Wright being put into the box:

Mr. A. Wyatt, P.M., said: "Wright, you and I have met before."

"Wild" Wright: "There is no fear of the Kellys killing me if I were out. You will not get the Kellys until Parliament meets, and Mrs. Kelly is let go, and Fitzpatrick lagged in her place. I could not have done much, as for four months before I was taken (arrested) the police had their eyes on me."

Mr. A Wyatt: "I WOULD GIVE YOU FAIR PLAY IF I COULD."

Wyatt was relieving Foster, who was on leave. Foster did whatever the police suggested, and Wyatt considered himself bound to do the same.

All the accused were again remanded for seven days.

Editorial in *O. and M. Advertiser,* 18/2/1879. — "The case of the men (Kelly sympathisers) now in Beechworth Gaol, however, is different . . . that they had been friends and even companions of the outlaws prior to the late outbreak, and that there is a strong probability that they would, if possible, aid the Kellys did opportunity offer. Others of them, however, are perfectly innocent of any such intention, and, as Mr. Zincke said in this particular, it is but fair that the wheat should be separated from the chaff, and these men set at liberty, unless it can be proved that there is aught against them. The proceedings last Saturday (15/2/79) were farcical in the extreme, and whilst we say by all means use every endeavour to capture the Kellys . . . still, in common fair play, let the men now confined on suspicion have a change of clearing themselves of an imputation, which, if not removed, must blast their lives and their reputation for ever."

The following week the sympathisers were again before the court. Four of them were formally discharged.

Supt. Furnell stated that one of the men, Joseph Ryan, had broken his leg. He intended to ask for his discharge, and requested Mr. Foster to visit him in gaol for that purpose.

Mr. Foster visited the gaol, and, on being discharged, Joseph Ryan was removed to the Beechworth Hospital.

Towards the end of March the Kelly sympathisers were again before the court, and Supt. Furnell applied for a further remand of seven days.

Mr. Bowman (on behalf of Mr. Zincke) said: "It was monstrous the way in which these arrest had been made, as according to what was being done they might have him (Mr. Bowman) arrested on the mere dictum of a police constable. Mr. Zincke had told him (Mr. Bowman) that when the accused Hart was let go he was almost apologised to; was told he had been arrested because his name was Hart, and had £1 given him. Not one reason had been assigned why these men were kept in confinement. It was easy enough to talk about Kelly sympathisers. No one hated Kelly crimes more than he did, and he protested against such a perversion of justice."

Kelly sympathisers were again remanded for seven days, notwithstanding Mr. Bowman's powerful appeal on their behalf.

APRIL 22, 1879

Kelly sympathisers were again presented before Mr. Foster, P.M. Supt. Furnell said he had been instructed to apply for a further remand of seven days on the ground that his witnesses were not available.

Mr. Bowman submitted that it was not the slightest use for Mr. Furnell to use such an argument as that, and he hoped that His Worship would act according to the dictation of his conscience.

Mr. Foster said: "I have felt it to be my duty to act independently, and to do that which, to my conscience, seems just and legal, and I do not feel justified in granting a further remand. I therefore discharge the accused."

All the sympathisers were then formally discharged.

It appears from the above statement that Mr. W. H. Foster, P.M., had not acted independently, and had not done that which seemed just and legal, from January 4 to April 22, during which period he deprived 20 law-abiding citizens of their liberty, and destroyed the confidence of at least 80 per cent. of the population in the Judiciary.

Some idea of the effect on the public mind of the foolish and illegal action of the authorities in keeping Kelly sympathisers in gaol for three months may be gathered from the following incident, which took place near Lake Rowan:—

The eight-year-old son of a well-to-do Lake Rowan farmer was sent on an errand to Benalla, a distance of 16 miles. The boy was mounted on a very fine pony, and when 12 miles from his destination he met an elderly gentleman, who, accompanied by his wife, was driving a buggy towards Yarrawonga. The following dialogue took place:—

Elderly Gentleman: How far are you going, sonny?

Boy: To Benalla, sir.

E.G.: That is a long way for a little boy like you to ride.

Boy: I have a first-class pony, and it will not take me long to get there.

E.G.: Are you afraid of the bushrangers?

Boy: The Kellys. They won't hurt me.

E.G.: If Ned Kelly meets you he will take that fine pony from you.

Boy: If Ned Kelly wants my pony I'll give it to him and walk to Benalla (12 miles).

TO JERILDERIE

The name of Jerilderie originated in quite a novel way. Mr. Gerald Wilson and his wife settled on the present site of the town, and the latter always referred to her loving husband as Jeril Dearie. She called her husband by no other name, so that the carriers and others gave their home the name of Jerildearies. When asked how far they were going to-day the invariable reply was, when going in that direction, "We'll go as far as Jerildearies." When the town sprang up it was called Jerilderie, a slight contraction of Jerildearie.

The New South Wales police had indulged a good deal of banter when referring to the inability of the Victorian police to capture the Kellys. If the Kellys were in New South Wales they said, they would soon have them in the prison cell. This was the usual boast of the average policeman over the border. The Kellys thought it a good thing just to show these gentlemen what they could not do with the Kellys. Plans were accordingly made for a visit to Jerilderie.

The Murray River was guarded by the united efforts of the border police of the two colonies, and the Kellys did not disturb them. They allowed the police to rest in peace. They heard of a crossing at Burramine, where they could swim their horses across, but they had no idea where to find a suitable landing place on the opposite bank. They sent their trusty providore, Tom Lloyd, to Burramine to discover the spot and report. He went, and not wishing to attract attention by making inquiries, he urged his black cob into the river and swam across, but the strength of the current carried him down the river and he could not land. He nearly got drowned. After a great struggle he succeeded in getting back to the Victorian side. He was defeated in his attempt to cross.

He then went up to Mr. P. Burke's Hotel, which was close at hand. He was wet through and told the publican that his name was Kain, and that he had sold a team of bullocks to a bullocky over the river, and wanted to go across to collect the cheque. The publican saw the prospect of a few pounds being spent in his hotel out of the bullocky's cheque, and being of a business turn of mind he said he would pull Mr. Kain across, and the latter could swim the horse behind the boat. Mr. Kain was very grateful. They both went down to the boat, which was secured to the root of a big gum-tree by a chain and padlock. The publican pulled to a recognised landing place, and Mr. Kain had no difficulty in getting his horse up the opposite bank.

Mr. Bourke said that if Mr. Kain would not be long away he would wait for him and pull him back again. Mr. Kain replied that he would not be absent for more than an hour. "Then I'll wait till you come back," said Mr. Bourke. Mr. Kain rode about a mile into New South Wales, then he dismounted and rested for some time. When the hour was nearly up he mounted his horse and returned to the river and found his good friend the publican waiting for him. Mr. Kain was pulled back again. He tied his horse up and assisted the publican to secure his boat to the root of the gum-tree.

They had a few drinks, and Mr. Kain returned to Greta, and reported to Ned Kelly how to cross the Murray without disturbing the rest or hurting the feelings of the border police of the two colonies.

"You'll have to take a small handsaw with you," said Mr. Kain, "in order to saw the root and get the chain free." Their horses were shod, and every detail of the expedition carefully attended to. A few days later the Kellys left Greta at dusk, and reached Burramine before daylight on Saturday morning, 8/2/79. They pulled across the Murray in two trips and swam their horses behind them. The swim refreshed the horses after their long ride.

They pushed on towards Jerilderie in the early morning and camped during the heat of the day, and reached Davidson's Hotel, two miles from Jerilderie, in good time for tea. Ned and Steve Hart rested off the track, while Dan and Joe went up to the hotel and had tea. They talked to the waitress and inquired if the Kellys were over there. They conveyed the impression that they (Dan and Joe) were afraid of bushrangers. "No, you need not be afraid of the Kellys, they won't hurt anyone," replied the waitress. With this assurance Dan and Joe settled down to a good meal. After tea they had a drink, and the waitress, who also served the drinks, sang one of the Kellys' songs and wished the Kellys, wherever they were, good luck:

We rob their banks,
We thin their ranks,
And ask no thanks
For what we do.

"How many police have you here in Jerilderie?" Dan inquired. "Only two, and they're enough — Senior-Constable Devine and Constable Richards."

Dan and Joe paid for their drinks and pushed on. Ned and Steve now rode up to the hotel, and they, as strangers, also made reference to their fear of the Kellys, but they were reassured by the waitress that the Kellys would not hurt them. They paid for their tea and pushed on to join Dan and Joe, who were waiting for them a little way along the road. The four horsemen reached the police station just as the coach was leaving Jerilderie for Deniliquin. As the coach was passing, one of the passengers was heard to say, "They might be the Kellys."

The police had just gone to bed. They had been very active during the afternoon and secured a drunk, whom they had placed in the lock-up.

Ned Kelly placed Dan, Joe and Steve in their positions around the police station. He then rode back towards Davidson's Hotel for about 250 yards. Ned turned his horse round and galloped on the metalled road up to the police station, yelling out. He pulled his horse up suddenly, and cried out excitedly, "Mr. Devine, there is a row at Davidson's Hotel; come down quick; there will be a murder there."

Ned talked excitedly. Richards jumped out of bed, and, pulling on his trousers, hurried around the house to the front, where Senior-Constable Devine had already appeared at the front door. The two policemen were now at the front together. Ned Kelly dismounted on the off side of his horse to show that he was not used to horses, while the police eagerly sought more enlightenment about the row at Davidson's.

Ned parleyed for a minute or two to see if there were any more police to come out. Then, when satisfied that there were only the two constables, he presented his revolver and announced the presence of "The Kellys." The other three had already closed in. The police surrendered and were handcuffed and taken inside. Ned Kelly inquired if there were any women inside. Devine replied that his wife and children were inside. Ned asked whether Mrs. Devine was in a delicate state of health, as he did not wish to give her a fright. Senior-Constable Devine replied in the negative.

Ned first secured the police firearms and ammunition, and placed the two policemen in the lock-up and brought the drunk out to sleep with them (the outlaws) in the dining-room.

These two constables were suspended from duty by Ned Kelly. Ned told Mrs. Devine that she had nothing to fear as long as she did not make a row or give an alarm. Mrs. Devine was required to show Ned over the house, so as to convince him that there were no more police in the place. Mrs. Devine was now told that she could go to bed to her children as usual.

Two of the Kellys slept while the other two kept guard. Early next morning, Sunday, Ned Kelly and Joe Byrne donned police uniform, ready for duty — the maintenance of order. They attended to their own and the police horses in the stables. Dan Kelly assisted Mrs. Devine to clean and dust the courthouse, which was on the opposite side of the street, and which would be used that Sunday by the priest who was due to celebrate Mass.

The Kelly Gang, photograph from 1878, produced as a postcard 1900.

10
ROBBING THE BANK AT JERILDERIE

MRS. Devine prepared breakfast for all hands, and in order to give the outside public the impression that the Devines had gone out for the day the blinds at the police station were drawn down, and everything appeared to be going on as usual. No one missed the police, Devine and Richards. People saw the new relieving police, Ned Kelly and Joe Byrne, and fine types of police they were, too. Dinner was served by Mrs. Devine, and everything in connection with "police protection" at Jerilderie seemed to the outside public to be in "order." During the afternoon Constable Richards was brought out of the lock-up, and, accompanied by the two new uniformed constables, Ned Kelly and Joe Byrne, patrolled the town. Richards was instructed to introduce Ned and Joe as visiting police to anyone to whom they chanced to speak. Ned took particular notice of the position of the Bank of New South Wales and Cox's Royal Hotel. The bank and the hotel were under the same roof.

It was fortunate that no one wanted police help that day, but if anything cropped up the four new constables were prepared to attend to it in an effective and intelligent fashion. They were determined to see that order was maintained. Senior-Constable Devine was kept in the lock-up. He was a determined character, and could not be trusted to "go quietly" if he were taken out to patrol the town. He was regarded as a man who would put up a fight and so disturb the peace as to imperil the success of the Kellys' mission to Jerilderie. For business reasons, therefore, it was considered safer for everybody to keep him in the lock-up.

The Kellys were about early on Monday morning. Joe Byrne, dressed as mounted trooper, took two of the Kellys' horses to the blacksmith to get their shoes removed and replaced with new shoes. The blacksmith promptly attended to this customer. The police horses were always shod there, and the blacksmith knew that his money was sure. He was struck by the superior type of these two "police" horses, and as he was looking over them took notice of their brands. These horses showed breeding. The horses were shod, and the cost charged to the New South Wales Government, whose police force had boasted what they would do with the Kellys. Joe Byrne took the horses back to the police station. Preparations were now made for the return to Burramine, but before starting they had to see the manager of the Bank of New South Wales. Senior-Constable Devine was still kept in the lock-up. Constable Richards was taken out, and accompanied Ned and Dan Kelly on foot to Mr. Cox's Royal Hotel shortly after 12 o'clock midday. Joe Byrne and Steve Hart rode on horseback. When they arrived at the hotel Constable Richards informed Mr. Cox by way of formal introduction: "This is Ned Kelly and this is Dan. That is Joe Byrne and the other young man is Steve Hart."

Ned informed Mr. Cox that he wanted the use of one of the large rooms of the hotel for a little while to have a "meeting."

The large dining-room was selected, and Cox was told to go in with Richards, the local constable. Everybody about the place was required to attend the "meeting" in the dining-room. The barmaid was told to remain "on duty." Dan Kelly went out to the backyard, where the servant girl was washing the clothes. She had not been long out from home, and had the company of a young man, who considered he was doing a "mash." Dan joined them, and, after a few remarks, invited the girl and her admirer to come in and have a drink. "No," replied this recent arrival from the old land; "I don't drink with strangers." "But," persisted Dan, "your friend here will come with you." "No, I won't drink with strangers," protested the girl. Dan Kelly could now see that his attempt at diplomacy had failed, and said, "Well, you'll have to come in; I am Dan Kelly; we have this place stuck up, and we must trouble everybody to come into the dining-room." At the same time Dan produced his revolver. The girl nearly fainted; she wiped her hands with her apron, and, with her admirer, walked into the dining-room, where they joined Mr. Cox and Constable Richards and many others. Dan now took charge of the bar, and talked to the barmaid. Joe Byrne went out the back, and, looking over the fence which divided the bank from the hotel, saw the bank teller, Mr. Living, enter the bank through the back door. Joe vaulted over the fence and followed the teller into the bank. Mr. Living heard someone coming in from the back, and was somewhat incensed with such rudeness, and said in a rather autocratic tone: "You have no right to come in that way; you should come in through the front door." Joe Byrne presented his credentials by covering Mr. Living with his revolver with a much more autocratic demand: "Bail up! Throw up your hands! We're the Kellys." Mr. Living promptly obeyed, and so also did Mr. Mackie, the junior clerk. The shock caused Living to stutter and it has been alleged that he stuttered for the rest of his life. Ned Kelly had already entered the bank by the front door. Ned and Joe collected the firearms and ammunition of the bank and demanded the cash. There was up one of the banks, but this Mr Nicolson denies, and adds that, coming something like £650 in the bank's drawers, and this was secured by Ned Kelly. Mr. Living put up a splendid defence on behalf of his employers, and tried to bluff Ned Kelly into the belief that that was the total amount the bank held. Messrs. Living and Mackie were taken next door to the hotel. Ned wanted to see the head, and inquired for the manager, Mr. Tarlton, who so far could not be found. Mr. Living was required to come back to the bank and search for the manager. After a little while Mr. Tarlton was discovered in the bathroom. He was requested to dress and come out, as the bank had already been stuck up by the Kellys.

Mr. Tarlton would not credit this statement, but, nevertheless, he hastened out of the bathroom, and was confronted by Ned Kelly holding a revolver levelled at him. Mr. Tarlton produced his key of the safe, and with the other key, secured from the teller, Ned opened the fireproof safe and collected the balance of the bank's cash, which made the total of £2300. The money was put into a seventy-pound sugar bag, and securely tied up. Ned now thought he would do a good turn for the poor struggling settlers in this district. He secured a package of mortgages held by the bank, and, taking them out the back, burnt them. He was not aware that copies of these documents were held by the Titles Office in Sydney. While Ned was in the bank, the local newspaper proprietor, Mr. Gill, and Mr. Rankin came into the bank, and were called upon to bail up. They did not wait to think, but ran out in great fear. Rankin ran into the hotel, and was secured. Gill ran in a different direction, and hid himself in a creek. Rankin was threatened with the supreme penalty, and in order to show the other prisoners what they escaped by their ready compliance with "orders," Rankin was stood apart from the others to be shot.

There was a general cry from the crowd not to shoot him, and with somewhat of a show of reluctance, Ned Kelly acceded to their request, and let the trembling Rankin off with a caution.

Ned now inquired who the other fellow was who had got right away. He was told that the runaway was Mr. Gill, who ran the local newspaper. Ned said he was sorry he got away, as he wanted him to publish a written statement which he (Ned Kelly) had prepared. Ned said he would pay Gill for publishing this statement. At this stage someone of the prisoners suggested to Constable Richards that a rush should be made on Steve Hart, who was guarding the prisoners, and overpower him. The constable replied that that would be too risky, as they were also covered by Dan Kelly.

The constable knew that so long as they "went quietly" no one would be hurt. A search was then made for Mr. Gill, so as to place an order for printing Ned Kelly's reply to police and press libels and misrepresentations. He was accompanied by Mr. Living. They went to Mr. Gill's home, but he was not there. Mrs. Gill did not know where he was. The bank teller then undertook to see Mr. Gill, and get Ned Kelly's side of the argument published. Ned said he would pay for it. Ned entrusted Mr. Living with the manuscript, on the promise of the latter to hand it to Mr. Gill. Mr. Living did not carry out his promise, but he handed the document to the police instead, and it was published in a very distorted and mutilated form after Ned Kelly had been executed.

In the meantime Joe Byrne attended at the post office, and compelled Mr. Jefferson, the postmaster, to cut the telegraph wires and also to cut down six or seven telegraph poles. Mr. Jefferson and his assistant were then taken to join the company at Cox's Hotel. After leaving Mr. Gill's house Ned and the bank teller called at McDougall's Hotel. Ned "shouted" for a crowd of about thirty people, and paid for the drinks. He then took McDougall's race mare out of the stable. McDougall protested that he was a comparatively poor man, and could not afford to lose the mare. Ned's socialistic principles came to McDougall's rescue, and the mare was handed back to her owner.

Dan was in the bar of the hotel, when a flash-looking young man, carrying a bowie knife in his belt, entered. He inquired of the barmaid when dinner would be on. The girl nodded towards Dan Kelly. The young man turned and looked at Dan and said, "What have you got to do with it, anyway?" Dan sat on the form, with his revolver in his right hand on his knee. He covered the revolver with his left hand, so that the newcomer did not see it. Dan replied that he had a great deal "to do with it." The flash man was becoming somewhat argumentative and defiant, when Dan stood up, and covering this insolent fellow with his revolver, said, "You go in there, and don't have so much to say." The knife man promptly obeyed, and, as they say in Parliament, the incident closed. Constable Richards was taken back to the lock-up, with the postmaster and his assistant, and lodged in the lock-up. Mrs. Devine was instructed not to let anyone out of the lock-up before 7p.m. that day, Monday, February 10, 1879.

Ned Kelly made a speech to the prisoners at Cox's Hotel before leaving. He told them of the way in which he and his family had been persecuted by the police, and how he himself had been sentenced to fifteen years by Judge Barry before he was arrested or charged with the alleged offence. He explained that any of his people who were arrested were treated in a prejudiced manner, and convicted without a trial. When any of them were tried it was really formal, as nothing could alter the verdict given before the case came into the court.

It was arranged by the outlaws that they should divide on their way back from Jerilderie, and meet on the bank of the Murray at the crossing place opposite Bourke's public-house, near Burramine.

Ned and Joe Byrne gave a splendid exhibition of horsemanship over stiff fences, and, then, waving a farewell to the crowd, left Jerilderie some time before Dan and Steve Hart. The latter got into some disgrace in the eyes of the other members of the gang by taking a watch from the local parson. Ned was angry with Steve, and ordered him to return the watch to the Rev. Mr. Gribble, from whom it had been taken. Dan and Steve rode about the streets before leaving, and threatened the prisoners with pains and penalties if they left the hotel before the time stated. The prisoners were told not to move for three hours. Dan and Steve left at 4p.m. The lock-up was to be opened at 7p.m.

The town was excited after the Kellys had left, and the wildest stories and rumours were in circulation. It was alleged that several of the Kellys' friends from Greta were in Jerilderie. Every strange face was supposed to be one of the Kellys' friends from Greta. From whispered conversations it would appear that Greta had migrated to Jerilderie. With this belief the townspeople were as circumspect in their words and actions, in reference to the Kellys, after the latter had departed as when the gang were in supreme command of the affairs of that town.

In addition to the £2300 taken from the bank, the Kellys also took the two police horses, revolvers and ammunition. These horses had been bred by Mr. John Evans, of Red Camp, near Moyhu, Victoria, and carried the breeder's well-known brand. Mr. Evans lost these horses some time previously. Of course, the New South Wales police department were not accused of stealing them. The Kellys brought the horses back to Greta, and turned them out at the head of the King River.

Some months later a cousin of the Kellys found one of the horses and identified John Evans' brand. The horses also carried the New South Wales Government brand, but the brand was on the neck under the mane, and was not easily seen. The Kellys' cousin returned the horse to the breeder.

The feelings of Senior-Constable Devine were so grievously wounded by the indignity of being locked up in his own prison cell at Jerilderie that he disliked to hear any reference to the Kelly Gang and their visit to Jerilderie. He afterwards went to West Australia, and obtained the position of racecourse detective. He remained in this position up to his death in 1927.

He was a spirited man, and was generally regarded as a man who would rather fight then run. It was because the Kellys recognised his courage that they did not take him out of the cell to parade the town. On the other hand, Constable Richards was much more docile, and would "go quietly" rather than take risks.

THE WELCOME HOME

The gang met, as arranged, on the banks of the Murray, where they had left the publican's boat in the early hours of the previous Saturday morning.

To their dismay, the boat was gone. They were unable to get across without a boat, and were forced to camp in a bend of the Murray all day Tuesday, February 11. They had six horses and the custody of £2300, and, therefore, they had to be careful. Joe Byrne strolled up the river, and discovered the boat used by the Boomanoomanah Station.

This boat was booked for their use, but it was not safe to commandeer it until after dark. Joe returned and reported his discovery. It was arranged that, after nightfall, Joe would go up for the boat and bring it down to their camp. The outlaws were anxious not to disturb or terrify the police, who were watching the crossings over the Murray.

During the day (Tuesday) Ned Kelly took a walk down the river,. He met a hawker who had camped there, some distance from the outlaws' resting place. Ned entered into conversation with him, and, as is the usual custom among country people, inquired if there was any news. The hawker instinctively took Ned to be a constable, and talked freely, especially about the Kellys, and replied, "Yes, the Kellys have been to Jerilderie, and robbed the bank, and terrified the people by threatening to shoot them." He said that he knew the Kellys well, and knew how they could be caught. He would go into their camp, he said, with two bottles of whisky, one bottle containing poison, and the other — the one the hawker would use — would be all right. Ned said that was a very good idea, but he, himself, could not give him permission to use the poisoned whisky. It would be necessary for him to get that from the sergeant at Mulwala. The hawker then went on to denounce the Kellys as a bad lot, and even said that their womenfolk were no good, either. Ned's blood was now boiling, yet he tried to restrain himself. He thought of putting a bullet through the head of this traducer of his family, and then asked him if he were married. The latter said, "Yes," but that he had lost his wife over a year ago. He had, he said, six children; the eldest was a girl, 14 years old. "A little mother," Ned thought as he decided that he could not deal with this slanderer in the drastic way that at first occurred to him.

At first Ned represented himself as a plain-clothes policeman, but now he decided to make known his identity. The hawker stated that he regularly visited Glenrowan, and bought cheese from a well-known dairyman in that district. He therefore enjoined Ned not to mention a word that he (the hawker) had said about the Kellys, because if the Kellys knew what he had said about them they would follow him up and murder him. Ned now told the hawker that he was "Ned Kelly," and that at first impulse he had intended to put a bullet through his head for slandering him and his people.

The hawker was visibly affected on account of the seriousness of the position in which he found himself, and begged for mercy. Ned said it was because of his little children, with that "little mother," that he had decided to let him go. He would not do anything that would make their lot harder than it was then.

Ned cautioned the hawker not to say a word to anyone that he had seen him there, and never again to speak disrespectfully of his family.

The hawker felt thankful to escape. The thought uppermost in his mind was that Ned Kelly was not such a bad fellow after all. Ned returned to his camp, and related the above news to his mates. After tea Joe Byrne went up the river for the station boat.

The Kellys got the six horses and themselves safely across the Murray, while the police of New South Wales and Victoria watched the public highways and bridges to intercept them. Before daylight on Wednesday morning, 12/2/1879, they arrived at Greta.

It is not possible to actually describe the heartiness of the welcome that greeted the Kellys at Greta. Their friends were illegally imprisoned without charge or trial, and some, who were not even known to the gang, were also illegally imprisoned as sympathisers. The satisfaction felt at the coup at Jerilderie and their safe return home was general among their friends and admirers throughout the North-Eastern district of Victoria.

The imprisonment of sympathisers did not prevent the successful operation of the Jerilderie bank by the Kellys, and the police were now more than ever subjected by the public generally to ridicule and contempt. The money was required to help the sympathisers and friends when they were attacked by the Government through the police. The gang went out to the hills for a few days' rest after their trip. Then they prepared for their accommodation at the old home, where, in spite of the army of police on "double pay," they rested in peace for over twelve months.

Dan Kelly, Ned Kelly and Joe Byrne, as photographed by Arthur Burrows, travelling Portrait Rooms 1878. Produced by his brother in Launceston.

11
THE SPIES

THE Victorian police were not only not sorry, but somewhat pleased, that the Kellys were so successful in locking up the New South Wales police at Jerilderie and assuming control of the town.

They recognised that, to some extent, the tables had been turned. Anyhow, they could say that notwithstanding their boast, the New South Wales constables had suffered greater humiliation than the Victorian police. The Kellys actually arrested the police, locked them up, and, by donning the police uniform, made themselves responsible for order in the town.

As police in charge of Jerilderie the Kellys were a huge success. There was no rowdiness or drunkenness from Saturday night till Monday afternoon; and, although, it may seem strange, it is nevertheless true that after the Kellys returned home they were not inconvenienced by the police, who were alleged to be pursuing them. In fact, it seemed that the Victorian police had an intuitive understanding with the Kellys to the effect that each should give the other as wide as berth as possible. They (the police) were afforded an excellent excuse for retiring from the pursuit, when the blacktrackers, refusing to continue to lead the police, announced that the Kellys were now close at hand. This was bad enough, but what the police really objected to was the cowardice of the blackfellows in ordering the police to go first: "Kelly very soon now, you go catch 'em." The police now decided to rely entirely on the employment of "spies." But as the word "spy" has a nasty sound, the police spies were called "agents." The first "spy" engaged was Aaron Sherritt.

When he was first approached by Supt. Sadleir, after the "Charge of Sebastopol," near Beechworth, Sherritt humiliated that officer by doubting his authority. Supt. Sadleir then called in Supt. C. H. Nicolson, Assistant Chief Commissioner of Police. Mr. Nicolson endorsed the promises made to Sherritt by Supt. Sadleir, but still Aaron Sherritt doubted the authority of both Sadleir and Nicolson. Then Sherritt was introduced to Captain Standish, Chief Commissioner of Police. The captain endorsed the promises made to Sherritt by Sadleir and Nicolson, and then Aaron Sherritt, who was at that time engaged to Joe Byrne's sister, was appointed as a police spy. His duties were to still pretend to be the most faithful friend of Joe Byrne and the Kellys, while he accepted service with the police to betray his intended brother-in-law for "blood-money." Sherritt fed the police with a constant supply of news of the outlaw's plans. Sherritt felt himself in very much the same position as some newspaper men. He felt that he had to supply facts if available, but if facts were not available then fiction. Sherritt displayed a good deal of skill in handling the police. He did not get on too well with Supt. Nicolson, whom he described as that "Crankie Scotchman." But he completely hypnotised Supt. Hare. It was quite true that the police officials did not like this method of capturing the outlaws, but their slogan at that time appeared to be "Safety first" — that is, their own personal safety. The Kellys were associated very little with Sherritt. He practically had nothing to do with them. But he had been the schoolmate and intimate acquaintance of Joe Byrne. While in the employ of the police Sherritt stole a horse from Mrs. Byrne — Joe Byrne's mother. He brought the horse down to Greta and sold it to Mrs. Skillion (Ned Kelly's sister), to whom he gave the usual receipt. Mrs. Skillion soon discovered that the horse she had bought from Aaron Sherritt belonged to Mrs. Byrne. The latter reported the matter to the police, and took out a warrant for the arrest of the police spy — Aaron Sherritt. This placed the police in an awkward predicament. If justice were done, Sherritt would be sentenced to gaol for a term of years. But as the police considered Sherritt's services as a police spy were indispensable, they apparently controlled the course of justice and secured Sherritt's discharge. A further example of police patronage in crime occurs in connection with John Sherritt Jr. A sheep owner at Woolshed, near Beechworth, reported to the police that he had been losing sheep, and that he suspected some of the Sherritt family of stealing and killing them. Constable Barry caught John Sherritt in the act of skinning a sheep, but no action was taken. The attitude of the police authorities in this connection suggested that the police and the Sherritt family had a licence to commit crime. This same sheep stealer was afterwards permitted, on the recommendation of Supt. Hare, to join the police force. In reference to this matter, Supt. Hare, on oath before a Royal Commission, said:—

Question by Superintendent Nicolson. — Do you not think that before you took Sherritt into the force you ought to have been very clear as to whom that sheep belonged that he was seen skinning by the constable? — No. I do not think so. My reasons are, for acting as I did, that through some means or other these men were thrown on the Government. I do not know how, but when I returned to duty I found they were there, and I had to find the best means of disposing of them. I made the suggestion, and Captain Standish said, "Find out everything you can." I did and reported to Captain Standish. That is all I had to do in the matter.

Question by Superintendent Nicolson. — Did you recommend their being taken into the force? — Yes, certainly, in the first instance; and when I made inquiries I could find nothing tangible against them, and two clergymen and other old inhabitants of the district, with Mr. Zincke, a member of Parliament, all gave these men (sheep stealers) an exemplary character.

Question by Superintendent Nicolson. — That is since I (Supt. Nicolson) spoke of it, and since you recommended them to be taken into the police force. Was it not your duty to make inquiries about this matter of sheep stealing? — All the inquiry was made that could be. Constable Barry saw Sherritt skinning sheep as he passed, and that was all. What further inquiry could be made?

Question by Superintendent Nicolson. — To whom did the sheep belong? — How could I specify to whom it belonged when it had been skinned and eaten? Whom could I have got information from?

Question by Superintendent Nicolson. — Could you not have used the police to ascertain for you who had lambs running about in that quarter? — Certainly that would be a gross injustice to imply that a man stole a sheep. There was no proof of it. Because a squatter ran sheep on the run this man lives on, and because this man is seen skinning a sheep, is it to be implied that he stole it?

Question by Superintendent Nicolson. — I did not say implied, I say inquiry — sufficient to prevent him getting into the force.

Question by Superintendent Nicolson. — No, but to make inquiries? — I did make inquiries.

Question by Superintendent Nicolson. — Did you make inquiries whether the Sherritts had sheep of their own? — No; they might have bought it.

Question by Superintendent Nicolson. — Would not the possession of this sheep be prima-facie evidence of his stealing it? — No.

Now let us look at the police attitude towards the Kellys.

Confidential.

"Forwarded for information of Mr. Nicolson and Mr. Sadleir. I address this to the latter, being uncertain whether Mr. Nicolson is still in Benalla. At all events, the information, which is important, should be communicated to him as soon as possible.

"The signals which Mrs. Skillion makes from her place clearly bring her within the reach of the new Act. It would be very desirable to commit her, if possible, or, at any rate, to prosecute her. — F. C. Standish, C.C. Police."

The above is one of the numerous examples which prompted Inspector Mountford, when giving evidence on oath before the Royal Commission behind close doors, to state: "I might say that a great deal of the trouble with these men (Kellys and their friends) would be got over if they felt that they were being treated with equal justice — that there was no 'down' on them. They are much more tractable when they feel that they are treated with equal justice."

The police had another spy, "Diseased Stock," whose activities were well known to the Kellys. They knew him well, and knew him to be a police spy. His name was Kennedy. This man was not a friend of the outlaws, and it was impossible for him to secure first-hand information. Kennedy was aware of that, but he knew also that the Government had plenty of money to spend, and he never failed to supply reports and draw his allowance. His reports and information, when submitted, were always stale, and usually second, and sometimes third and fourth hand.

The spy business was regarded by some as a new industry, and the "official spy" frequently worked with some of his friends to concoct likely stories of the plans, intentions, and whereabouts of the outlaws. A fair specimen of this class of concoction was responsible for the taking of Supt. Nicolson and Supt. Sadleir to Albury while the outlaws were, without opposition, securing £2000 from the bank at Euroa. The letter was written in New South Wales, and bore the postmarks of Bungowannah and Albury, December 3, 1878.

It was received by one of the police spies at Greta, and handed as something extra special to the senior constable at Edi. The latter sent it to Supt. Sadleir at Benalla. This letter was handed to Supt. Nicolson by Supt. Sadleir, both of whom took the next train to Albury. Here is the letter as quoted by Supt. Sadleir when giving evidence on oath:—

"Sir, — I have been requested by E. and D. Kelly to do what I could to assist them in crossing here, I am to write to you to let you know the arrangements. They are to be at a time to be named at the junction of the Indigo Creek and the Murray, and there is to be a password. It is this:— 'Any work to be had?' 'Yes'. 'Where?' On the New South Wales side one shall meet you. I will have a boat ready. There must not be any horses come to the river. If you should have horses they must be led by the bridge to a safe place already prepared for them. I will have four on each side on the river to watch upper and lower sides. I have a place fixed where you will be safe. If you should want horses there will be some got for you. There are two who say they will join you if requested. You must mind it will want money, and I have got none. When you write, direct to Howlong for the signature."

After quoting the above, Supt. Sadleir continued:— "It is not out of sympathy I do not mention his name, but it is sent by a person well known and suspected in that neighbourhood. I made a note of it at the time to this effect, amongst other matters, that the envelope showed the Bungowannah and Albury postmarks of the 3rd inst."

This letter was responsible for diverting the attention of the heads of the police force at Benalla to Albury while the Kellys entertained the Euroa bank manager and his wife and family and staff with tea at Faithful Creek homestead.

"Renwick" was the alias of another spy named Lawrence Kirwan, of Carbour, near Oxley, farmer, who on oath stated:—

(1) That in April, 1879, I was employed by Mr. Hare as a scout and guide to assist the police in the pursuit of the Kellys, at the rate of £1 per day.
(2) That I acted as scout or guide for different parties of police for thirteen days and received in payment therefor the sum of thirteen pounds.
(3) That I was instructed by Mr. Sadleir to go out and seek information on the gang, and, acting on those instructions, I went to Benalla, round Mt. Emu and Dondongadale River, where I met Mr. Furnell and party; thence back to Carbour, and then up the Mitta River to Beechworth, where I met Detective Ward, who approved of what I was doing. I went next to the Little River, and then to the Upper Murray by way of Cotton Tree Hill, but found no traces, and returned to Benalla and reported where had been, and that I had found no traces of the gang.
(4) That when I sent in claim for payment for the time I was out seeking information, Mr. Sadleir declined to pay me, as he said he did not know I was out; and I was left by this decision without a shilling and had to borrow ten shillings to take me home.
(5) In September or October, 1879, I got a written message from Mr. Assistant Commissioner Nicolson to meet him at Wangaratta. I went in on Monday to Wangaratta and saw Mr. Nicolson, who asked me to go out and seek traces of the gang. I refused to go on the ground that I had a claim against Mr. Hare and Mr. Sadleir for services which they declined to recognise. Mr. Nicolson pressed me to go out, but I several times refused to go. I explained to Mr. Nicolson my claims, and he said he would do his best to get the amount for me. Mr. Nicolson said he had heard of the disputed claim at Benalla, and that he knew he would be handicapped over it. I understood that Mr. Nicolson meant that this disputed claim would prevent my working for him. I afterwards saw Mr. Nicolson; three days after I agreed to go out under him. I went out alone the following day. I was out four days on the King River. I went out with

specific instructions to see if there were camps or traces of camps in certain localities on the river. I found no traces. I found an old saddle, which afterwards proved to be one of the saddles belonging to the police murdered at the Wombat. There were floods in the King River, which interfered with the search I was directed to make. I returned to Wangaratta and saw Mr. Nicolson and reported to him.

(6) That I remained in Mr. Nicolson's service until the first day of June, 1880. That I was paid for all the time I was working for him. I was paid all the time I was out, whether I got information or not. I never had a dispute with Mr. Nicolson. I was paid by Mr. Nicolson the sum of twenty-six pounds, fifteen shillings. When not employed by Mr. Nicolson I was idle, so that I received only twenty-six pounds, fifteen shillings in twenty-seven weeks.

(7) That when Mr. Nicolson was leaving the district I saw him near Beechworth. He told me he was about to leave and paid me three pounds which were due to me. He told me that Mr. Hare was coming to take charge and that he (Mr. Nicolson) would like me to go on working for him. I told Mr. Nicolson I did not think I would, and added that if he was going to leave I would knock off working. Mr. Nicolson pressed me to stay on, and I at last said I would go down to Benalla and see Mr. Hare on the subject.

(8) That what I said might have led Mr. Nicolson to believe that I intended to go on working for Mr. Hare.

(9) That Mr. Nicolson could not have said more than he did to induce me to remain working for Mr. Hare. I did not mention my claim to Mr. Nicolson on this occasion.

(10) I never spoke to Mr. Nicolson again until August, 1880.

(11) I went to Benalla and saw Mr. Hare. He asked me to work for him. He said: "I want you to keep on working for me the same as you have been doing for Mr. Nicolson, as you know the locality and the whole affair." I said I wanted my disputed claim paid before I would do any more work. He said: "Can't help that; it is nothing to do with me." I said that I had asked Mr. Sadleir and he gave me the same reply, and if that was the way of it I was quite full of it and would work no more. I went home by train.

(12) That I met Detective Ward afterwards, and he told me that when Mr. Hare complained to him of my refusal to work he (Ward) said I had a disputed claim with the department for work performed, and that Mr. Hare had said in reply: "If Kirwan had told me that I would have made it all right."

(13) That from the information I was supplying and from the movements of the gang and police, I am sure that Mr. Nicolson and his party must have encountered the gang within a few days of the time Mr. Nicolson was removed. An encounter could not have been postponed for ten days, and might have occurred in four or five.

— LAWRENCE KIRWAN. Sworn at Wangaratta, in the Colony of Victoria, this fifth day of September, one thousand eight hundred and eighty-one, before me, Fred J. M. Marsden, a Commissioner of the Supreme Court of the Colony of Victoria for taking Affidavits.

Towards the end of 1879 each of the permanent police spies developed the spirit of prophecy to a very high degree. They always reported that the Kellys were starved out; that they were very thin, and would soon be caught. Dan Kelly, as a matter of fact, had developed into a fine, well-made man, although he was only nineteen years old when he died at Glenrowan. Constable Bracken, who had been arrested by the Kellys at Glenrowan, said that the four bushrangers were in the pink of condition; that Ned Kelly was fit to win the Melbourne Cup.

Supt. Nicolson loudly proclaimed his great faith in the spies he employed, and, on the other hand, the spies proclaimed their great faith in Mr. Nicolson's ability to capture the outlaws.

From the spies' stories of the starving bushrangers it would appear a wise policy that Mr. Nicolson should remain at the Benalla police barracks, so as to be on hand when the outlaws would come in to give themselves up. They were a happy family — Mr. Nicolson and his spies.

Pat Quinn joined in the crowd of spies. He was not on friendly terms with the Kellys, and would willingly give them away if he could. He was not related to the Kellys, but his wife was Mrs. Kelly's sister.

The friends and sympathisers of the Kellys kept Mr. Pat Quinn well supplied with mythical movements of the outlaws, and Quinn lost no time in communicating these mythical movements to the police officials. On one occasion he was told in the deepest and most intense confidence that the Kellys were at the head of the King River, where they were to rest for a few days. Quinn rushed to the Benalla police barracks, where he met Supt. Nicolson, who had just returned after a long wild-goose chase. Mr. Nicolson did not have any confidence in Quinn, and made a legitimate excuse that his men and horses were worn out, and were unable to undertake a 70-mile ride without a rest. Paddy was somewhat annoyed at his failure to arouse Mr. Nicolson's enthusiasm. Actually at the time that this news was given to Mr. Nicolson the Kellys were introducing themselves to the foreman and his wife at Younghusband's Faithful Creek station, near Euroa. This was the end of Quinn as a police spy.

On still another occasion Quinn was anxious to "discover" reliable traces of the outlaws. While his wife was away from home he took some of the contents out of a bag of flour he had recently brought home, and putting it into a sugar bag took it over to a spot near his front slip rails. He dumped the sugar bag of flour on the ground and led his horses around the bag several times. Some of the flour sifted out of the sugar bag, and left clear evidence that a quantity of flour had been placed there. The tracks of horses about this spot indicated that the outlaws had been there and received provisions from Mrs. Quinn during her husband's absence. He then planted the sugar bag of flour in a shed. When Mrs. Quinn came home he was angry. He accused his wife of giving flour and other provisions to the Kellys. She denied the charge, whereupon her husband took her over the spot where the flour had sifted out of the bag, and called her attention to the tracks made by the horses. After hearing her denials, Paddy ordered her to go to the house and see if any flour was gone. She went, and to her astonishment a quantity of flour was missing. "They must have been here while we were away!" she said. Quinn rode with all speed to report this positive evidence of the outlaws' visit, and when the police party arrived and saw the evidence they too were convinced that the outlaws had been there. This incident somewhat revived official confidence in Quinn as a genuine friend of "law and order."

A schoolmaster named Wallace offered his spying services to the police. He was, he said, in close touch with the outlaws and held their complete confidence. His services were readily accepted. He undertook to get hold of Joe Byrne's diary, under the pretence of licking it into printable shape. He was in reality not in close touch with the Kellys at all, but he was in financial difficulties, and drew large, and regular sums from the police department. He wrote very voluminous reports, which contained no news of any value. He drew £180 in about seven months.
Eventually the police officials woke up and came to the conclusion that this pedagogue was either a financial expert or a faithful worker for the outlaws.

In his reports he disclosed his disapproval of the character of some of the police officials stationed at Beechworth. On November 26, 1879, he wrote to Supt. Nicolson as follows:— "Met . . . Junior and P. . . . I had a long and interesting conversation with these worthies, who manifested much pleasure in meeting me. I wondered at the marked change in Jack's manners towards me, as, on two or three previous occasions, he carefully avoided me. I soon ascertained the reason. It appears by their account that the virtuous detective who is standing the season at Beechworth had stated a day or two previously that my name had been added to the black list at the office; that he believed that 'bloody' W. . . . was in constant communication with the outlaws."

In giving evidence before the Royal Commission, the following statements were made by the schoolmaster on oath:—

Question (by Commission). — What did you mean by "The virtuous detective" who is "standing the season" at Beechworth? — That is exactly what I meant. He had the reputation of acting immorally, "putting it in a mild form."

Question (by Detective Ward). — Do you know anything personally about it? — I know no one in the North-Eastern district who bore a more unenviable character for immorality, than you yourself.

Question (by Ward). — Can you give any instances? — Tampering with the pupil teachers (the girls) in the State School.

Question (by Commission). — Was there any stir made about that at the time? — I believe so. I believe Captain Standish made an inquiry into the matter, but it was hushed up.

Question (by Commission). — Did you hear anything of the result of that inquiry? — I did not.

Question (by Ward). — Any other person? — I have heard you are the father of several illegitimate children.

Question (by Ward). — Will you give me just one if you can? — It is currently reported in the North-Eastern district that you were the father of the illegitimate child of Miss ——, of ——.

The character of some of the police and police spies had a good deal to do with deciding a very large section of the community to become Kelly sympathisers. The moral character of the four outlaws was admired by the respectable section of the community. Even the police had so much confidence in their chivalry that when two or three of the police were under the bed after the shooting of Aaron Sherritt they pulled Mrs. Sherritt under the bed with them, saying, "The Kellys won't fire when they know that there are women here."

What a striking contrast to the action of the police at Glenrowan, where the police shot down innocent men, women and children!

12
SUPT. HARE IN CHARGE

THE Kellys arrived home from Jerilderie on February 12, 1879, and on that date a report was sent to the police that Dan Kelly was seen at Taylor's Gap, near Beechworth. This report was not true. Other reports came in that the Kellys were at Urana, New South Wales, and at Rutherglen, in Victoria. The police were very much hampered by the numerous wild reports of the imaginary appearance of the Kellys in the most unlikely and impossible places. After the haul at Jerilderie the Victorian Government increased the reward to £4000, or £1000 for each of the outlaws. The New South Wales Government also offered £4000 reward for the outlaws, alive or dead. That made the sum total of the money on the heads of the outlaws £8000, or £2000 for each or any of them. The two Governments thought this huge sum would induce those who were in close touch with the Kellys to inform on them. It is an extraordinary fact that, notwithstanding this large reward, the Kellys lived at home on the Eleven-Mile Creek in comparative peace and security from the time of their return from Jerilderie to their destruction at Glenrowan.

Even at Glenrowan it is generally admitted that Mrs. Jones' whisky was the major factor in the capture of the Kellys, yet, strange to say, Mrs. Jones not only received none of the reward, but she was arrested and charged with harbouring the Kellys. She was not their friend, and the Kellys knew it. As the Outlawry Act had lapsed before the alleged offence was committed, she was discharged.

The offer of the Queensland Government to send six blacktrackers, in charge of a senior constable, under Inspector O'Connor, was, after a good deal of delay, accepted. Captain Standish held the opinion that a subject race, such as the blacks, could not be superior to the white man in tracking. Now, however, he gave way, and the blacks arrived at Albury on March 6, 1879.

Mr. O'Connor gave an exhibition of the skill of his trackers to Captain Standish at Albury. The latter appeared to be fully convinced that the blacks were wonderful trackers. On March 8 Mr. O'Connor, Senior-Constable King, and his six trackers — Corporal Sambo, Troopers Hero, Johnny, Jimmy, Barney and Jack — arrived at the Benalla police barracks, which were to be their headquarters while tracking the outlaws.

The usefulness of the blacktrackers was destroyed by the absurd policy of the "Board of Officers" at Benalla, which effectively defeated Inspector O'Connor and his trackers, and crushed the ambition of those rank and file members of the force who had courage enough to encounter the Kellys to effect their arrest or destruction.

This position was made quite clear when Supt. Hare gave evidence on oath before the Royal Commission on March 31, 1881.

Question. — While you were in charge of the parties that were in pursuit of the Kellys can you say what were the instructions to the out-stations, such as Wangaratta? Could the men act on their own responsibility and go and follow any traces when they got them, or had they to remain in till they got instructions giving permission to go out? — No, their duty was to report the information they received to Benalla, where we had a "Board of Officers," and it was referred to all of us. We considered what was best to be done, and if we so decided the men who got the information were sent off to inquire into it at once.

If the Wangaratta police were informed that the Kellys were at North Wangaratta, two miles away, the police were required to first consult the "Board of Officers" at Benalla before taking any action to capture the outlaws and earn the reward. If the "Board of Officers" decided that nothing should be done, as this Board frequently did, then the Wangaratta police could do nothing, and were expected to be contented with their "double-pay" as sufficient compensation for the ridicule and scorn heaped on them by the public.

DOG POISONERS

Superintendent Hare, continuing his evidence on oath, said. — I may say that sympathisers' dogs and dogs of relations were a great nuisance to us. . . . . The next time I went to the spot I appointed a man with a few baits in a bag, and told him to drop a bait here and there and let any animal that liked pick it up.

Question. — Baits to destroy dogs? — Yes.

Question. — Strychnine on a bit of meat? — Yes, but after that many of the dogs about the place you could not poison if you tried. They always had muzzles on day and night, and used to come into Benalla with the muzzles on. I have seen Mrs. Skillion and Kate Kelly come into Benalla with their dogs muzzled.

Question. — What you want to convey to the Commission is this: That the Kellys were so supported by the sympathisers and actually the dogs were so trained that if strange horses came the dogs would look out for the trackers and boys follow them up? — Yes, that is it.

From the above it appears that even the dogs in the Greta district had no confidence in the police.

Superintendent Hare. — I wish to state another great difficulty we had to contend with — the want of young, smart and intelligent officers. We have plenty of officers in the force, but I think there is not one of them five years under my age. The junior officers are older than the seniors on the list, many of them; they have only been appointed these last four or five years. I myself, for instance. I do not think I should have been sent out on those parties; but I had a good knowledge of the country and was a fair bushman, and there was no one to take my place. My experience of twenty-seven years was surely likely to be of more service than being stuck in the bush, where, perhaps, a young officer would have done even better than I could do, because he was younger and had more dash in him; and I should have been left behind at headquarters to assist and to arrange things there. I felt myself when I was out that I should not have been out — that my services should have been more valuable inside.

This appears to be a candid admission that Supt. Hare was not fit to lead in the Kelly hunt.

Mr. Hare was very much under the influence of Aaron Sherritt. The latter told Hare that Joe Byrne had written to him (Sherritt), asking Aaron to meet him at the Whorougly races to ride Byrne's black mare in the hurdle race. Supt. Hare was much impressed by this letter. Aaron Sherritt had arranged with some of his intimate friends to remain on the hill some distance from the racecourse, so that if Aaron signalled his friends could show themselves, and then disappear, while Aaron pointed them out to Supt. Hare as being the outlaws.

Supt. Hare, before the Commission:—

I will tell the Commission the exact facts of the case. The letter was written in peculiar phraseology that none of us here could understand, and it had to be interpreted by Aaron Sherritt himself before we knew what it meant; but the purport of it was asking Aaron Sherritt to go over to Whorougly races — this is a small country racecourse on the Ovens — and to meet him (the writer, Joe Byrne) at a certain place, as he wanted him to ride his black mare in some hurdle race. I saw the letter, and beyond doubt in Byrne's handwriting, because we had seen a great many of his documents. I communicated with Captain Standish on the subject, and we (the officers) decided what was to be done. We arranged that I should take three of my best riders and pluckiest men and go to the races myself. I selected three men unknown to the public in that part of the country, viz., Senior-Constable Johnson, Constable Lawless and Constable Falkner. I told them what duty they would have to perform and the information that I had received, and directed them to ride singly, as if unknown to each other, on to the racecourse. Lawless I set up with an under-and-over table and dice. Johnson was got up as a bookmaker, and Falkner was to act the "yokel" and patronise the other two — the under-and-over place and to make bets on the races. I myself drove them down on to the course in a buggy and mixed among the people, and the ordinary police in uniform attend the races. I took all these precautions for the purpose of preventing anyone knowing.

Question. — Did Sherritt know? — Of course, he was there.

Question. — The police did not arrest your three-card trick man? — No; in little country racecourses they are not so particular about little things of that sort; there is no money made.

Many of the outlaws' greatest sympathisers were on the Whorouly racecourse, and knew the three constables — the "Bookmaker," the "Spieler," and the "Yokel." There is no doubt that there was a great need of young, intelligent officers with some dash. However, Supt. Hare's "spielers" provided the Kellys' sympathisers with a great deal of amusement, and these sympathisers were able to assure Ned Kelly and his mates that as long as Supt. Hare was in charge of the Kelly hunt the outlaws had nothing to fear and very little inconvenience to endure. The Kellys felt very comfortable as long as the "Board of Officers" had supreme control. Ned Kelly's opinion of his pursuers was that an inquiry would soon be held, and that Captain Standish and Supt. Hare, Inspector Brook-Smith and Supt. Sadlier would be dismissed from the police force. He said that Supt. Nicolson was the only man who would survive such inquiry. It is interesting to know that as the result of the report of the Royal Commission, held after the execution of Ned Kelly, Captain Standish and Supts. Hare and Nicolson and Inspector Brook-Smith were retired from the force. The £8000 reward offered for the capture of the Kellys had a very demoralising effect on the "Board of Officers." The capture of the Kellys was desired by these officers, but they were very jealous as to where they themselves would come in when the reward money would be allotted. This led to very serious quarrels among the heads, and, as the Kellys were not then stealing horses and were not injuring their neighbours, there was no local demand for greater police efficiency or activity. The results of these quarrels increased the public contempt for the valour of the police.

In those days the favourite game played by school children was "the Kellys and the police," and it happened that the Kellys invariably won.

After the arrival at Benalla of Inspector O'Connor and his party of blacktrackers a fresh start was made. The "Board of Officers" now comprised Captain Standish, Supt. Hare, Supt. Sadleir and Mr. O'Connor. These officers were now stationed at Benalla and the employment of an increased number of police spies was a special feature of the Board's activities.

On March 11, 1879, Mr. O'Connor and his party of blacktrackers were out after the Kellys. They were accompanied by Supt. Sadleir and about six or seven Victorian police, making a party of about fourteen in all. Mr. O'Connor objected to so many being in the party. He wanted only two Victorian policemen who knew the country to accompany his party of trackers, but Captain Standish insisted on at least six or seven Victorian police going with the blacktrackers every time they went out. This large party could not move quickly, and the pack-horses required were a considerable hindrance. After being out for a week the whole party returned to the barracks on March 18. They did not come across the Kellys or their tracks, though they went up the Fern Hills and Holland branch of the Broken River. They came across some tracks which the trackers followed, but these tracks turned out to be the tracks of local stockmen in search of sheep and cattle.

The party returned on account of not being sufficiently supplied with necessaries, and one of the blacks — Corporal Sambo — had become very ill. The necessaries were food, blankets and clothing.

The next move by Mr. O'Connor and the blacks was not made till April 16, when they were accompanied by Supt. Sadleir and five or six white police. The whole party numbered sixteen men. This party went up the King River, and after being out for five days came to De Gamaro Station. Mr. O'Connor was there informed that one of the police horses taken from the police at Jerilderie had been discovered on the Black Range. The trackers were about to search for the tracks of this horse when a constable galloped up with a letter from Captain Standish, saying that if they were not on "anything good" it would be better to return. Mr. O'Connor and Supt. Sadleir conferred, and they decided to follow up the tracks of the Jerilderie police horse. They advised Captain Standish to this effect. Next day Captain Standish sent yet another message recalling the party to Benalla.

Mr. O'Connor and Supt. Sadleir both complained of the lack of interest taken by Captain Standish in the Kelly hunt.

In May, 1879, Captain Standish in official matters began to show his dislike to Mr. O'Connor, and wanted to take the blacktrackers from his command and place them in different townships — to split up the blacktrackers. Mr. O'Connor would not agree to this, and received the following wire from the Queensland Government:—

To Sub-Inspector O'Connor:— The Colonial Secretary desires that you will not separate yourself from your troopers, nor allow any to be detached from you. — C H Barron, pro Commissioner, May 13, 1879.

Shortly after this there was a breach between Captain Standish and Mr. O'Connor. The leading officers took sides. Captain Standish and Mr. Hare were on one side, and Supt. Nicolson and Mr. O'Connor were on the other side. Supt. Sadleir tactfully took a neutral position.

The Kellys also adopted a neutral attitude and successfully evaded contact with either of the two factions in the police force.

As a result of official disagreements, Mr. O'Connor and his blacktrackers were not allowed to go to the races — the Whorouly races, where Supt. Hare's "Bookmaker," "Spieler," and "Yokel" were doing good business to the immense enjoyment of the friends and sympathisers of the Kellys.

Portrait of Tracker Johnny from Maryborough.

13
JOINING THE BENEDICTS

MR. O'Connor arrived at Benalla on March 8, 1879, and boarded with the other officers at Craven's Commercial Hotel.

He met there the sister-in-law of Supt. Nicolson. It was a case of love at first sight; but the parties were evidently not ready to make elaborate preparations for their marriage. It was decided that they should get married quietly, and still live as Mr. O'Connor and Miss Smith.

One morning the happy couple appeared at the Church of England at Benalla, in company with Mr. James Knox, Benalla shire secretary, as best man, and were married by the Rev Mr. Scott.

This marriage was a great secret, and both parties continued, as far as the public were concerned, as unmarried people. However, a great public wedding was arranged six months later at Flemington. Many guests were invited. The four who figured at the secret marriage at Benalla were there, and retired to a room in one part of the house where the marriage ceremony was supposed to be performed. The guests were in another part, in a big room, and were waiting till the clergyman, Mr. Scott, and Mr. Knox, the best man, and the bridegroom and the bride would emerge and receive their congratulations. This farce was successfully staged, and the guests, except Mr. Knox and the clergyman, were in complete ignorance that the happy couple had been lawfully married six months before.

Captain Standish heard the full account of the secret wedding, and his dislike to Mr. O'Connor was considerably intensified, and, when giving evidence before the Royal Commission on March 23, 1881, he was cross-examined by Mr. O'Connor as follows:—

Mr. O'Connor. — Do you ever remember saying to me that you would endeavour to get the Kellys without my valuable assistance?

Captain Standish. — I never said any such thing.

The Chairman (to Mr. O'Connor). — You had better for the present confine your questions to any personal matters you wish dealt with at this sitting. The witness (Captain Standish) stated he had heard things about you he would not like to mention.

Mr. O'Connor. — He made some reflections about my private character, but I do not care a fig about it from a man of his private character, but I should like him to state what he alluded to.

The Chairman. — Captain Standish referred to your letter, in which you said you have been treated in an ungentlemanly, ungenerous, and discourteous manner by him throughout the whole sixteen months you were under his command, and he said he gave that the lie direct, and further, that he found out things that made him keep out of your company. Do you desire to say anything about that?

Mr. O'Connor. — Captain Standish's knowledge of my private character is very limited, and all I can say is that, if he has so low an estimate of my character, I care very little about it, considering the character of the man who judges. He said I was not a fit and proper person; I say that of him. (Under such circumstances it was natural that at least 85 per cent of the public took the side of the Kellys.)

By Mr. O'Connor, to witness (Captain Standish). — Did you allude to my private character? — No; I said things came to my knowledge that shook my faith in you.

By Mr. O'Connor. — Let him say it.

By Commission (to the witness). — I think, in fair play to Mr. O'Connor, you ought now to state what you refer to? — You (Mr. O'Connor) told several people that you were engaged to be married to a certain lady, and I remember asking what day and you said on the anniversary of your birthday, the 10th of February; and I found that you were married all the time.

Mr. O'Connor. — I give that the lie direct. I say that is a falsehood, and I am ready to prove it. On one occasion, when I dined with Captain Standish, he said, "I noticed you making love to a certain young lady," and I said, "That is nonsense, it is only fun," and I thought nothing more about it until I received a letter congratulating me. I immediately wrote back and said there was not a word of truth in it.

The witness. — I was driven to say this, and Mr. O'Connor was married a few days after he came to Benalla.

Mr. O'Connor. — But everything was quite correct.

Captain Standish. — May I ask for all that to be withdrawn? I request, as a particular favour, that you allow the whole of that to be expunged from the evidence.

Mr. O'Connor — I am sorry for my loss of temper, and will be glad if this matter be not reported.

The Chairman observed that, as the earlier statements of Captain Standish had already been reported in the "Herald" newspaper, he did not see how the later remarks could be withdrawn.

Mr. O'Connor told the Royal Commission on March 30, 1881, that Captain Standish often spoke of Mr. Nicolson in the most disparaging terms. On one occasion Captain Standish, referring to the death of the Hon. John Thomas, said, "Now Mr. Nicolson's billet as Assistant Commissioner will soon be done away with, as the Hon. John Thomas Smith got it for him; the billet is a farce, and it will be all up with him now, as he has not another friend left."

Mr. Nicolson was the son-in-law of the late Hon. J. T. Smith.

Mr. O'Connor and his trackers went out on two occasions with Mr. Hare, but with no results. At the end of June, 1879, Mr. Hare acknowledged himself badly defeated by the outlaws. His health began to fail, and he asked to be relieved.

Supt. C. H. Nicolson was sent to Benalla early in July, 1879, and was given a free hand in controlling the pursuit of the Kellys.

On taking over the Kelly hunt, Supt. C. H. Nicolson decided to alter the plan of campaign. Supt. Hare rushed parties of police around on any rumour, and had his men and horses worn out after their return from some of their trips. Mr. Nicolson changed all this. He decided to lie in wait until some really good information came to hand, and to push forward with both men and horses in the pink of condition.

The Kellys, on the other hand, had developed a great fear of the blacktrackers. They had been pursued very closely on one or two occasions, and they were very much struck with the accuracy and speed of the blacktrackers when following them. On one occasion they saw a party of police in search of them. Supt. Hare was in charge, but he had no blacktrackers. The police camped for the night. One of the constables moved some distance away from the others to camp. The Kellys, who were not very far away, approached the police camp cautiously, and took stock of the police horses and the number of men in the camp. The Kellys would have annihilated the whole police party if they had been even one per cent. as bloodthirsty as the daily papers had represented them to be.

This was shortly after the Jerilderie bank robbery; the Kellys did not want to disturb the peace, or to give definite information where they had been putting in their time, so they left the police to rest undisturbed.

On one of their expeditions with the blacktrackers the police were in hot pursuit, but had no idea they were so close to the Kellys.

The backtrackers were working with great enthusiasm. The Kellys knew the police were in pursuit. After they had travelled a long journey the trackers picked up their tracks. The Kellys pushed on as fast as they could with their jaded horses; one horse knocked up, and had to be abandoned. They pushed forward for about a quarter of a mile, and tied the rest of the horses up. They gave these horses the balance of the horse feed which they had carried with them. Having secured their horses, then they prepared to meet their enemies — the police — in a desperate fight for life. They had one great advantage — the selecting of their battleground. They decided to double back about twenty yards from the track by which they had come and parallel to it, and take up their position behind a big log about twenty-five yards from their disabled horse. Their position gave them a good view of the disabled horse, and the track coming to him. Ned gave instructions how they were to pick their men in the event of the police refusing to throw up their hands. The outlaws were now ready. They did not have to wait long to learn their fate. They heard the blacktrackers coming, with about eight or nine policemen following close up. The tracker who was about a dozen yards in the lead pulled up as he came to the abandoned horse. The police looked surprised, and the tracker exclaimed, "Kelly very soon now, you go catch 'im." The officer in charge said quickly, "We'll go back to the camp, and come out to-morrow," and already started back with all possible speed. Before the outlaws recovered from their surprise the police had retreated a good distance, but were still within range of their (the outlaws') rifles. "Well," said Ned, "that beats Banagher!" The Kellys fully expected to either have the pleasure of disarming the police and taking their horses, or putting up a real good fight. Of course, they recognised that they had a great advantage over the police, who would not know in their surprise where the challenge came from when called upon to surrender.

The police duly reported that they were on the outlaws' tracks sure enough, but owing to the cowardice of the blacktrackers, who refused to go on any further, they were very reluctantly compelled to return to their camp.

The Kellys paid a visit to the police paddock at Benalla and examined the police horses, but they did not come up to the outlaws' requirements, and were not taken by them. The Kellys wanted horses with some blood and breeding; the police horses were big, upstanding crossbreds that could show neither pace, nor endurance, and were described by Ned Kelly as a lot of scrubbers.

On Mr. Nicolson taking over the management of the Kelly hunt he relied almost exclusively on the spies he employed. He had to deal with a large volume of correspondence from these spies, and decide whether or not action should be taken. The following were a few of his most prominent spies:— "Renwick" — Lawrence Kirwan, of Carbour; "Diseased Stock" — D. Kennedy: Greta — "Tommy" (Aaron Sherritt); Moses (J. Wallace), a school teacher. The latter, after drawing £180 from the Police Department, was looked upon as a genuine friend of the outlaws, to whom it was alleged he regularly communicated full particulars of the police plans and movements. This spy wrote volumes of reports, but they contained no tangible information of the whereabouts of the Kellys. The spies, through their reports, were very optimistic, and continually promised the early capture of the outlaws.

These spies also reported that the outlaws were starved out, and that Dan Kelly was seen somewhere, and that he was very thin and starved-looking. Mr. Nicolson reported these optimistic records to the Chief Commissioner of Police as the justification of his policy of patience — to lull the outlaws into a feeling of false security so that they may become reckless and venture out into the open, and be easily captured or destroyed.
The Kellys took full advantage of the immunity they now enjoyed from pursuit, and settled down in their old home at Eleven-Mile Creek. They put a ceiling of bark in the house, and the four outlaws slept there in the attic, and seldom ventured out during the day. Their friends kept a close watch on all the movements of the police, and advised the outlaws if there was any danger of police invasion.

A party of twelve mounted police were sent from Benalla to Greta. They were on some "good information," and were out to pick up the tracks, and, if possible, capture the Kellys. The four outlaws were sitting inside taking things easy. Suddenly one of Mrs. Skillion's children rushed in, and then exclaimed that there was such a lot of men coming from Benalla on horseback. There was no time for the four men to get away

Ned told Mrs. Skillion to take the children into the back

room, and lie down flat on the floor with them. Mrs. Skillion said she would get the children out of the way as suggested, but that she herself would remain beside them and hand them the cartridges. The police were coming on at a walking pace. Ned was a bit worried, as the women and children might get shot. Each of the outlaws took up his position in readiness for the battle. The usual position was, however, altered in this case. It was the police who would come up and challenge the outlaws. But then the police might just ride up and bully the women to show them over the house. In that case they would be called to "bail up" and throw up their arms. There was great excitement in the old home; the police were now almost up to the sliprail, and the four outlaws had the leading four covered. With good shooting, it would take three shots each to account for the twelve policemen. The tension was suddenly relieved when Mrs. Skillion exclaimed, "They're off; they're off to Greta!" The police as they came to the sliprails started off in a canter, quite oblivious of the reception that was in store for them if they had attempted to call at the homestead.

The police went on to inquire into the "good information" sent in by one of the spies. They found some tracks, and after following them for some time came to the conclusion that the tracks were not those of the outlaws.

The Kelly armour following the Glenrowan seige, by James Bray.

14
THE ARMOUR AND AMMUNITION

SO quietly did the Kellys live at their old home that the general opinion of the public and some of the police was that the Kellys had gone to one of the other colonies. Sergeant Steele held this view right up to the shooting of Aaron Sherritt. The Kellys wanted more money, but the sticking up of the banks was not so easy now, on account of the preparations of defence made by the bank officials. It was stated that the manager was secured behind a stout wall, which had a porthole in it, and through which he could shoot an intruder without exposing himself to view.

The Kellys decided to get some kind of covering that would resist a bullet at the close range of ten yards. They had heard that an indiarubber coat would do this. After a trial the rubber coat was declared to be ineffective. Then they tried sheet iron. This would resist a revolver, but would not stop a rifle bullet.

The next material to suggest itself was steel. But where could they get steel in suitable sheets? There was a difficulty about this. After some discussion it was decided to test the resisting qualities of the mould-board of their own single-furrow plough. The mould-board stood the test and stopped the bullets of their best rifle at ten yards. This removed their difficulty. It was then decided to commandeer twenty mould-boards from their enemies — police agents or spies — and make a suit of armour for each of the four outlaws. Four mould-boards were required for the body of each armour. The next difficulty was how to make the mould-board straight; how could they take the twist out of it? This was quickly solved by Dan. It was decided that as Dan was a handy man with blacksmith's tools, he and his cousin Tom Lloyd should make the armour. They secured a big green log and stripped the bark off. They then simultaneously heated the mould-boards in a great hot fire, big enough to get all the mould-boards red hot. They then placed each mould-board in turn on the green log and beat it straight. This was done in a very short space of time. The green sappy log was necessary, because a dry log would become alight from the red-hot sheets of steel.

One mould-board after another was straightened on the bank of the Eleven-Mile Creek near Skillion's. Then the rest of the work was done on the anvil at the old homestead. Each suit of armour had to be made to measure. Great care had to be taken with the first suit. When Ned Kelly had a "try-on" it was considered a great success. The next suit was for Joe Byrne. This suit did not take nearly as long as Ned's. The armour for Steve Hart was easily done, and Dan's was the last one to be made. There was only one helmet made, and that was for Ned Kelly. The weight of Ned Kelly's armour complete was 95 lb., and resisted Martini rifles at ten yards. It is remarkable that the armours were made at Kelly's homestead, on the Eleven-Mile Creek, while Supt. C. H. Nicolson, having given up active pursuit, was lulling the outlaws into a sense of false security.

It was thought by the police that the armours were made by a Greta blacksmith. This was only a guess, which was made on the assumption that such work could only be done by a qualified tradesman. However unintentional, this was quite a compliment to Dan Kelly and his youthful cousin, Tom Lloyd, who assisted him.

Two full-sized mould-boards were required for the front body piece and two equally large mould-boards were required for the back body piece of each suit of armour. The mould-boards were riveted together down the centre of the front and back. The shaping of the body pieces was carried out on a small green log. The back and front body pieces were held together over the shoulders by strong leather straps, and were fastened together at the sides with bolts and straps. A steel apron protected the thighs in front, and was hung from a bolt in the centre. This allowed the apron to be easily swung to one side or the other, but could be kept in a fixed position, when required, by a bolt on each side. Only one helmet was made, and that was the one worn by Ned Kelly at Glenrowan. This helmet has been identified by Police-Inspector Pewtress as the one now exhibited at the Aquarium, in the Exhibition Buildings, Melbourne. All other helmets exhibited are very rough and clumsy imitations of the original. The helmet made by Dan Kelly and Tom Lloyd rested on the shoulders of the armour, and was high enough to protect the top of the head.

A large sized mould-board was cut to the size required, and an opening was cut out the full width of the face from the eyes down. The narrow strip passing over the forehead was bolted to the other end of the mould-board. A piece of steel was fitted to protect the face and was secured on each side by hinges, leaving a very narrow opening for the eyes.

After the siege at Glenrowan, when raking over the ashes, which was all that remained of Mrs. Jones' hotel, the police failed to discover the three missing helmets, and three imitations were made at a blacksmith's shop in Collins-street, Melbourne. It is a matter for regret that these spurious helmets were exhibited to the public and passed off as genuine. It is alleged that a police official, apparently without authority, gave Ned Kelly's armour with a bogus helmet to a titled millionaire at Sunbury. After completing the four suits of armour, all pieces, cuttings, and trimmings left over were very carefully buried alongside the forge, and within 30 feet of the back door of the old homestead.

MORE POLICE DECEPTION

Assistant Chief Commissioner of Police Supt. C. H. Nicolson on oath stated on the 7th September, 1881:—

"On my return to that district in June, 1879, I did not discourage the popular fiction that the Strathbogie Ranges were favourite haunts of the outlaws, as I desired to draw public attention from their real haunts, and also to flatter the gang that the police were as ignorant as the public. It was the policy of Mr. Sadleir and myself to keep up this idea of the Strathbogie Ranges, so as to draw them away; but we knew perfectly well they could not make that their haunt — it is not country fit for it."

The Kellys were now well provided with guns, rifles and revolvers. They also had four suits of armour; all they now wanted was a good supply of ammunition. The "Outlawry Act" made it a little difficult to buy ammunition in a country town. It was therefore necessary to go to Melbourne to get a supply. Rosier's was the recognised gunshop in Bourke street, Melbourne, and it was arranged that the cousin who helped to make the armour should go with Mrs. Skillion and a friend from Glenrowan way. The three were to go down together. Mrs. Skillion and her cousin blacksmith met the Glenrowan man at Benalla railway station and secured three first-class return tickets to Melbourne. The three called at Rosier's in the afternoon; they wanted ammunition; they said they were going on a shooting trip on the Phillip and French Islands in Western Port. Rosier had all the ammunition they ordered except that required for a certain rifle. He had some of this class, but not enough. The party paid for the ammunition and said they would call back again next morning at 11 o'clock, as Rosier promised to have the extra quantity in for the rifle by that time to complete their order. In order to establish their bona fides, Rosier was paid £2 deposit on the further supply, for which they would call next day. The Glenrowan friend took the ammunition already secured and left by train that afternoon for Benalla. He disembarked at Benalla, and that night the ammunition was handed over to the outlaws.

As soon as the party left Rosier's the latter reported to the police the sale of a large parcel of ammunition. "They are coming back again to-morrow morning," said Rosier; "they are sure to return, because they paid me £2 as a deposit on the further supply of rifle cartridges they want."

Mrs. Skillion and Tom Lloyd had tea at the Bobby Burns Hotel, and, engaging rooms for the night, they paid for them in advance. They did not intend to return to this place, but in the event of the police following them to this hotel they would doubtless wait for them to return, just as the police were doing at Rosier's. They stayed at another hotel. Next morning the police came to Rosier's and planted themselves in the shop ready to pounce upon these unarmed simpletons from the country. They waited till 11 o'clock in their cramped positions, but as country people are not always punctual, the police made allowances, and waited on and on, but the owner of the £2 deposit did not turn up. Again and again Rosier assured the police that his country customers would return, as they had paid £2 deposit.

Mrs. Skillion and her cousin boarded the evening train at Essendon for Benalla.

By this time the police woke up and wired to Supt. Sadleir at Benalla to watch the evening train for the Kelly friends and relatives, and to search the train for ammunition, which under the War Precautions or "Outlawry Act" was contraband of war. When the train drew into the Benalla railway station Mrs. Skillion and Tom Lloyd were detained by the police, while the latter searched the train for ammunition. No ammunition could be found. The police then jumped to the conclusion that the packet must have been dropped from the train between Violet Town and Benalla. Mrs. Skillion's friend had left his horse in a small paddock near the Benalla pumping station. The police seized this horse as soon as Supt. Sadleir received the wire from Melbourne and stabled him in Cobb & Co.'s stables. When their search of the train failed, the police, feeling somewhat ashamed, told Tom Lloyd that they found his horse wandering in the street and "kindly" took charge of him on account of their "good will" for the owner. The outlaws were now fully equipped with arms and ammunition and with armour; but they were in no hurry yet awhile to levy tribute on the banks.

They attended socials and dances among their friends. On one occasion the outlaws were resting near the Strathbogie Ranges and had arranged with Ben Gould to have a supply of provisions for them when he attended a picnic some distance from Violet Town. Ben Gould had his tent on the picnic grounds and sold hot saveloys to the public. Ned Kelly and Joe Byrne walked into his tent. Ben was thunderstruck when Ned Kelly arrived and said to Ben, "Have you got anything in the back, Ben?" Without answering Ned's question Ben whispered, "Good gracious, man, don't you know that there is £2000 on your head?" "Never mind that, Ben, old man," said Ned, "we're all right here." Ben did happen to have "something" in the back and he gave each of the two outlaws a glass of whisky. Ned and Joe mixed with the crowd. Some of the Kellys' friends recognised Ned, and busied themselves in showing their appreciation of the local constable, who, having come from the city, was a stranger in these parts.

The Kellys' friends flattered the constable and shouted freely for him. The constable thought that these were the nicest people he had ever met; they were so sociable. He got pretty full, and as the afternoon advanced, someone suggested dancing on the green. Good music was available, and Ned Kelly took the merry constable as his partner in a buck set. Ned thoroughly enjoyed himself, and as the constable had never seen a photograph of Ned Kelly except distorted and extravagant press pictures, and knew for a certainty that the outlaws would not be there, he also enjoyed himself. The constable had not the slightest suspicion that his arms had been around an outlaw on whose head there was a reward of £2000. Towards evening the people began to drift away from the grounds. The constable went home, and Ned and Joe Byrne had a meal with Ben Gould, and then went off with a good supply of rations. Dan Kelly and Steve Hart could hardly credit Ned's account of the fun that Joe and himself had had at the picnic.

As a neighbour and her two daughters were returning one night from a dance at Greta they felt somewhat scared on suddenly meeting four horsemen, and in the confusion she pulled up her buggy horse. One of the horsemen said: "I suppose you thought we were the Kellys?" The lady replied, "We're not afraid of the Kellys, they would do us no harm; the Kellys are all right." "You're right, old woman, the Kellys won't harm you." She then recognised the spokesman to be Ned Kelly. Although police parties were for a time constantly watching the homes of Joe Byrne, Steve Hart and the Kellys, they never seemed to get into close quarters with the outlaws, and if they had been in close quarters with the Kellys the police did not know it. On one occasion, while watching Kellys' homestead on a moonlight night, the police heard someone playing the concertina, and noticed several horses tied up at the yard and the house lighted up. Suddenly the dog barked, and as suddenly the music ceased and the lights went out. Men were seen moving about. In making a hasty retreat one of the police, Constable Graham, tripped over a log and dropped his rifle, which he did not wait to pick up. He feared the Kellys were after him, and consequently time was more precious than the rifle; it was the essence of the "contract."

CONSTABLE FITZPATRICK'S DISMISSAL

Shortly after the passing of the Outlawry Act Constable Alex. Fitzpatrick was transferred to the police depot, and from there he was sent to Lancefield, where he was under Senior-Constable Mayes.

After being only nine months in Lancefield, Fitzpatrick was charged by Senior-Constable Mayes as follows:—

"That he was not fit to be in the police force; that he associated with the lowest persons in Lancefield; that he could not be trusted out of sight, and that he never did his duty."

As the result of these charges Fitzpatrick was dismissed from the Victorian Police Force.

When giving evidence before the Royal Commission on July 6, 1881, Fitzpatrick was cross-examined as follows:—

Question: How long were you in the police force?

Fitzpatrick: Over three years.

Question: Did you plead guilty to charges of misconduct during that time?

Fitzpatrick: I did, foolishly.

Question: How often?

Fitzpatrick: I could not tell you how many times, but they were very trifling offences.

Question: Did you plead guilty to neglect of duty during the three years?

Fitzpatrick: Yes, for missing the train once or twice in Sydney.

Question: Are you aware that the Inspector-General of Sydney wrote to complain of your misconduct in Sydney?

Fitzpatrick: Yes.

Question: Were you never told in Sydney, by any officer of police there, that they complained of your conduct?

Fitzpatrick: I was.

Question: You had the opportunity of answering the charge at Sydney?

Fitzpatrick: I did write out a report in reference to that. In completing his answer to another question, Fitzpatrick said:— "There are many constables in the force who have done more serious things than I did, and have remained in the force and got promotion."

In this latter statement, Fitzpatrick was corroborated by Ned Kelly, who stated that there were men in the police force who were not fit to be there.

From the time Mr. C. H. Nicolson took charge in July, 1879, the only activity on the part of the police was among the police spies. The Kellys handled the police spies very wisely, and through their friends kept them supplied with something new. This was an easy matter, owing to the bitterness of the quarrels which continued between the heads of the police department engaged in the Kelly hunt.

In July, 1879, Supt. Hare returned to Melbourne a broken man; he was completely baffled by the outlaws. The blacktrackers were the only section of the Kelly hunters who were taken seriously by the outlaws. But as the Kellys put in their time between their old home on Eleven-Mile Creek and certain week-end resorts or camping places which they had established in the ranges, they were not troubled by the Queensland blacktrackers. Still, the outlaws held a somewhat exaggerated idea of the tracking powers of the blacks. These trackers were kept under close police supervision, and the Kellys, not being able to get in touch with them, were unable to square them. The sympathisers did not know enough of the habits of the Queensland blacks to attempt to get in direct touch with them. Otherwise the Kellys would have secured their services just as effectively as the services of many spies who joined the "spy brigade" for the purpose of supplying the outlaws with most reliable inside police information.

"THE GREATEST MAN IN THE WORLD."

Aaron Sherritt regarded Ned Kelly as the greatest man in Australia for clean dealing as a mate and for his extraordinary powers of endurance. Supt. Hare, giving evidence before the Royal Commission, said of the endurance of Aaron Sherritt and the outlaws:— "I say he (Aaron Sherritt) was a man of most wonderful endurance. He would go night after night without sleep. In the coldest nights in winter he would be under a tree without a particle of blanket of any sort, in his shirt sleeves, whilst many of my men were lying wrapped up in furs in the middle of winter. This is an instance that occurred actually: I saw the man one night, when the water was frozen on the running creeks and I was frozen to death nearly. I came down, and said, 'Where is Aaron Sherritt?' and I saw a white thing lying under a tree, and there was Aaron without his coat. The men (police) were covered up with all kinds of coats and furs and waterproof coatings, and everything else, and this man was lying on the ground uncovered. I said, 'Are you mad, Aaron, lying there?' and he said, 'I do not care about coats.' I said to him (Aaron Sherritt) on one occasion, 'Can the outlaws endure as you are doing?' He replied, 'Ned Kelly could beat me into fits.' He said, 'I can beat all the others; I am a better man than Joe Byrne, and I am better than Dan Kelly, and I am a better man than Steve Hart. I can lick these two youngsters into fits. I have always beaten Joe, but I look upon Ned Kelly as an extraordinary man; there is no man in the world like him — he is superhuman. I look upon him as invulnerable; you (Supt. Hare) can do nothing with him,' and that was the opinion of all his (Aaron Sherritt's) agents. Nearly every one in the district thought him invincible. When the police had a row with any of the sympathisers they would always finish off by saying, 'I will tell Ned about you; he will make it hot for you some day'; never speaking about the others at all."

(Is it any wonder that the police, on "double-pay," instinctively avoided coming into contact with this Napoleon of the Southern Hemisphere?)

Commissioner to Supt. Hare:—

Question: Did you ever ascertain what those traces were on the Warby Mountains? — No, never to this day; and I believe it was the men (Kellys) flying before us. They were as wonderful as everyone said they were; they could fly before us; but if we had had some of Mr. O'Connor's men on that day we could have got them, I believe.

15
FORMULATING A CAMPAIGN POLICY
SHERRITT SENTENCED TO DEATH

ON one occasion the four outlaws were camped in a dry lagoon near the Broken River, below Benalla. Two contractors, Riggleson and Graham, were working on a big gum-tree which they had felled the previous day. The contractors were visited by two young men, one of whom was recognised as one of the outlaws. The young men chatted with the contractors for some time, and incidentally inquired if they (the contractors) had seen the police about lately. The reply was no, they had not seen any police in that quarter. The two young men were Joe Byrne and Dan Kelly. They kept looking about while conversing with the contractors. Quite suddenly Dan and Joe said, "So long," and disappeared over the bank into the dry lagoon. A few minutes later the contractors saw four horsemen coming towards them from the direction of Benalla. They rode up to where these two men were working.

The four horsemen were now recognised as policemen. They inquired if the timber workers had seen any horsemen about. The contractors truthfully replied, "No." Although they knew the Kellys were in the lagoon — within speaking distance — they had not seen them mounted, and although there was a reward of £8000 for their capture, the contractors, who were almost unknown to the Kellys, would not assist the police, even with the £8000 inducement. The police, after a few commonplace remarks, turned back to report at Benalla. The Kellys in their lagoon could have shot the four policemen, but instead of shooting they started off in the opposite direction mounted on four splendid horses. The contractors went down into the dry lagoon and saw that the Kellys had fed their horses on oats and chaff, but principally raw oats. This was the period when the average policemen felt convinced that the Kellys had left Victoria for one of the other colonies. On another occasion while the heads of the police department were at loggerheads the Kellys came into Benalla en route for the police paddock, and as the police officials were sampling well-matured whisky in Craven's Hotel on one side of Bridge-street, the Kellys were also enjoying themselves in another hotel on the opposite side of the street.

They frequently discussed their plans for the future. The providore suggested that they should go on to Queensland. He would get them there one at a time. When they were safely landed in Queensland they could come together again. Dan Kelly was now about nineteen years of age and had already developed into a broad-shouldered young man. A few years retired from observation would so change his appearance and also that of Steve Hart, who was now twenty years of age, that neither of them would be easily identified. Joe Byrne was now just on twenty-three years, and with a few years in the tropical climate he, too, would not be recognised. Ned Kelly would only have to clean shave to defy the keenest eye to identify him. The Kellys took time to talk over this suggestion. They looked at it from various points of view, and finally it was turned down, on the ground that they would be strangers in a strange land. If they or any of them should be recognised they would not have the same whole-hearted support from the people in Queensland as they had where they were best known. It was better to work with the object of forcing the Victorian and New South Wales Governments to come to peace terms with them. They decided on the following programme:—

They should do some banks first. The Bank of New South Wales at Benalla was mentioned, and also the Dookie and Lake Rowan banks. The police would not expect an attack on any of the Benalla banks, and if the outlaws could so arrange their plans to draw practically the whole of the Benalla police away, the proposition would be as simple as shelling peas. After doing these banks, or at least two of them, they should try and capture the superintendents of police and take them to the ranges, and ask for an exchange of prisoners. The first thing was to secure their mother's freedom, and also that of the others, Skillion and Williamson, who were unjustly convicted. Having secured their mother's freedom by an exchange of prisoners, their next move would be for their own pardon. They would get some of their friends to remove to Melbourne and learn of the habits and customs of Lord Normanby, the Governor of Victoria. With this information their next move would be to kidnap the Governor, take him away to the ranges and hold him as hostage for a peace parley with the Service Ministry. These plans were well thought out, and their successful execution would have completely changed the history of Victoria and probably that of the other colonies also. The Kellys considered that if they could put their case before the Governor, while he was their prisoner, he would be converted into a sympathiser.

Everything looked favourable for an active campaign. Nicolson was to be recalled, and Supt. Hare would take his place. The Kellys knew that their friends would have very little difficulty in keeping Supt. Hare galloping about the country on a wild-goose chase. The feud that had now developed between Captain Standish and his favourite, Supt. Hare, on the one side, and Supt. Nicolson and his brother-in-law, Mr. O'Connor, on the other, would materially assist the friends and sympathisers of the Kellys in keeping the police department fully occupied in the North-Eastern district, while they (the Kellys) operated in the south and secured control of the Queen's representative.

Joe Byrne now paid one of his numerous visits to Woolshed, and, notwithstanding that a party of police were there watching his mother's house, he went home. His mother had some startling news for him. She said that, a few days ago, she had met Aaron Sherritt, and called him a traitor.

"What will Joe think of you now?" she said to Sherritt. She was very angry with Sherritt on account of his acting for the police against her son Joe. Sherritt said in reply, "I'll shoot Joe Byrne, and I'll . . . him before his body gets cold!" This threat to shoot Joe Byrne was not enough, but Sherritt used the foulest and most indecent expression he knew of as to what he would do with Joe Byrne's dead body. Mrs. Byrne hastened away.

Joe was nettled somewhat on receipt of this information; but he quickly controlled himself, and said that he would take care Sherritt would not get the chance to shoot him and then commit an abominable outrage on his body. After getting a change of clothing and some refreshments, Joe Byrne left his mother's house. He made for the camp, and on arrival there informed his mates of what Aaron Sherritt had said. Joe continued: "We will have a brush with the police some day and I may go out, but I do not want to leave that scoundrel behind me, to heap insults on my dear old mother. I say that Aaron Sherritt must be shot dead."

Ned Kelly said that he never went anywhere with the intention to shoot anyone; but in a fair fight he was prepared to shoot and shoot to kill. "But in this case, Joe," added Ned, "you may do as you like." Dan Kelly agreed with Joe Byrne's view. He was prepared, he said, to go with Joe and give Aaron Sherritt a dose of his own medicine, by shooting him, not only because he was a traitor, but because he was a low immoral scoundrel as well. Steve Hart took no part in discussing this sentence of death on Aaron Sherritt. It was now decided to start on their active campaign. Joe and Dan would go to Sebastopol on the following Friday night to locate Sherritt; stay all day Saturday in the neighbourhood of Sherritt's and deal with this spy on Saturday evening. They would then hasten back and join Ned Kelly and Steve Hart at Glenrowan.

The shooting of Sherritt would create a great stir at Beechworth, and the police from Benalla would be sent up there by special train. Ned Kelly and Steve Hart would go down to Glenrowan, and with their own screw wrenches and spanners remove the rails at the curve just on the Wangaratta side of the Glenrowan cutting, a quarter of a mail from the railway station. Having removed the rails, they could then compel the stationmaster to stop the train at the platform. They then would await the arrival of Dan Kelly and Joe Byrne. The four outlaws would next get ready to capture the police train at Glenrowan railway station.

Dan Kelly was opposed to the Glenrowan visit and the lifting of the rails. He said it would be better to let the police go right on to Beechworth, while their Beechworth friends would supply numerous reports that the Kellys were not far away, and thus keep the police concentrated on Beechworth while they (the Kellys) operated at Benalla through the Bank of New South Wales.

16
SHERRITT EXECUTED

THE Kellys were in no way harassed by the policy pursued by Supt. Nicolson, and as long as the police kept out of their way no one in the district was hurt. It was the general belief that the Kellys had left the North-Eastern district. Even Sergeant Steele was under that impression. On his oath on May 31, 1881, Sergeant Steele said, "I was under the impression that they had left the district altogether."

Supt. C. H. Nicolson was recalled on account of his inability to get into touch with the Kellys. He found it easier to write a report in 1877 suggesting that the Kellys should be rooted out of Greta than to arrest them now that they offered armed resistance. He had no scruple in harassing the Kellys by a most diabolical system of official tyranny and persecution. But for the past eleven months he preferred to draw his salary of £500 per year, with £1 per day expenses, or a total of £865 per annum, without exposing himself to the risk of being either wounded or captured by the Kellys. Supt. Hare took charge of the Kelly hunt on June 2, 1880, and on account of the strained relations existing between Captain Standish and Supt. Hare, on the one side, against Inspector O'Connor and his brother-in-law, Supt. C. H. Nicolson, on the other side, it was decided to get rid of the Queensland blacktrackers. Mr. H. M. Chomley, who shortly after the capture of Ned Kelly succeeded Captain Standish as Chief Commissioner of Police, had already been sent to Queensland to secure about half a dozen blacktrackers for the Victorian police force. Mr. O'Connor and his "boys" left Benalla for Melbourne on Friday, June 25, 1880, en route for Brisbane, Queensland. The new blacktrackers had not yet arrived. Supt. Hare decided to continue Supt. Nicolson's policy of spying on the Kellys, and those spies who had been paid off by Supt. Nicholson were reappointed.

Aaron Sherritt expected trouble after his quarrel with Mrs. Byrne and his threat to shoot and outrage Joe Byrne. Supt. Hare decided to take ample steps to protect this spy, and sent four policemen to protect Sherritt by day and night. The four policemen who were to protect Sherritt were Constables Armstrong, Alexander, Duross and Dowling.

These four constables stayed with Sherritt and his wife all day, and Sherritt used to accompany them at night to watch Mrs. Byrne's home. The avowed object of this watch was to come into contact with the wanted Joe Byrne. It was thought by Supt. Hare that if only these four strapping young constables could get near the outlaws there would be something doing — something out of the ordinary. The constables were armed to the teeth, and were selected for this special duty so that they might retrieve the somewhat besmirched reputation of the Victorian police force.

The Outlawry Act lapsed with the dissolution of the Berry Parliament on February 9, 1880. Now that there was no "Outlawry Act" the two Kellys stood before the law just the same as any other men for whose arrest warrants had been issued. But the case of Joe Byrne and Steve Hart was different. The only warrants issued for their arrest were contained in the "Outlawry Act," and now that that Act had lapsed there was not even a warrant in existence for their arrest.

THE OUTLAWRY ACT
ANNO QUADRAGESIMO SECUNDO
VICTORIAE REGINAE

An Act to facilitate the taking or apprehending of persons charged with certain felonies and the punishment of those by whom they are harboured.

Whereas of late divers persons charged with murder and other capital felonies availing themselves unduly of the protection afforded by law to accused persons before conviction and being harboured by evil-minded persons remain at large notwithstanding all available attempts to apprehend them and some of them being mounted armed and associated together have committed murders and have resisted and killed officers of justice whereby the lives and property of Her Majesty's subjects are in jeopardy and need better protection by law: Be it therefore enacted by the Queen's Most Excellent Majesty by and with the advice and consent of the Legislative Council and Legislative Assembly of Victoria in this present Parliament assembled, and by the authority of the same as follows (that is to say):

1. This Act shall be cited as the "FELONS APPREHENSION ACT 1878" and shall apply to all crimes committed and evidence taken and warrants issued and informations laid relating thereto as well before as after the passing of this Act.

2. Whenever after information made on oath before a justice of the peace and a warrant thereupon issued charging any person therein named or described with the commission of a felony punishable by law with death any judge of the Supreme Court on any application in chambers on behalf of the Attorney-General and upon being satisfied by affidavit of these facts and that the person charged is at large and will probably resist all attempts by the ordinary legal means to apprehend him may forthwith issue a bench warrant under the hand and seal of such judge for the apprehension of the person so charged in order to his answering and taking his trial and such judge may thereupon either immediately or at any time afterwards before the apprehension or surrender or after any escape from custody of the person so charged order a summons to be inserted in the "Gazette" requiring such person to surrender himself on or before a day and at a place specified to abide his trial for the crime of which he so stands accused. Provided that the judge shall further direct the publication of such summons at such places and in such newspapers and generally in such manner and form as shall appear to him to best calculated to bring such summons to the knowledge of the accused.

3. If the person so charged shall not surrender himself for trial pursuant to such summons or shall not be apprehended or being apprehended or having surrendered shall escape so that he shall not be in custody on the day specified in such summons he shall upon proof thereof by affidavit to the satisfaction of any judge of the Supreme Court and of the due publication of the summons be deemed outlawed and shall and may thereupon be adjudged and declared to be an outlaw accordingly by such judge by a declaration to that effect under his hand filed in the said Court of Record. And if after proclamation by the Governor with the advice of the Executive Council of the fact as such adjudication shall have been published in the "Government Gazette" and in one or more Melbourne and one or more country newspapers such outlaw shall afterwards be found at large armed or there being reasonable ground to believe that he is armed it shall be lawful for any of Her Majesty's subjects whether a constable or not and without being accountable for the using of any deadly weapon in aid of such apprehension whether its use be preceded by a demand of surrender or not to apprehend or take such outlaw dead or alive.

4. The proclamation as published in the "Government Gazette" shall be evidence of the person named or described therein being and having been duly adjudged an outlaw for the purposes of this Act and the judge's summons as so published shall in like manner be evidence of the truth of the several matters stated therein.

5. If after such proclamation any person shall voluntarily and knowingly harbour conceal or receive or give any aid shelter or sustenance to such outlaw or provide him with firearms or any other weapon or with ammunition or any horse equipment or other assistance directly or indirectly give or cause to be given to him or any of his accomplices information tending or with intent to facilitate the commission by him of further crime or to enable him to escape from justice or shall withhold information or give false information concerning such outlaw from or to any officer of the police or constable in quest of such outlaw the person such offending shall be guilty of felony and being thereof convicted shall be liable to imprisonment with or without hard labour for such period not exceeding fifteen years as the court shall determine and no allegation or proof by the party so offending that he was at the time under compulsion shall be deemed a defence unless he shall as soon as possible afterwards have gone before a justice of the peace or some officer of the police force and then to the best of his ability given full information respecting such outlaw and made a declaration on oath voluntarily and fully of the facts connected with such compulsion.

6. In any presentment under the last preceding section it shall be sufficient to describe the offence in the words of the said section and to allege that the person in respect of whom or whose accomplice such offence was committed was an outlaw within the meaning of this Act without alleging by what means or in what particular manner the person on trial harboured or aided or gave arms sustenance or information to the outlaw or what in particular was the aid sustenance shelter equipment information or other manner in question.

7. Any justice of the peace or officer of the police force having reasonable cause to suspect that an outlaw or accused person summoned under the provisions of this Act is concealed or harboured in or on any dwelling-house or premises may alone or accompanied by any persons acting in his aid and either by day or by night demand admission into and refused admission may break and enter such dwelling-house or premises and therein apprehend every person whom he shall have reasonable ground for believing to be such outlaw or accused person and may thereupon seize all arms found in or on such house or premises and also apprehend all persons found in or about the same whom such justice or officer shall have reasonable ground for believing to have concealed harboured or otherwise succoured or assisted such outlaw or accused person. And all persons and arms so apprehended and seized shall be forthwith taken before some convenient justice of the peace to be further dealt with and disposed of according to law.

8. It shall be lawful after any such proclamation as aforesaid for any police officer or constable in the pursuit of any such outlaw in the name of Her Majesty to demand and take and use any horses not being in actual employment on the roads arms saddles forage sustenance equipments or ammunition required for the purposes of such pursuit. And if the owner of such property shall not agree as to the amount of compensation to be made for the use of such property then the amount of such compensation shall be determined in the Supreme Court according to the amount claimed in an action to be brought by the claimant against Her Majesty under the provisions of "THE CROWN REMEDIES AND LIABILITIES STATUTES 1865."

9. No conveyance or transfer of land or goods by any such outlaw or accused person after the issue of such warrant for his apprehension and before his conviction if he shall be convicted shall be any effect whatever.
10. THIS ACT SHALL CONTINUE IN FORCE UNTIL THE END OF THE NEXT SESSION OF PARLIAMENT.
By Authority: John Ferres, Government Printer, Melbourne.

The Berry Government passed the above Act on November 1, 1878, and the end of the next session of Parliament was 9/2/1880, when Parliament was dissolved. Therefore there was no Outlawry Act after February 9, 1880.

****

Dan Kelly and Joe Byrne left Greta on Friday night to go to Sherritt's at Sebastopol. They knew that Sherritt had police protection, and knew the risk they were running in meeting superior numbers. But somehow the Kellys had formed a very low estimate of the courage and fighting qualities of the police. Ned Kelly estimated that one Kelly equalled forty policemen. In the opinion of the Kellys, the attitude of the police changed from savage cruelty to arrant cowardice. Dan and Joe took up their position in the ranges close by, and remained there all day Saturday, June 26, 1880.

They had tea early, and, as darkness set in, they came down and tied their horses up at a convenient distance from Sherritt's house; they also had a pack horse carrying their armour. As they issued forth they came across a German named Anton Weekes. They handcuffed Weekes, and told him as long as he obeyed their instructions he would not be hurt; but if he refused then they would deal with him in a most drastic fashion. Weekes said he would do what they wanted, but he could not do much. Joe Byrne told Weekes to go up to Sherritt's house, knock at the back door, and say that he had lost his way, and ask Aaron Sherritt to show him the way to his hut. Weekes readily agreed, and was somewhat surprised at the simplicity of the task imposed on him. He went up to Sherritt's, but never suspected that Joe Byrne intended to do something to Sherritt. He and Joe Byrne went to the back door, and Dan Kelly went to the front door. The house was a two-roomed wooden slab building with kitchen and bedroom only. Weekes knocked at the back door, and Joe Byrne stood a little distance from him. They heard a shuffling of feet inside and Aaron Sherritt called out, "Who is there?" Weekes said, "It's me, I loss my vay." Mrs. Aaron Sherritt came to the door, and opening it said, "It's Anton Weekes; he has lost his way." Aaron Sherritt then came to the door, and opening it said, "It's Anton Weekes; he has lost his way." Aaron Sherritt then came to the door, the light fell on Anton Weekes, and Joe Byrne stood close by in the darkness. Aaron Sherritt in a joking way said, "Do you see that tall sapling over there?" As he uttered these words Aaron shrank back a little as if surprised at what he saw. Just then Joe Byrne fired, and stepping quickly into the room fired a second shot, and Sherritt fell and died without uttering a word.

When Weekes first knocked at the door Constable Duross was in the kitchen with Aaron Sherritt, his wife, and his wife's mother, Mrs. Barry, who had arrived about fifteen minutes before Weekes. Duross immediately went to join the other constables in the bedroom. That was the shuffling of feet that Joe Byrne had heard. The four constables were very much scared by the report of Joe Byrne's gun so close at hand. They were all armed, but were very much afraid of getting hurt.

Aaron Sherritt's mother in law — Mrs. Ellen Barry — giving evidence before the Royal Commission on July 20, 1881, said:— "I was just about a quarter of an hour inside when a knock came to the door, and Aaron asked who was there. His wife asked who was there first, and the German answered, and she said, 'It is Anton Weekes; he has lost his way.' Aaron went to the door, and Weekes said, 'Come and show me the way; I have lost my way.' Aaron opened the door and I went to the door with him, and he mentioned a sapling as he was going out, but that was out of a joke. I went with him just to the door behind him. I heard Aaron say, 'Who is that?' and as he said the words he seemed as if inclined to come in again. He just had that word out of his mouth when a shot went. I just stood on one side of Aaron and stepped backwards into the middle of the room, and there was another shot fired through the door, and my daughter was standing just behind the door, and the shot passed her face, and she went back into the bedroom. Aaron stood on the middle of the floor and I was looking at him, and could see no mark on his face, and I heard no noise. I turned round, and there was a man standing with his back to the door, and he fired a second shot at Aaron, and he fell on the floor. He never spoke, not a word. I did not know at the time who fired the shot. He (Aaron) stumbled some time before he fell, and then he fell backwards. I went and stooped down, and knelt down just by his head, and I could see that he was dying. This man (Joe Byrne) called me by my name, and he said he would put a ball through me and my daughter if we would not tell who was in the room. Duross was in the sitting room when the knock came to the door, and he walked into the bedroom then, and I was thinking he might have heard the man's step going into the room, as he asked who was the man that went into the bedroom. I asked Byrne would he let me go outside. He gave me orders to open the front door directly after that, and as I did I saw another man in front of the door with a gun. Byrne was at the back door, and this other man at the front. I asked him (Byrne) to let me outside, and he said, 'All right.' So when I went outside I saw Weekes standing by the side of the chimney. He was handcuffed, but I could not see at the time, it was too dark; but I could see Byrne taking them off. Byrne said to me outside, "I am satisfied now, I wanted that fellow' — that was Aaron. 'Well, Joe,' I said, 'I never heard Aaron say anything against you.' And he said, 'He would do me harm if he could; he did his best.' He (Byrne) told me to go in and bring the man out of the bedroom, for my daughter had told him it was a working man looking for work, and said his name was Duross. I went into the bedroom and told the police to come out. They were looking for their firearms. When I went in the room was dark; in fact, it would be very hard to know what they were doing; they were stooping looking for firearms, and beckoned me to go outside. They did not want to make a noise. The police could have shot Joe Byrne when he stepped inside to fire the second shot if they had their firearms ready. He used to place me in front of him, and when he sent me in he used to put my daughter in front of him — that was Byrne, but Kelly did not do that; and he went round soon after that to look for bushes to set fire to the place. Byrne sent in my daughter after some time and she was kept inside. I went in afterwards, and they (the police) just got me by the clothes and one of the men, Dowling, said, 'Stop inside, and if they set fire to the place, they (the police) would let both of us out.' They (the police) said they did not think the outlaws would set fire to the place while women were inside, so I stopped in. Before I came in the last time, Dan Kelly had the bushes outside the room where the men (police) were. He took out a box of matches and struck a match and the wind blew it out; when I saw him strike the match, I said, 'If you set fire to the house, and the girl get shot or burnt, you can just kill me along with them.' Dan said nothing at the time, but some time after he sang out to Byrne to send me inside, and I said it was no use my going in — that I would be burned with the rest; and he said he would see about that. So I went in, and we all remained inside till daylight. The first time I went into the room the men (police) appeared as if they were bustling about looking for their firearms, and the second time I went into the room Alexander and another man were sitting on a box in front of the door with their 'possum rugs around them, and I could not see the other men; I did not notice them in the room. I could not say where they were at the time. The third time I went into the bedroom they had my daughter kept in (this was the last time Byrne sent me in). Alexander was at one side of the room and the other constables were under the bed. Constable Alexander was at one side of the room where the bed was not. Constable Duross and Constable Dowling were under the bed, and their head and shoulders out at the side of the bed. I went to the two men, and they caught me by the clothes and pulled me to the ground. I remained lying on the floor; they did not put me underneath the bed. Duross just tried to shove me in slightly, but I remained where I was; in fact, I do not think that I could get under the bed.

"At the time that Byrne was standing at the door no doubt if the police had come to the side of the door they could have fired at him right enough. Of course, I know that we cannot do without police in the country, for any honest person could not live, but they ought to speak the truth. My opinion of some of them is they are not particular what they say. I am quite certain about the two men, Duross and Dowling, being under the bed and their heads out, and the guns facing them by the door, and that was when they pulled me down, and Dowling said if I did not keep quiet they would have to shoot me. He said, 'You have better stop in, Mrs. Barry, and if you stop in the outlaws will not set fire to the place while there are women in the place.' That might be about nine o'clock. Of course, it has been said that there were voices outside during the night, but I did not hear any, and I can hear as well as anyone."

Mrs. Aaron Sherritt, on July 21, 1881, on oath said: "When her husband, Aaron Sherritt, was shot she saw Dan Kelly about a quarter of an hour after the shooting standing inside the front door; he had his elbow leaning on the table. The men (police) could have shot him there if they tried; if the police had been looking out of the door or keeping an eye on the division — the partition that was between the two rooms — they could have had Dan Kelly very easily; but I do not think they were prepared at the time."

Question (by the Commission): It would not take them all that time to look for their arms? — "Not at that time; there were two of them under the bed. I am quite certain that there were two under the bed and two lying on top; so it was impossible to have either of the outlaws in the position the men (police) were in. They (the police) were in that position when Dan Kelly was in the room. I was put under the bed. Constable Dowling pulled me down, and he could not put me under, and then Armstrong caught hold of me, and the two of them shoved me under, and they had their feet against me. They remained in that position for two or three hours. I do not remember hearing voices outside after I was put under the bed, only the dog howling. I heard no voices outside after my mother came in, and remained — not after that — I did not hear anything.

The second time I came in Dan Kelly was by the table, and then when I went out again he was gone to get bushes to set fire to the house."

ANTON WEEKES

On July 20, 1881, Anton Weekes on oath said: "I remember going up to Sherritt's door and asking the way the night Aaron Sherritt was shot. I was stuck up by Byrne and Dan Kelly. They asked me my name. Then they put handcuffs on me and made me go up to Sherritt's door, and ask him to show me my way. I was there about six o'clock, and I left the place about nine o'clock. I then went home. I live a quarter of a mile from Sherritt's. After Sherritt was shot I stood an hour or two with the people outside. Byrne was with me, and Dan Kelly was at the front door. I did not hear any conversation with Mrs. Sherritt or Mrs. Barry. They came out and went in again. I had no chance of escaping.

"At about nine o'clock Byrne took the handcuffs off me and left me standing. I stayed there by myself for 15 or 20 minutes, and then I went round home through the bush. I was so frightened I ran directly home and stayed at home. I did not see any others there, only Joe Byrne and Dan Kelly. I heard Byrne call out, 'Dan, stand and watch the window.' That is how I knew it was Dan. They were on horseback when they stuck me up, and Byrne was leading another horse. I do not think they had armour on, not Byrne — I think Kelly might; he looked very stout. He had nothing on his head (no armour). I could see his face. I did not see them try to set the house on fire. Byrne always called out for two men to come out, and said, 'Mind, I will set the house on fire if you do not come out.' But he never began to do it while I was there. Byrne did not say there were police in the house; always two men he wanted out. I knew Byrne since he was a child. He was a neighbour of mine half a mile away. I heard Byrne and Mrs. Sherritt talking and crying, I heard Byrne ask who was there, and she said, 'A man in there looking for work', and he said always, 'Bring the man out,' and he sent Mrs. Sherritt in to bring the man out. I did not know that there were police in the house, and never heard it. I did not hear anyone say there were policemen about there till after the murder."

The four constables in the bedroom had more confidence in the chivalry of the Kellys than in their own courage. These "heroes" put Mrs. Sherritt between them and the wall under the bed. She would stop a bullet if one came through, but they were very confident that the Kellys would not fire a shot through the wall while there were women inside. It is perfectly clear that no attempt had been made to set fire to the house. Next day, Sunday, the four constables remained inside until six o'clock on

Sunday evening. If the order were reversed and two outlaws were in the bedroom and four constables outside, what a different state of affairs would have prevailed! The four constables would, undoubtedly, have been captured. Later, at Glenrowan, there were fifty police to Dan Kelly and Steve Hart, and then the police were not confident of success.

Supt. Hare agreed with Joe Byrne that Aaron Sherritt was better dead than alive. He (Supt. Hare) wrote as follows:— "It was doubtless a most fortunate occurrence that Aaron was shot by the outlaws; it was impossible to have reclaimed him, and the Government of the colony would not have assisted him in any way, and he would have gone back to his old course of life, and probably become a bushranger himself."

Portrait of Steve Hart by Barnes.

17
GLENROWAN

THE conduct of the four constables who were entrusted with the protecting of Aaron Sherritt was officially described by the Royal Commission as follows:— "That the constables who formed the hut party on the night of Aaron Sherritt's murder, viz., Henry Armstrong, Wm. Duross, Thomas P. Dowling, and Robert Alexander, were guilty of disobedience of orders and gross cowardice, and that the three latter — Constable Armstrong's resignation having been accepted — be dismissed from the service."

The evidence of these four men was not believed by the Royal Commission, but if either of them gave similar evidence against the Kellys the evidence would have been considered sufficient for a conviction and a heavy sentence.

After taking the handcuffs off Anton Weekes, Joe Byrne and Dan Kelly hastened to join Ned Kelly and Steven Hart at Glenrowan, where they arrived early on Sunday morning. Ned Kelly and Steve Hart had already arrived at Glenrowan and went down to where the rails were to be lifted from the railway line. They applied their own spanners and screw wrenches to the nuts, but could not take a budge out of them. After working for some time to unscrew the bolts they had to give up in despair. This failure necessarily caused a serious alteration in their plan of campaign. The Kellys at first intended to capture the train quietly. By breaking the line at the curve, the stationmaster would be required to stop the train at the Glenrowan station, and as the police and trackers would not have expected such an attack they would not be in close touch with their guns and ammunition. The four outlaws in armour could, if resisted, rake the train from end to end. It the train refused to stop when a danger signal was flashed, then it would go over the bank; if the driver tried to run back, a quantity of blasting powder and fuse was supplied to blow up portion of the line in the rear of the train.

Ned and Steve first bailed up a number of navvies who were camped in tents near the stationmaster's house at the railway gates, as they suspected there were detectives amongst them. They then bailed up Mrs. Jones' Hotel. Joe Byrne and Dan Kelly had not yet arrived from Sherritt's. The Kellys then stuck up the stationmaster, Mr. Stanistreet, and asked him if he could stop a special train with police and blacktrackers.

The Kellys were not aware that the blacktrackers had already left Benalla en route for Queensland. Mr. Stanistreet replied that he could stop any passenger train, but would not guarantee to stop a special train carrying police and blacktrackers exactly where the Kellys might want it. This reply made it clear that there was no means of capturing a trainload of police unless the line was broken. Ned then went with Steve Hart and called up the platelayers. They roused Sullivan up, and met Reardon, who got up to see what was wrong, and ordered them to pull up the line a quarter of a mile from the railway station on the Wangaratta side of Glenrowan so that the train could go no further. Ned intended that the stationmaster should flash the danger signal to stop the train near the station, and tell the police to leave their firearms and horses in the train; that it was no use fighting, as the Kellys were in steel armour and could rake the train from end to end, and everything in it; that the best thing for them (police) to do was to walk out with their hands up and their lives would be spared. The plan was to capture the leaders and hold Supt. Hare and other leaders, such as O'Connor and the blacktrackers, as prisoners of war, and then request an exchange of prisoners. The Kellys would give up Hare and O'Connor upon the release of Mrs. Kelly, Mr. Skillion, and Williamson, the three who were innocent of the charge on which they had been convicted. This plan had to be abandoned on account of the difficulty of keeping their presence at Glenrowan a secret from the police. The alternative plan was to bail up everybody who happened to be in Glenrowan on Sunday, and get the train stopped about a mile on the Benalla side of Glenrowan, opposite the Glenrowan police station. The police were to be told by Curnow, the schoolmaster, that the Kellys were in the police barracks, so that while the police rushed to surround the police station the train would have to go on to Glenrowan to unload their horses, and the Kellys would capture the train and compel the engine driver to take the train back to Benalla and take the Kellys down the line to rob the banks. The police surrounding the barracks would be without horses and would be fairly stranded while the Kellys successfully carried out their plans. Ned Kelly had arranged that their (the police) horses, which they had brought to Glenrowan, were to be driven into the hills, and thereby effectively cut off means of transport for the police at Glenrowan. The four members of the Kelly gang drank freely, and it was this free indulgence in bad liquor that was responsible for their destruction.

SUNDAY AT GLENROWAN

It was not until Sunday afternoon about 2.30 that the police headquarters in Benalla received word that Aaron Sherritt had been shot by Joe Byrne on Saturday evening at about 8. On receipt of this information Supt. Hare sent for Supt. Sadleir, and they held a consultation as to what was the best thing to do. Supt. Hare wired to Captain Standish, who was at Melbourne headquarters, requesting that Mr. O'Connor and his "boys" be sent up that Sunday night to get on the Kellys' tracks while they were fresh. Captain Standish got in touch with the Chief Secretary (Mr. Ramsay), who in turn wired to the Queensland Government to allow Mr. O'Connor and the backtrackers to return. The Queensland Chief Secretary agreed, and Mr. O'Connor was at the Essendon railway station with his blacktrackers and equipment at 9.45 p.m. on Sunday, 27/6/1880. The train bringing Mr. O'Connor, his wife and her sister and a number of press representatives arrived at Benalla about one o'clock on Monday morning, June 28, 1880.

The Kellys took complete possession of Glenrowan and almost everybody in the town except their special friends. There were two hotels in Glenrowan, viz., McDonald's, on the Greta or eastern side on the railway station, and Mrs. Jones' hotel, on the western side of the railway station. McDonald was a genuine friend of the Kellys, and therefore his place was not utilised to stick up the town. Mrs. Jones, on the other hand, was an enemy; she was regarded by them as a police spy. It was therefore necessary to take charge of her and her hotel. The men and women at first were sent to the stationmaster's house, and then after the rails were taken up the men, women, and children were imprisoned at Jones' hotel. The full list of prisoners totalled 62. On Sunday morning Steve Hart was much the worse for liquor, but late on in the day he sobered up. He was in charge of the stationmaster's wife and children at the gatehouse.

The Kellys treated the prisoners well, and the day was put in with sports in the hotel yard. Ned Kelly joined in hop, step and jump with the prisoners, and used a revolver in each hand as dumbbells. Others whiled away the time card-playing. At night a room was cleared for a dance, and "all went as merry as a marriage bell."

Between 9 and 10 p.m. Ned Kelly, Joe Byrne, Thomas Curnow, the schoolmaster, and his brother-in-law, Dave Mortimer, E. Reynolds, and R. Gribbens, went down to the police barracks to "arrest" Constable Bracken. The police barracks were situated a mile from Glenrowan towards Benalla on the main Melbourne-to-Sydney road.

Ned and Joe rode and wore their armour; Reynolds, the postmaster, and Gribbens, who was staying at Reynolds', walked. Dave Mortimer also rode. The post office was close to the barracks. When they got near the barracks Curnow, who was driving his buggy, in which were his wife and sister and little Alex. Reynolds, aged seven, the son of the postmaster, and the others were told to remain about 30 yards away. Ned dismounted and told Mortimer to do the same. Dave Mortimer was told to go up to the door of the police barracks and knock. He did as directed. Joe Byrne remained some little distance away. Knocking and calling failed to attract the constable's attention. Ned consulted with Joe Byrne for a few seconds, and then took little Alex. Reynolds and his father to the back of the barracks. Mr. Reynolds called Constable Bracken, and after a while the latter came to the door with his double-barrelled gun in his hand ready for action. As Bracken opened the back door he was covered by Ned Kelly and ordered to throw up his hands. Bracken obeyed, and Ned took charge of Bracken's gun, revolver, and horse. Bracken was ordered to mount the horse, which Ned, riding his own horse, led by a halter. Ned told Curnow that he may go home with his family, and he was also told to stop the train. Curnow was ordered when he stopped the train to tell the police in the train that the Kellys were in charge of the police barracks. The rest of the party, with Ned and Joe Byrne, went back to Mrs. Jones' hotel. It was now between 11 and 12 o'clock midnight. Mrs. Jones was overheard by Ned telling one of the line repairers to be a man and escape, while she would keep Ned Kelly engaged. The railway line repairer refused to take the risk. Although there was no actual drunkenness, still the Kellys and some of their prisoners spent a good deal of money at Mrs. Jones' on drink, most of which was considered as dangerous as "chain lightning," and the Kellys were somewhat muddled. The Kellys now decided to let their prisoners go home, as they themselves intended to prepare for action. Dan Kelly told their prisoners that they could now go. Just then Mrs. Jones said, "You are not to go yet; Kelly is to give you a lecture." So the people who had got up to leave turned back into the hotel again. Mrs. Jones came in and said, "Kelly will give you all a lecture before you go."

While in conversation with some of the men Ned was interrupted by Joe Byrne, who came in and said, "The train is coming." The Kellys had one room reserved for themselves, in which they kept their armour. They now entered this room and hurried to dress in their armour. The prisoners could hear the rattle of steel. Mrs. Jones' interruption for a lecture prevented the civilians from getting away.

18
EVIDENCE

Constable Bracken had seen where the Kellys had put the key of the room in which he and others had been imprisoned, and watching for his opportunity, while the Kellys were getting into their armour, opened the door and escaped from the hotel. The other prisoners feared being shot if they followed Bracken, and so decided to remain in the hotel. He rushed over to the railway station, into which the train had just come. Supt. Hare had already given orders to unload the horses, but on hearing from Constable Bracken that the Kellys were in Jones' hotel, and that the place was full of people bailed up there by the Kellys, he then called his men to let their horses go and follow him. Supt. Hare led the way, followed by Constables Kelly, Barry, Gascoigne, Phillips, Arthur, Inspector O'Connor, and five Queensland blacktrackers.

Before Constable Bracken left the hotel he told the civilians held up there to lie flat on the floor if there was any firing. Ned Kelly mounted his horse and rode round to the station; when close to the station he hurriedly jumped off his horse to take charge of the train. In doing so he broke a bolt in his armour and had some delay in repairing it. By this time the police had rushed over in front of the hotel and fired a volley. The women and children screamed, and Ned, thinking the screams came from the gatehouse, where Steve Hart had been, hastened down to their assistance. He got half-way between the gatehouse and Jones' hotel when he was shot in the foot, and almost immediately afterwards he received another shot in the arm. Ned then fired four shots from his Spencer rifle. He fired at the flashes made by the firing of the police at the hotel, which they (the police) knew was full of innocent men, women, and children. One of these four shots hit Supt. Hare. Ned's hand was so badly injured that he was unable to use either rifle or revolver effectively.

The Kellys did not fire a single shot until Ned was wounded, which was the third volley from the police. Ned went to the hotel and called out to those inside, "Put the lights out and lie down." He then went around the back of the hotel and met Joe Byrne, who informed Ned that Constable Bracken had escaped. Ned told Dan and Steve to go into the hotel and to pull up the counters and barricade the sides of the building. The police now kept up the continuous fire at the hotel. The bullets went through the weatherboard walls as if they were cardboard. Ned then retired to a spot some distance from the hotel in the direction of the Warby Ranges, and lay down. He was bleeding freely. There was still one cartridge in his rifle.

Supt. Hare retired after being shot in the wrist. He called out to O'Connor to surround the house, and he told Senior-Constable Kelly to do likewise. Hare continued: "Come on, O'Connor, the beggars have shot me; bring your boys with you and surround the house." Supt. Hare then retired from the field. He went over to the railway station and ordered the train back to Benalla so that he could receive medical attention. He did not offer to take the women, Mrs. O'Connor and her sister, Miss Smith, back to Benalla with him; they were left to take their chance of being shot. Hare appeared to be bent on self-preservation. His wound was dressed by Dr. Nicholson, but he (Supt. Hare) also sent for his cousin, Dr. Chas. Ryan, of Melbourne. Hare did not return to the fight. The screaming of the women and children in the hotel was heartrending, but the police, as if craving for someone's blood, kept up a continuous and murderous fire on them. It was a bright moonlight night. Mrs. Jones' boy was shot by the police early in the encounter. Some of the civilians got out during a short lull in the murderous fire on the women and children from the ranks of the police. Mr. James Reardon and his wife and children tried to escape from the hotel about daybreak, but were driven back by the volleys of hissing bullets directed towards them. They went into the hotel again. Mrs. Reardon saw Byrne, Dan Kelly, and Steve Hart in the passage. She said to them, "Will you allow us to go?" One of the three replied, "Yes, you can all go, but if you go out the police will shoot you." Mrs. Reardon put her little girl out in the yard and she screamed, and she herself followed and screamed. Dan Kelly said, "If you escape — —" "What will I do?" said Mrs. Reardon. He replied, "See Hare and tell him to keep his men from shooting till daylight, and to allow these people all to go out, and then we shall fight for ourselves."

Mrs. Reardon, in giving evidence on oath before the Royal Commission, said: "I came into the yard and screamed for the police to have mercy on me. 'I am only a woman; allow me to escape with my children. The outlaws will not interfere with us — do not you.'"

"I could see the men behind the trees. A voice said, 'Put up your hands and come this way, or I will shoot you like — — dogs.' The voice came from a tree behind the stable on the Wangaratta side. I did not know at the time whose voice it was. It was Sergeant Steele, but at the time I did not know who it was; I saw him afterwards. I put my baby under my arm and held up my hand, and my son let go one hand and held the other child by it, and we went straight on. The man commenced firing, and he kept firing against us. I cannot say he was firing at us, but against us. He was firing in my direction, and I got close to the fence, and the tree stood some distance from the fence of Jones' yard, and as I did I saw a gun pointed at me. I then turned round and went down along the fence towards the railway station, and two shots went directly after me, and two went through the shawl that was covering the baby. I felt my arm shaking, and I said, 'Oh, you have shot my child!' I have the shawl here with two bullet holes in it. (Shawl produced and the holes in it examined). I do not know whether it was two shots or one, and the holes have got a good deal larger since. The shawl was doubled and wrapped round the baby. There were two holes in the shawl when I first looked at it. It came from a gun, for I was very close to it. My son was close behind me, coming about a yard away from me, and he said, 'Mother, come back; you will be shot'; and I said, 'I will not go back; I might as well be shot outside as inside'; but I said, 'I do not think the coward can shoot me.' My son turned away and walked back towards the house, pulling the little child by the left hand, and with the right hand up. I looked round and saw him going, and that was the last I saw of him. It was quite bright; I cannot say whether it was daylight or moonlight. It was sufficiently light to tell a man. I heard the police call to Sergeant Steele, saying, 'Do not shoot her; you can see it is a woman with a child in her arms.' It came from a policeman close behind Sergeant Steele. I found out afterwards that it was a constable named Arthur. My son was two yards from me. My son was two yards from me. Just as I turned two shots went past me. I did not see my son shot. He got shot when retreating to the hotel. He said it was just as he was going to the door, and he fell against the door. No one called out to me to stop or they would fire before the shots came. Only one called out what I have said, 'Put up your hands or I will shoot you like —— dogs'; and we went where the man called us. I could not be mistaken for a male. I was dressed in my ordinary female attire, and not only that, but they had been firing from the station at me. There was a gutter along there, and when Steele commenced shooting at me they all began shooting at me from the other place. I cannot say the exact words Constable Arthur used. I heard him say at the first set-out, 'Do you not see it is a woman with a child in her arms?' — and when those two shots were fired at me I heard him (Constable Arthur) speaking very angrily, and then the firing ceased. I know that Ned Kelly was captured after what I am now relating. I walked straight on to the slip-panel, and I got behind a tree, and, when all the firing had ceased, I called out for them (the police) to spare my life — that I was but a woman, and for a long time nobody spoke. And then Guard Dowsett came out from the railway station, and, as I was not able to get there alone, he helped me to the station. I do not know how he got me there, whether it was over the fence or through. I did not see my son (wounded) until about ten o'clock in the day. He remained at the hotel after being shot, until the male prisoners were released. That was the first time I knew he had been shot in the morning. I was very much excited when I attempted to leave the hotel a second time, when I got into the yard and found how I was treated by the police. I thought my life was in danger. I knew it was in danger. I knew it was a constable who shot at me from behind a tree, for there were no others there. I found out who it was that shot at me by inquiring. I know I am speaking very strongly against that man (Steele). I found out particularly that same afternoon Sergeant Steele told my second eldest boy, some sixteen years of age, that it was he (Steele) who shot him (my eldest son). Another lad from Winton — I think a son of Mr. Aherne — was speaking to my second boy about the shooting affair. The latter said, 'My brother was shot,' and the other lad asked by whom, and Sergeant Steele made answer and said, 'It was I who shot him' — so I think that is plain enough. I stated that Constable Arthur remonstrated with him (Steele) for shooting. I did not know him (Arthur) at the time, but two months afterwards I saw him and recognised him, and inquired as to his name, and found it was Constable Arthur."

CONSTABLE JAMES ARTHUR

On June 9, 1881, Constable James Arthur, giving evidence on oath before the Royal Commission, said:— "I remember Mrs. Reardon coming out, and her son and Mr. Reardon. It was near daylight. I was thirty yards from the house on the Wangaratta side of Jones' Hotel. I was stationed between the back and front, opposite in a line with the passage, about due north from the house. I heard Mrs. Reardon cry out. When she came out she

Steele sang out, 'Throw up your hands or I will shoot you like a —— dog,' and the woman was coming towards him and he fired. He fired direct at her; we could see it in the moonlight, and then she turned round, and then he fired a second shot, and then I spoke to him and told him not to fire — this was an innocent woman. I could see her with a child in her arms; and then afterwards he turned round and said, 'I have shot the mother Jones in the ——.' Constable Phillips was on his right, on the right hand behind, and I heard him make some remark about a feather. I could not say what it was. I told him (Steele) not to fire — it was an innocent woman. I said I would shoot him if he fired. I was about twenty yards from him (Steele). They came out of the back door of the hotel, out of the passage, and just as she came out of the passage Steele fired. Right behind the hotel I saw her (Mrs. Reardon's) son coming out. I saw the young fellow coming out, leading a child. I could distinguish it was a figure of a man. I could see it was a young man. It was quite light. He was walking, leading the child. I could not be positive that Steele deliberately fired at that young fellow, because he (young Reardon) was nearest to me and Steele had to fire past me. I have no hesitation in saying Steele deliberately shot at the young fellow. He shot at him. I did not see him fall with the shot Steele fired, but with another shot he fell in the doorway. I would not swear it was Steele who fired the second shot. Steele made no remark then. After the youth a man came out with a child in his arms, and Sergeant Steele sang out to him to hold up his hands. The man threw up his arm, and he (Steele) fired at him. The man (Reardon) crept on his stomach, and crept into the house. He (Steele) seemed like as if he was excited. He fired from the tree when he first was there. He fired when I could see nothing to fire at. I did not see that he had been drinking. When he came first in the morning he came to where Constable Kelly and I were standing, and we went to tell him about the outlaws being in the house, and he would not wait; he rushed over to a tree close to the house, leaving his men to place themselves. He did not place his own men or anything — he would not wait."

Question (by Commission): Who placed his men? — The senior constable took two, and the others went by themselves.

Question: You recollect you are on oath; are you quite positive in those statements you have made? — I am.

Question: And that young Reardon was not crawling? — He was not, not when he came out.

Question: And the man that held up his hands after, you say Steele fired at him? — Yes.

Question: We have it in evidence that the elder Reardon fell on his knees and belly and crawled in? — That is what I say. I would not swear it was Reardon, or young Reardon, but those that came out after Mrs. Reardon.

Question: You have no doubt in your mind that this was a woman? — Any man could see her and hear her voice.

Question: You had no suspicion in your mind that it was one of the outlaws? — None at all.

Question: You could tell the voice? — Yes.

Question: Sergeant Steele had the same opportunity of knowing that as you? — Just the same.

Question: Did he make any remark when you said you would shoot him if he fired again? — No; the only one was that he had shot Mrs. Jones in the — —.

CONSTABLE WILLIAM PHILLIPS

On oath on June 9, 1881, said:— "I saw Mrs. Reardon come out of the house."

Question: The first thing I heard was Steele challenging somebody and firing, and then I heard a woman screaming; and with that, from the front of the house several shots came up. I heard Constable Arthur say, "Do not shoot — that is an innocent woman," or "That is a woman and children" — something to that effect.

Question: Was there any difficulty in yourself, Arthur, or Steele knowing that is was a female? — Not the slightest.

Question: Before he fired you could see distinctly it was a woman and children? — Yes, it was bright moonlight.

Question: Did Steele shoot immediately he challenged them? — Immediately.

Question: Did you hear him (Steele) say anything? — First, I asked him what he was shooting at, and he said, "By Christ, I have shot old mother Jones in the — —"; and I said, "It is a feather in your cap."

Question: Did you see what happened after? What did the woman do? — She was singing out and went out of the place. Steele was at some (one) of the trees there, and she walked down. The fence was between her and Steele, and that was what saved her, no doubt. After he fired there was loud talking going on and screaming, and I do not know who took her away.

Question: She was taken away, at all events? — Yes, and did not go back to the house.

Question: Did you see any other figure besides her? — No, only the boy.

Question: Where was he? — He was following her, and all at once I saw him run back to the house.

Question: Did you not see that he had hold of a child? — No, I could not swear that.

Question: Did you hear anyone challenging the boy? — Sergeant Steele was the only one who challenged them.

Question: Did you see whether the boy was crawling? — Walking.

JAMES REARDON, RAILWAY LINE REPAIRER

On May 14, 1881, on his oath, stated to the Royal Commission:— "Shortly after two o'clock on Sunday morning, June 27, 1880, I heard the dogs barking, making a row, and I got up and dressed myself and went outside the door and heard a horse whinnying down the railway line, and went towards where I heard the horse. I thought it was the horse of a friend, and I went down, and Sullivan was coming through the railway fence, and I said, 'What is the matter?' and he said, 'I am taken prisoner by this man.' Ned Kelly came up and put a revolver to my cheek and said, 'What is your name?' and I said, 'Reardon,' and he said, 'I want you to come up and break the line.' He said, 'I was in Beechworth last night, and I had a great contract with the police; I have shot a lot of them, and I expect a train from Benalla with a lot of police and blackfellows, and I am going to kill all the ——.' I said, 'For God's sake do not take me; I have a large family to look after.' He said, 'I have got several others up, but they are no use to me,' and I said, 'They can do it without me,' and he said, 'You must do it or I will shoot you' — and he took my wife and seven or eight children to the station.

"When we came to the small tool-house the chest was broken and the tools lying out on the side of the line. He said, 'Pick up what tools you want,' and I took two spanners and a hammer, and I said, 'I have no more to take,' and he said, 'Where are your bars?' and I said, 'Two or three miles away'; I said, 'In front of my place,' and he sent Steve Hart for them, who came in a few minutes after himself. When I went on the ground I said to Hart, 'You have plenty of men without me doing it.' 'All right,' he says, and he pointed to the contractor from Benalla, and said, 'You take the spanner.'

"That was Jack McHugh, I think. He took the spanner and I instructed him, on being made, how to use it. Ned Kelly came up and said, 'Old man, you are a long time breaking up this road.' I said, 'I cannot do it quicker.' And he said, 'I will make you do it quicker; if you do not look sharp, I will tickle you up with this revolver.' And I said, 'I cannot do it quicker, do what you will'; and he said, 'Give me no cheek.' So we broke the road. He wanted four lengths broken. I said, 'One will do as well as twenty.' And he said, 'Do you think so?' And I said I was certain. I said that, because I thought if only one was off, the train would jump it and go on safely. Hart pointed out the place.

"He then brought us all up to the station and remained at the gatehouse, where the stationmaster lived, for perhaps two hours. There were about twenty of us. All who came along were bailed up, and on Sunday evening he (Ned Kelly) had 62 which I counted.

"At the hotel he did not treat us badly — not at all. They had drink in them in the morning. When I first saw Steve Hart he was pretty drunk. I saw some people offer drink to Dan Kelly and Byrne, I believe, and they said, 'No'; but if Ned Kelly drank I cannot say, for he was in the kitchen in the back. When it came night we were all locked in and kept there. There was no opportunity of escaping at all — not the slightest. No chance. I was there when the police came. I was still there when he went for Bracken between nine and ten o'clock on Sunday night. They took him prisoner also. There was only one constable here at the time. During the night before the police came they were very jolly, and the people and Mrs. Jones cleared the house out. They would not have it without a dance. She wanted me to dance, and I said, 'No, something is troubling me besides dancing.' Mrs. Jones said, 'We will all be let go very soon, but you may thank me for it'; and my missus asked Dan Kelly to let me go home with my children and family. 'We will let you all go directly,' she (Mrs. Jones) said. That would be two o'clock, about an hour before the police arrived.

"There was a dance got up in the house; there were three of the Kellys, Ned, Dan and Byrne danced, and Mrs. Jones and her daughter, and three or four others I did not know. Mrs. Jones praised Ned Kelly; she said he was a fine fellow. Dan Kelly said, 'Now you can all go home,' and I stood up and picked up one of my children in my arms, and we were making for the door when Cherry picked up Ryan's child, and Mrs. Jones stood at the door and said, 'You are not to go yet; Kelly is to give you a lecture,' so we all turned back into the house again, and Mrs. Jones came in and said, 'Kelly will give you all a lecture before you go.' A little later Byrne came in and said, 'The train is coming.' That stopped all the discourse. They turned into the back room — the three bushrangers; there was one (Steve Hart) taking care of Stanistreet's family. Then they went into one of the back rooms, dressing themselves in their armour. I could hear the armour rattling. We could have got clear away if we had been allowed to go when Dan Kelly said we could go.

"Mrs. Jones seemed to be very pleased that the outlaws were there. Bracken saw where they planted the key, and at the time they went to put their armour on he went and took the key. He put the key in his trousers pocket and came back to the door and stood there till he got his opportunity, and opened the door and turned the key in the lock. When the police came the outlaws went round the house and fired. There were three (Dan, Byrne and Steve Hart) who came in again. I do not believe Ned came in at all. The police fired at once. There was a return shot immediately. There were two or three hot volleys very quick. We could see the light (outside). There was no light in the house. We were all frightened, and Bracken told us to lie down on the floor as flat as we could before he went away. The Kellys said they would allow us all to go if the police would. There was a tall chap — I forgot his name — he put a white handkerchief out of the window, and there were three bullets sent in at once. The shots went straight from the drain into the window. He threw himself on the floor. After the second or third round was fired things got quiet for a bit, when Hare said cease firing. Ryan and his wife and three or four children and three of mine, and a strange woman from Benalla, then rushed out, and the firing was on them as hard as it could be blazed from the drain, and I could not say where, and I rushed out and my son with me. It was just daylight. My wife and I got out, and we had to go back into the house because of the firing. The firing was from all directions. The most part of it was from the drain. The fire was strong up from the drain, and Mr. O'Connor popped his head up from that drain and said, 'Who comes there?' with a loud voice. I recognised the voice. Ryan sang out, 'Women and children,' and the firing still continued.

"We went back again and said to Dan Kelly, 'I wish to heaven we were out of this.' Byrne said, 'Mrs. Reardon, put out the children and make them scream, and scream yourself, and she was coming past the rifles in the passage, and one of the rifles tangled in her dress, and Dan Kelly said to Byrne, 'Take your rifle, or the woman will be shot'; and I came out and she screamed, and the children, and they came out. The fire was blazing and a policeman called out — I thought it was Sergeant Steele — 'Come this way'; and he still kept firing at her — at my wife with the baby in her arms. (He was not covering her.) Firing at her and covering her are two different things. She has a shawl with a bullet hole through the corner of it which she can show you. I heard a voice saying, 'Come this way.' Constable Arthur was standing close to Sergeant Steele, and he said, 'If you fire on that woman again, I am —— if I don't shoot you, cannot you see she is an innocent woman?' These were Arthur's own words, and I did not believe that the man would do that. Then I had to return back; there were bullets flying at me, and I crept on the ground, and went back to the house with the children, and as my son returned he got wounded in the shoulder, and fell on the jamb of the door, and he has got the bullet yet, and he is quite useless to me or himself. I would sooner have seen him killed. He is getting on to nineteen. I returned back to the house then and lay down among the lot inside, and put the children between my knees, when a bullet scraped the breast of my coat and went across two other men, and went through the sofa at the other end of it. We remained there expecting every minute to be shot, until we heard a voice calling us to come out, about half-past nine in the morning (Monday). We got ten minutes. I think it would be Mr. Sadleir's voice, to the best of my belief. I cannot say for certain. Mr. Sadleir was the first I recognised after I came out. We all came out. I was the last, for I had the two children, one in each hand, and as I was coming down there was a constable named Divery, and he said, 'Let us finish this —— lot,' or something like that. Then the terror of that drove me — I ran to the drain. A blackfellow there cocked his rifle at my face, and I did not know what to do with the children, and I ran away up to where Mr. Sadleir was."

By the Commission: That was hot work. — Hot work! You would not like to be there, I can tell you.

"Byrne had been shot at the end of the counter, going from the passage. He was standing still. I only heard him fall. I heard him fall like a log, and he never groaned or anything, and I could hear a sound like blood gushing. That was about five or six in the morning; but when I was coming out, the other two (Dan Kelly and Hart) were both standing close together in the passage, with the butt end of their rifles on the ground (floor). They were struck while I was there; I could hear the bullets flying off the armour several times. Their lives were saved for the time being by the armour. They fired many shots before that in the early part, but I believe from the time it became daylight they did not fire but very few times that I could notice."

Question by Commission: At the time that Steele, you say, was firing upon you, and your wife escaping, were the outlaws firing from the hotel? — No, I am positive they were not.

Question: Why? — Because they were standing still, and I could hear if they did. They (Dan Kelly and Hart) said they would not fire until we escaped. Sergeant Steele told me and several others that he had shot my son.

Supt. Hare went to Benalla shortly after he received a wound in wrist. In his absence Senior-Constable Kelly was in charge.

Sergeant Steele seemed to be too intent on shooting at women and children to take command. At about six o'clock Supt. Sadleir arrived from Benalla with reinforcements, and he was from that hour in supreme command. There was no order or discipline among the fifty policemen and several civilians who were assisting the police. At about seven o'clock a figure like a blackfellow appeared up in the bush. Someone called out, "Look at this fellow." Senior-Constable Kelly called out to Guard Dowsett to "Challenge him, and if he does not answer you, shoot him." Ned Kelly, who in armour and helmet looked like a blackfellow, pulled out a revolver and fired at Constable Arthur. Three or four constables fired at him, and he advanced. On coming towards the house in the direction of Jones' there were several shots fired at him; they had no effect. Constable Kelly sang out, "Look out! he is bullet proof." Ned Kelly was coming towards the position which Sergeant Steele had taken up. Dowsett fired at him with a revolver. Ned Kelly was behind a tree, but one hand was projecting outside the tree. Constable Kelly fired at the hand and missed; he fired again and hit the hand. Ned still advanced and moved over to a fallen log at Jones' side of the log. Ned was coming from the Wangaratta side of the hotel, and was coming from the direction of the Warby Ranges. Several policemen fired at him. Senior constable Kelly said, "Come on, lads, we will rush him." Ned was firing under great difficulties. He appeared to be crippled; he was holding up his right hand with his left hand; consequently his shots fell short and struck the ground half-way. Steele now came close up behind Ned and fired at him. Constable Kelly fired two shots, and Steele also fired, and Ned Kelly dropped on his haunches. Steele ran and caught him by the wrist and under the beard. The helmet was on. Steele had one hand on his neck. Constable Kelly pulled the helmet off and said, "My God, it is Ned!" Constable Kelly threw Ned over on Steele.

Constable Dwyer rushed up and kicked the captured bushranger while he was held down. Steele was about to shoot him with his revolver, when Constable Bracken prevented him. Steele seemed thirsting for blood — someone's blood. One of the police thought Ned Kelly was a ghost; some thought it was the devil. They were all in a state of great excitement, and Ned Kelly was taken to the railway station and examined by Dr. John Nicholson. It was now known that Joe Byrne was dead. There were only Dan Kelly and Steve Hart left. As the day wore on the fifty policemen continued to fire at the hotel.

Dr. John Nicholson, of Benalla, made history by suggesting to Supt. Sadleir that the latter should wire to Melbourne for a field gun (cannon) in order to make sure that these youthful warriors should not outwit the police and escape.

Supt. Sadleir sent a wire to headquarters in Melbourne for a cannon to be sent up to blow up the hotel. It was also known to the police that Martin Cherry was lying dangerously wounded in the detached back room of the hotel.

Wire sent to Supt. Sadleir to police headquarters, Melbourne:—

"Glenrowan, June 28, 1880.

Weatherboard, brick chimney, slab kitchen. The difficulty we feel is that our shots have no effect on the corner, and there are so many windows that we should be under fire all the day. We must get the gun (cannon) before night or rush the place."

The cannon had reached Seymour when the hotel was burnt down, and, on this information being received, it was returned to Melbourne.

The odds of 25 police to one youth was not considered sufficient. The valour of 50 policemen to two youths, one nineteen years of age and the other twenty years old, would be equalised if the 50 policemen also had a cannon with which they could stand off and blow the two bushrangers and Martin Cherry, a wounded civilian, to pieces. The police now had Ned Kelly's armour and helmet, and could have used it on a constable to enter the house. But the police seemed to be short of one important part of the necessary equipment — courage

Affidavit of John Nicholson, Doctor of Medicine, and legally qualified to practise in Victoria.

I, John Nicholson, Doctor of Medicine, and legally qualified to practise in Victoria, make oath and say as follows:—

I reside in Benalla. I was called early on Monday morning, 28th June, 1880, by Superintendent Hare, who said that he had been shot by the Kellys, and wanted me to go on to Glenrowan, where the police had them surrounded in a house. I wanted him to wait a minute or two until I put on some clothing and I would dress his wound. He would not wait, but said he would go on, and I was to follow him over the bridge. Mr. Lewis, Inspector of Schools, was with him. I shortly afterwards went to the post office, which is about three-quarters of a mile from my residence. I met Mr. Sadleir, who told me Mr. Hare was at the post office, and he said he would wait a quarter of an hour for me, and I was to go with him to Glenrowan.

I then went and saw Mr. Hare, who was lying on some mail bags in the post office. I ascertained that he had been wounded in the left wrist by a bullet, which had passed obliquely in and out at the upper side of the joint, shattering the extremities of the bone, more especially of the radius. There were no injuries to the arteries, but a good deal of venous haemorrhage in consequence of a ligature which had been imprudently tied around the wrist above the wound. I temporarily dressed the wound, during which he fainted. He did not complain of being faint when I first saw him at my residence. Seeing that the wound, although serious, was not dangerous to life, I made all haste to the railway station and accompanied Mr. Sadleir and party to Glenrowan. Mr. Sadleir asked me what I thought of Mr. Hare's wound, and I told him that it would be a question whether amputation of hand would not be the best course to adopt, as the wound was of such a nature that recovery would be very protracted, and might endanger life.

We arrived at Glenrowan before daylight, but the moon was shining. The men, under Mr. Sadleir's instructions, then immediately spread, having first ascertained from Senior-Constable Kelly where the guard was weakest. A party headed by Mr. Sadleir went up the line in front of the house, and were immediately fired at. Three shots were fired in one volley at first, and immediately afterwards a volley of four. The fire was sharply replied to by Mr. Sadleir's party, and also from other quarters where the police were stationed. I did not see anyone come outside, and thought the return fire was at random. The firing on the part of the police was renewed at intervals and replied to from the house, but never more than a volley or two after this. Mr. Marsden, of Wangaratta, Mr. Hawlins, several gentlemen, reporters for the press, some railway officials and myself were on the platform watching the proceedings, sometimes exposed to the fire from the house, in our eagerness to get a clear view of everything. Things remained in this state for about an hour, when a woman with a child in her arms (Mrs. Reardon) left the house and came towards the station, crying and bewailing all the time. She was met by some of the police and taken to one of the railway carriages.

From her we learnt that the outlaws were still there, and at the back part of the house, but she was too much excited to give any definite information. About 8 o'clock we became aware that the police on the Wangaratta side of the house were altering the direction of their fire, and we saw a very tall form in a yellowish-white long overcoat, somewhat like a tall native in a blanket.

He was further from the house than any of the police, and was stalking towards it, with a revolver with his outstretched arm, which he fired two or three times, and then disappeared from our view amongst some fallen timber. Sergeant Steele was at this time between him and the house, about forty yards away, Senior-Constable Kelly and Guard Dowsett nearer to him on his left, and

Constables Dwyer, Arthur and Phillips near the railway fence in his rear. There was also someone at the upper side, but I do not know who it was.

Shortly after this a horse with saddle and bridle (Ned Kelly's bay mare) came towards the place where the man (whom we had by this time ascertained to be Ned Kelly) was lying, and we fully expected him to make a rush for it, but he allowed it to pass, and went towards the house. Messrs. Dowsett and Kelly kept all this time stealthily creeping towards him from one point of cover to another, firing at him whenever they got a chance. The constables in his rear were also firing and gradually closing in upon him. At last he laid down, and we saw Sergeant Steele, quickly followed by Kelly and Dowsett, rush in upon him, and a general rush was made towards them by the spectators and the other police who had been engaged in surrounding him. When I reached the place, probably two minutes after he fell, he was in a sitting posture on the ground, his helmet lying near him. His face and hands were smeared with blood. He was shivering with cold and ghastly white, and smelt strongly of brandy.

He complained of pain in his left arm whenever he was jolted in the effort to remove his armour. Messrs Steele and Kelly tried to unscrew the fastenings of his armour, but could not undo it on one side. I then took hold of the two plates, forced them a little apart, and drew them off his body. While doing this we were fired at from the house, and a splinter struck me in the calf of the leg. He was then carried to the station, and I examined and dressed his wounds. Mr. Sadleir came after Kelly was brought to the station and asked him if he could get the other outlaws to give in, but he said it was no use trying, as they were now quite desperate. After dressing the wounds I saw Mr. Sadleir, and he asked me whether I thought he was justified in making a rush upon the house. I said to do so against men in armour, such as we saw, was certain to result in several men being severely, if not mortally, wounded, and as the day was young it would be best to wait some time before attempting anything, as there was no possibility of their escape. I then said: "It is a pity we have not got a small gun with us; it would made them give in pretty quick, as their armour would be no protection to them, and the chimney would be knocked about their ears." Mr. Sadleir said that Captain Standish was starting from Melbourne and would be up a little after mid-day, and he would immediately telegraph to him and mention the matter; but as no time could be lost he would send a telegram at once. The telegram was sent about five minutes after the gun was first mentioned. Possibly if there had been time for mature consideration it would not have been sent at all.

Mr. Sadleir was particularly cool and collected all the time I saw him, but events were not under his control. The crowd which had collected made anything like order utterly impracticable. The position was one of great difficulty, and I do not think anyone would have managed much better. The place might have been rushed, but to unnecessarily risk men's lives would have been foolhardy however brilliant it would have looked.

I attribute most of the want of concerted action on the part of the police to Mr. Hare leaving the ground before Mr. Sadleir had arrived and relieved him. There was evidently no necessity for his doing so, because he would not wait at my residence to have his wound dressed, which he would undoubtedly have done had it been at the time greatly inconveniencing him.

I have known Mr. Sadleir for several years, and have invariably found him a painstaking, trustworthy and capable officer. I may add that a great deal of my knowledge of his character has been obtained in my capacity as Justice of the Peace. And I make this declaration conscientiously believing same to be true, and by virtue of the provisions of an Act of Parliament of Victoria rendering persons making a false declaration punishable for wilful and corrupt perjury.

JNO. NICHOLSON.

Declared before me at Benalla on the 16th day of September, One thousand eight hundred and eighty-one. — Robt. McBean, J.P.

THE GREEN SILK SASH

While the Kellys were living at Wallan, Ned Kelly saved the life of a boy who had fallen into a flooded creek. The boy's father was so grateful for Ned's heroic rescue of his son that he decided to make Ned a present of a very valuable "Green Silk Sash with a heavy bullion fringe."

At the siege of Glenrowan, Ned Kelly received five bullet wounds, and while bravely attempting to rejoin his comrades he fell, overpowered by numbers. He was captured and removed to the stationmaster's office. While Dr. John Nicholson, of Benalla, was removing Ned's clothing, he saw the beautiful Sash, and, removing it, rolled it up and put it into his pocket.

Having fainted, Ned was quite unconscious while the doctor secured the sash. After the siege was over the doctor said nothing about the sash, and neither the police nor the public were aware of its existence. But in the year 1901 the doctor's son, Richard McVean Nicholson, took the sash with him to England.

In 1910 the young Mr. Nicholson was drowned in the Firth of Forth, and the sash was handed over to his sister, Mrs. R. Graham Pole, to whom application has been made for its return to Mr. Jim Kelly, Ned Kelly's sole surviving brother.

Mrs. R. Graham Pole is the second daughter of Dr. John Nicholson who attended college at Benalla with the Author. Mrs. Graham Pole sent the sash back to Australia with a cousin who was returning to Melbourne. All trace of the sash has been lost.

Still more important than the green sash referred to, is the confiscation by the police officials of the four suits of armour used by the members of the Kelly Gang. The armour of Dan Kelly, Steve Hart, and Joe Byrne is still in official custody, and is in Melbourne. Ned's armour, with a bogus helmet, is said to have been simply given away to a titled millionaire. The original helmet is still in Melbourne. As Ned had ceased to be an "outlaw," before he was arrested, and afterwards tried, convicted and hanged by process of law, there was no legal justification for confiscating his effects, and these should now, as an act of very tardy justice, be obtained by the present Government and handed over to Mr. Jim Kelly, as Ned's sole surviving next of kin.

It is to be hoped that, though belated, retribution will yet be made to the next of kin — Mr. Jim Kelly, of Greta, the only surviving brother of Ned Kelly. It may incidentally be mentioned that Mr. Jim Kelly is a well known and very highly respected resident and farmer of Greta, and the author has the greatest possible pleasure in having produced this book, vindicating the memory of his famous brothers and all the members of his family.

THOMAS CARRINGTON, ARTIST

Mr. Thomas Carrington, before the Royal Commission, was sworn and examined:—

By the Commission: What are you? — Artist.

Question: You are connected with the press? — Yes.

Question: Were you present at Glenrowan when the Kelly Gang was caught? — Yes.

Question: Is it a fact that the impression you formed from the early portion, say from 3 o'clock till just before the firing of the hotel, was that there was no superior officer taking command and giving any instructions to the men? — That is what it seemed to me.

Question: Did you see Mr. O'Connor at that time? — No.

Question: If you did not see Mr. O'Connor or Mr. Sadleir giving instructions between the hours you speak of, did you see any constables or men giving orders or doing anything as if they were under orders?

Answer: No; I saw Mr. Sadleir during the day, but he was always, when I saw him, in the room with Ned Kelly, cutting up tobacco and smoking, standing by the fire and talking to others. I was in the room three times.

Question: Do you know what time the cannon was sent for?

Answer: I do not. I heard a rumour of a cannon being sent for, but I thought it was a joke; that someone was amusing himself. The idea of a cannon to blow two lads out of a house seemed to me something very

Question: You say lads — how do you know there were but two?

Answer: We were told that Byrne had been shot while drinking whisky, and Ned Kelly was a prisoner.

Question: Who told you Byrne was shot?

Answer: Nearly everyone that came out of the hotel.

Question: Did you hear Ned Kelly say so?

Answer: No.

Question: Was it generally believed by those present that Byrne had been shot?

Answer: Yes.

Question: It was an established fact?

Answer: Yes, it was circumstantially told that he was shot, drinking a glass of whisky, and that the other two were standing in the passage — that was what twenty or thirty men said coming out, that the other two were cowed — were standing in the passage frightened, and then when I heard about the cannon to destroy those two lads I looked upon it as a joke.

Question: Is the Commission to understand that really your impression is that had any officer been present after Mr. Hare had to retire, in consequence of the shot, those outlaws could have been captured much earlier in the day, and without the burning of the hotel?

Answer: My idea is this, that if anybody had been there to take up the command, after those four outlaws had come out and emptied their weapons, and called on his men to rush in, they could have taken them easily. They were all outside the hotel when Kelly was wounded.

Question: What was your impression later on in the day after the civilians were released? — Were you then under the impression that if any officer had been there to have commanded the men to make a rush they could have been taken easily?

Answer: I am perfectly certain they could, because the house towards the Benalla end was a blank wall. There was a door here and there, a small passage and a blank wall the other side. The men could have come up to this side and rushed round simultaneously.

Question: Those blank sides are the chimney end?

Answer: One is the chimney end; they are both blank ends. They could come up this way, open out and take the house in front and rear (pointing to the plan), besides there was (Ned) Kelly's armour on the platform. If it was good enough for him to face the police with, surely someone could have put it on and have gone in, besides with the knowledge that the only two left in the place were the youngest, and they were both cowed and frightened, and both in their armour.

Question: From what you have seen, did you approve of that action of burning the hotel?

Answer: Certainly not — most ridiculous. I never heard of such a thing in my life. Of course, I do not know much about military tactics, but it seemed to me almost as mad as sending for a cannon. If the police had joined hands round the hotel the outlaws could not have got away; they (the police) could have sat down the ground and starved them out.

Question: Did you hear any civilians say they were willing to do it (rush the hotel)?

Answer: I heard two or three working men say, "I would do it if I had some firearms myself. I would rush the hotel myself."

Question: Did those uncomplimentary remarks apply to the police as policemen or to the officers and their discipline?

Answer: To the police generally — spoke of them as they, "Why do not they rush the hotel?" "Why do not they put on the armour?" and so on.

Question:— About what time in the day did you see the last shot come from the hotel?

Answer: Well, I do not think there were any shots fired after ten. I am not sure, but you could not very well tell, because there was more danger from the police scattered round. The police on the hill might have fired a shot and people have thought it came from the hotel.

Question: Was there danger of the police shooting each other?

Answer: Undoubtedly. I went down during the day to the Beechworth end and knelt behind a log with one of the police, and while we were sitting there — I was making a drawing — a rifle ball came over our heads. I will swear it was not fired from the hotel, because I was looking at the hotel at the time. It must have come from the ranges at the back — the south end.

Dave Mortimer's Statement.

Statement made, immediately after the burning of the hotel, by Mr. David Mortimer, brother-in-law of Mr. Thomas Curnow, State school teacher, who stopped the police train:

"Our feelings at that time were indescribable. The poor women and children were screaming with terror, and every man in the house was saying his prayers. Poor little Johnny Jones was shot almost at once, and I put my hands in my ears so as not to hear the screams of agony and the lamentations of his mother and Mrs. Reardon, who had a baby in her arms. We could do nothing, and the bullets continued to whistle through the building. I do not think the police were right in acting as they did.

We were frightened of them and not of the bushrangers. It was Joe Byrne who cursed and swore at the police. He seemed perfectly reckless of his life. . . . We frequently called on the police to stop firing, but we dared not go to the door, and I suppose they did not hear us. Miss Jones was slightly wounded by a bullet."

When the midday train arrived from Melbourne it brought many passengers from Benalla and other stations. One passenger, the Very Rev. Dean Gibney, who joined the train at Kilmore East, en route for Albury, also alighted from the train.

Dean Gibney came to Victoria collecting for an orphanage in Perth, and when he heard of the siege at Glenrowan he inquired if there were a Catholic priest there, and on being answered in the negative, he decided to get off at Glenrowan and attend to Ned Kelly, who was said to be dying.

It was Dean Gibney who entered the burning hotel and saved Martin Cherry from being burnt alive by police who had set fire to the hotel.

19
THE HERO OF GLENROWAN

VERY Rev. Dean Gibney gave evidence on oath before the Royal Commission on June 28, 1881, as follows:—

Question by the Commission: What are you? — I am the Vicar-General of the Roman Catholic Church in Western Australia.

Question: We just want the few things you know yourself at Glenrowan. — Yes.

Question: Do you remember the taking of the Kellys at Glenrowan? — I came there by train. I do not know the exact hour the train arrived, but I believe it was the first ordinary train from Melbourne. I was staying at Kilmore the previous night and started then with the train.

Question: It would be about twelve o'clock? — Coming on twelve, I think.

Question: Did you take any particular notice of what was going on at the time? — I had not heard previous to my getting into the train of the Kelly capture or that the police had found them, but when I came to Benalla I was told there that Kelly was taken, that he was wounded, that the others were stuck up at a place which I could not remember the name then — that was Glenrowan. I inquired myself if there was a Catholic clergyman there, and I was told no; and then I made up my mind if there was not I would stop to attend first to Kelly, and then to any others I might be called on to.

Question: You were a witness of what occurred after twelve o'clock? — I was a good deal of the time.

Question: Where were you principally stopping? — I made my way into where Ned Kelly was lying. I understood he was in a dying state at the time.

Question: That was in the station? — Yes.

Question: Did you notice anything that occurred at Mrs. Jones' hotel? — I observed that the police stationed round were firing into the hotel just as the train came up; in fact, the firing seemed to be then vigorously carried on.

Question: All round? — All round. It took me some considerable time to get into where Ned Kelly was lying. There seemed to be a great press of people about the windows and door, curiously trying to see him; but I think one there was Dr. Nicholson, to whom I am very thankful for the manner in which he assisted me to get to Kelly, and attended to any call now and then when, as I thought, Kelly was in a dying condition — he was fainting. He was always ready to attend to any call to give me any assistance he could.

Question: Did you hear anything during the afternoon about the proceedings of the police with reference to the Kellys? — Well, just some few incidents came under my notice that I do not think were stated, as far as I could see, correctly. That is, I was told that Kelly's sister was coming on the scene. It would be some considerable time after I had attended to Ned Kelly.

Question: Some time in the afternoon? — Yes, and I was then glad to find that, because I thought she could proceed to Mrs. Jones' house safely to speak to the men. I stepped forward and asked her would she go to her brother and tell him there was a Catholic priest here who was anxious to come and see him, and to ask him would he let me in. She said, "Of course, I will go up and see my brother." She was very excited. She started then for the house, but was stopped.

Question: By whom? — I could not say. I did not know any person on the scene. By some police authority, I suppose, so I was told. The officer in charge of the police was off in one direction of the semicircle which the police formed, standing in different groups here and there behind trees. I was told he was off in that direction, so I went on from one group of police to another to find the officer in charge, and when I had gone to the extreme end there I was told he was not there, so I was directed then on to the other end, and when I came to the last body I was told that was he — I think Mr. Sadleir — and then I sent the girl to ask (I did not go myself) for permission for her to go up to the house, mentioning that I advised her to go; and she went and she was told she would not be allowed to go. I was strongly inclined to go myself prior to that, but when I had been with Ned Kelly, after I had attended to him, I asked him did he think it would be safe for me to go up to the house and get this man, his brother, I think, to surrender. "I would not advise you to go; they will certainly shoot you!" I said, "They would not shoot me if they knew I was a priest or a clergyman"; and he said, "They will not know who you are, and they will not take the time to think!" I saw that I could not justify myself in going up as long as I did not see the probability of doing any service. That alone was what kept me back during the course of the day. I was surprised a good deal that there seemed to be no sign of truce at any time offered; there was no signal given that the men might see, that they might have the idea their lives would be spared if they came out. I was rather surprised at that, and remarked it repeatedly, but still I did not know whether it was to anyone in authority or not, because there seemed to be an incessant feeling of anxiety in the minds of those men that were around.

Question: Did they (police) seem to be under any control? — I could not say that they were guided by any others. I could not make a statement on that subject.

Question: Did they seem to have the appearance of being guided by orders? — I do not think they had. I do not think really that there was any disciplinary order guiding them, as far as I could judge.

Question: In point of fact, that there was a want of generalship? — Oh, that was evident.

Question: They seemed just to be shooting away at random? — Firing at the house was the only thing that anyone could say there was any uniformity about.

Question: Just firing at the house? — Yes

Question: Did you hear any shots fired from the house after you arrived? — I repeatedly tried to ascertain for myself whether there were, and I could not. Sometimes there would be shots fired that I could not really say whether it would be from the house or not, but the reason of that was that sometimes, in my position, the police were above and beyond the house, and I could not really say then whence the sound came.

Question: So far as you know there was no further attempt made to communicate with them after Mrs. Skillion and the sister came? — No further attempt was made to communicate with them that I saw or heard of, only that until the house was set fire to.

Question: Did you feel it your duty to rush in to see them when the house was fired? — It was at that particular time that the crisis occurred that then buoyed me up to do what I did when the house was being set fire to. My feelings revolted very much from the appearance it had, and I was wishing in my heart that it might not take fire. That was my own feeling in the matter; and then I said to myself, "These men have not five minutes to live. If they stop in they will be burned, and if they come out they will be shot." That was what decided me, and I thought then they will be very glad to get any service now — they will be glad to see anyone coming to them.

Question: Did you go in at the front door? — I was then close down to the gate at the railway crossing, and I started from there direct for the front of the house. I think I might have been about half the distance between where I started from and the house when I was called to. I was told afterwards it was Mr. Sadleir who called to me not to go there without orders, without consulting him — that I should not go there without consulting him.

Question: You were told afterwards it was Mr. Sadleir? — Yes; so I stopped then a few moments, and stepped towards him, perhaps two or three paces, to remonstrate with him. I said something to this effect, "I am not in the police service, I am going to my duty, and there is no time to lose." So he did not interfere with me further, and I walked on. As I was going on towards the house there was a large number of people about. I am not a very good judge of numbers that way, but I thought there could not be less than 500 or 600 people.

Question: They had collected from all parts of the country about? — They were coming in from various directions.

Question: Did you see the two young men when you went in? — When I was going up towards the house the excitement of the people was very great, and they clapped their hands as if I was going on a stage, as their excitement was high at the time. I went in then on what I think was the room on the right-hand side, and it was quite vacant or empty. It was the other end of the house the fire was set to, and then when I came inside I called out to the men that I was a Catholic priest, and came to offer them their life, and asked them, for God's sake, to speak to me. I got no answer, of course, but I thought to myself that they might be on their guard watching to see if I was what I said I was.

Then I found first the body of Byrne. There was a door leading out of this room towards the door. His body was lying there where he had fallen in a straggled kind of way. He seemed to have fallen on his back, like on his hip. He must have died soon, because he was just in the position as he fell; he was still lying, and his body was quite stiff.

Question: Did you see him fall? — No, he had fallen in the morning. I heard when I came there that he was shot, and that he could not have lived long after he fell. When I found this man's body, that part of the house was blazing furiously just before me. I did not think that I would go in then if I got any other passages round, so I went to another back room that was off the one I entered first, and there was no exit out of that — no door — so I had to come back to the same spot again, and the place was blazing considerably. I was afraid at the time that I might be caught with the flame; I just blessed myself in the name of God and rushed through. Then when I came in the passage down from the bar towards the back of the house there was a little room to the left hand, and I spoke again to the men inside. I got no answer, of course, and I looked in upon the floor and found two corpses lying together.

Question: Both dead? — Both dead. The room was small.

Question: At the time you saw the two corpses lying in that room had the fire taken sufficient hold of the building to have destroyed those two corpses by fire, or are you under the impression they were dead prior to the fire? — Oh, I am certain they were dead.

Question: But we want your own impression whether their death was caused by the fire, or suffocation, or by any other means? — My impression is that they were certainly not killed by the fire — were not suffocated by the heat of the fire. I myself went in there and stopped there safely, and just when I came into their presence they were very composed looking, both lying at full stretch side by side, and bags rolled up under their heads, the armour on one side of them off. I concluded they lay in that position to let the police see when they found them that it was not by the police they died; that was my own conclusion.

Question: You concluded they committed suicide? — Yes, that is my own belief.

Question: At the present time? — Yes, I took hold of the hand of the one that was near me to see whether or not they had recently killed themselves — whether there was life in them, and I found it was quite lifeless. Then I looked at his eyes, and I found that his eyes showed unmistakable signs that he was dead for some time; and then I went to the other to touch him. I was satisfied that life was completely extinct in both of them before I left; and at that time in this little room they were in, the fire was just running through it. I saw that the roof itself was sufficiently safe, that I was in no immediate danger. It was very hot, but still I saw I was not in any immediate danger of being caught.

Question: At the time that you entered the little room at the back of the building where the two corpses were lying, had the two men been living there was sufficient time for them to have escaped with their lives from the fire? — Oh, yes there was, if there had been life in either of them. I would have had them out myself, and I was perfectly satisfied that they would be taken out. I looked upon it that my own purpose was realised, that I had satisfied myself that what I came to do was over, that it was too late, and then I said I would give word to the police, of course, as soon as I found how they were. I walked out of the back of the house, that was the nearest way then, and I called out to the police that the men were all dead inside.

Question: Did they (the police) rush to the building then? — There came two or three running up very soon after. The first man — I suppose he was a policeman — that came up, it appeared to me, was determined to have a shot into one of them. That was just the impression I had at the moment.

Question: He had his revolver ready? — Yes, he had his revolver ready, and especially so it appeared to me. I laid my hand upon his arm that way, and said, "Do not fear; they are both dead!" That was Byrne's body; he could not see the other two from there. So then I believe it was the time they rushed in and pulled out the body of Byrne. Of course, the crowd came running then quickly, and I was certain they would have taken out the bodies. I was perfectly satisfied they would have done so, and there was plenty of time; but then I did not make sufficient allowances for appearances, or of the fact that I had an advantage over the police just then. I knew that the room had not been burnt through; though burning, it was not burnt through.

Question: Then from the way in which they were lying, with a pillow of bags under their heads, you came to the conclusion that it must have been arranged before? — That they laid it out, and that they could not have been laid in such a position except by design.

Question: Did you notice if they had any weapons in their hands? — I did not see any, and I cannot say that I saw any sign of blood; in fact, my impression was that they must have laid the pistol under their breasts and fired into their hearts; but that is only conjecture, for I did not see the wounds about them — about the bodies or on the bodies.

Question: I think you said you went in at the front door, that is the door facing the railway line? — Yes.

Question: And then you went out at the back door? — I went out the back after having found the three bodies.

Question: Did you come through again out of the front door? — No, I went into the room off the first room, and thence into a room off that, thinking I could get out that way without passing through the flames, because that was the end of the house fired first, and the fire was worst there, and the spirits might have caught fire, I thought; there was a sheet of fire.

Question: About how long were you in the house altogether? — I could not really say. Perhaps I might have been from eight to ten minutes; I think so.

Question: Would the time not seem to be longer than it really was? — It might appear to me to be longer, because all that I did, when I found Byrne was dead, was to pass on to get the others. I went into the back room, as I said, off the one that I entered first, thinking to go out that way.

Question: You could have done all that in five minutes? — I dare say I could.

Question: How far were the police from you when you came out and said the men were dead? — There were none of them I saw nearer, I should say, than between twenty or thirty paces.

Question: There was no effort made by them to come up until you told them? — No, there was no man that came up with me, or that I saw, till the first man that reached me after I came out of the back, and called out to them. He was the first man I saw come to the house. I think that there were three that ran up after that. That was after I came out. My great object is going, of course, was to see to get those men time for repentance; and I would have preferred much to have seen them executed rather than to have seen them destroyed in that manner.

Question: Although you saw no firearms about them, you still think they committed suicide? — I could not judge of anything except from the position in which they were lying. They lay so calm together, as if laid out by design.

Question: It had all the appearances of a prearrangement? — It had. I saw some time in the press different remarks about casting censure upon the Police Commission — that they had not given me any portion of the reward. Now I wish to make a statement on that matter. From the first I never intended to receive anything of that reward, though I might be considered entitled to it. I never thought myself for a moment that I would accept any portion thereof; and my reason for that is simply this — that it is better for society at large that we should be (the Catholic priesthood, I mean) free from any charge of taking any money that is offered as a reward, because we can more readily move in that matter; we can approach them with some amount of confidence on that account. Of course, I merely make the remark with your permission that it was my own determination; and if you had not given me the opportunity of saying so, of course, I would never make such a remark, because it might not be understood in the way I intend it.

Question: This is not the Commission that allocated the reward? — Indeed!

Question: That was a Board appointed for the purpose; but your object in stopping at Glenrowan that day was in your capacity as a Catholic priest? — As a priest.

Question: Your duties as a priest were paramount to all other considerations? — It was only that that kept me there and actuated me at all. There was another thing I thought I might as well remark. I thought it strange, as I was the principal witness in finding those bodies, that I had not been in any way consulted in the matter, that I had not been referred to at all as a witness. I did not see any reason at all why I should not be, at least so far, consulted in the matter, or spoken to, to hear what I had to say on that. Of course, I was the witness of the manner in which those bodies were found, and the first witness.

Question: We fully intended to call you, but we did not know at first you were in the colony? — I referred simply to the inquest.

Question: And you were on the ground at the time? — I went on to Albury.

Question: But they could have found you? — Yes. I think I might say, too, with your permission, that in order that it may not appear strange why I should be so far from my own place, my object in visiting Victoria has been collecting for the orphan institution of which I am the certified manager myself in my own colony. It might appear a strange thing for me to be away so far from my own duties.

Question: Did you tender any advice or suggestion to the police officers during the day in any way? — Well, I did not find or see any of them. I exposed myself very considerably in trying to find one of them, because in going from tree to tree, if the parties had been alive inside, as was supposed, they might have said, "He is one making himself very busy giving general directions, going from place to place, from one officer of police to another." They might have picked me off; but still I was very intent on trying to have the sister go there, seeing no one else would be safe to go, and it was then I sought for the officer in charge.

Question: You did not find him on the scene of the fight? — He was with the party at the opposite end.

Question: Did you notice the blacktrackers there? — Well, as I was passing along in the front of the house, along by the railway line like — I was questioning myself afterwards about that — I think I saw some of them lift their heads and look up to me from a kind of gulf or hole they were in. I could not say for positive now; I did not pay any particular attention to that.

Question: You did not notice whether there was any particularly heavy shooting from there or not? — No.

Question: Is there anything further you wish to add? — I do not think there is.

20
THE CHARRED BODIES

VERY Rev. Dean Gibney's evidence continued:— "There is one thing which is hardly relevant to the matter. There was a report spread at the time after I had been attending to Ned Kelly. Of course, I was a very considerable time with him before I moved out at all, trying to prepare him for his last hour, because I thought he was in a dying state — the doctor could not give a deciding opinion as to the result. After that I came out and heard there was a report he was cursing and swearing just soon after I came out. I said, 'My labour is lost if that is the case,' and I made my way back and asked the policeman in charge of him to tell me was he making use of any bad language or was he disturbed. He said, 'No,' and I asked Kelly himself, and he said, 'No.' Then I came out and challenged the parties, and said the man was bad enough, and not to tell lies about him, and afterwards I found it had been telegraphed, but these are points that are of no importance. I forgot to mention anything about Cherry, the man that was taken out of the house. I was aware that he was wounded in the house almost from my going there. Some parties met me and told me this man, a platelayer, was shot by the fire of the police upon the house and he was wounded, and I knew from their information that he could not possibly come out, that he was inside incapable of moving himself, and yet they said he had not died. Well, I did not find him in any of these three rooms. I came to where the bodies of the outlaws were, and I had already passed through the house, and it was a party who had been bailed up with him who knew where he was and ran and took him out."

Question. — From an outhouse? — I fancy so. I believe he would have been burned; that he is the only one that would have been burned alive if I had not come up.

Question. — You mean that he was the only one whose life would have been sacrificed by the effects of the fire? — Yes.

Question. — You saw him when he was brought out? — Yes; I attended to him as well as I could, and administered the sacrament of my own church to him as far as I could.

Question. — He made some remarks? — Not to me. He seemed to be conscious, but not able to speak.

Question. — You said you went in at the front and not at the back; did you not afterwards appear at the front door, and hold up your hands in this manner (explaining by gesture)? — No; it was at the back. When I was going in I held up my hands, and kept my hands in such a position going into the house, so that the parties observing me might perhaps be justified in saying that I came back from the fact that I turned back from the room I first entered, because I was standing between the people and the blaze, and every movement of mine, I believe, they could see with the strong light that was beyond me. They might in the excitement of the time think I came out. I did not come out of the house at the front.

Question. — Did you appear at the door? — No.

Question. — What intimation had the police from the front that it was all over that caused them to go up to the house? — When I saw the others running to the other side, I suppose I called out to the police. They were on my right hand as I went up. After I came out I turned to them and called out. I dare say they were watching anxiously, and the first of that party then came running, and they all rushed after. I did not come outside the house until I came out of the back. The witness withdrew.

The Very Rev. Dean Gibney Further Examined July 6, 1881.

Questioned by the Commission: — Mr. Sadleir, who had charge of the police at the taking of the Kellys, thinks that some of your statements might be prejudicial to him, and he desired some questions to be put to you; and he has given the written questions here so as to elucidate his meaning in any possible way that can be done? — I may remark that if any word of mine would wound, which is not necessary for truth, I hereby desire to record my wish to blot it out.

Question: The Commission considers that you did exactly what was your duty in everything that you said, even if a wrong impression has been created. Mr. Sadleir was not present, and he desires that these questions may be put. That is the whole thing, and we thought it well to have the matter brought under your notice; and we are much obliged to you for coming again. I will just put the questions as they have been written down, and those are the questions you are supposed to reply to.

The first question is: Were you aware before your arrival at Glenrowan on June 28, 1880, that all the innocent persons except Cherry had left Mrs. Jones' two hours or so before? — I was aware on my arrival there. I became aware of it soon — at least that the innocent people had been allowed to remove from the house some time about half-past nine or ten o'clock — some two hours before I came that would be; but I heard there was one wounded man there. I believe it was Cherry.

The second question is: When did you learn that I was (that is, Mr. Sadleir) the principal officer on the ground, and where was I then? — I could not say for certain whether I learned the name of the officer in charge before the time the Kellys' sister came on the ground. Then I knew for certain, as I made inquiries in order to find the officer in charge.
The second portion of the question is: And where was Mr. Sadleir then — I was directed to Mr. Sadleir then by parties on the cordon, the line of the police in the direction in which I found that Mr. Sadleir was not then.

The third question is: Where were you mostly from your arrival at twelve o'clock until the time approached when the house was set fire to? — I might have been perhaps an hour, or it may be more — an hour and a half, perhaps — in attendance on Ned Kelly. In my endeavour to get to him I was, perhaps, ten or fifteen minutes before I could get in, and then I was, I dare say, three-quarters of an hour with him, attending to him with my own duties. It might be more, but I believe it was not short of that time. After that time I went over to the hotel on the opposite side and spent about perhaps five or seven minutes there; it might be more. I met a reverend gentleman there of the Church of England (Rev. Mr. Rodda), and we walked down to where the line of railway had been torn up, and then came back to the railway station.

The fourth question is: Do you remember seeing me (Mr. Sadleir) about the platform? — After the house had been set fire to, I believe I saw you twice. I said I saw you. I believe it was pointed out that that was Mr. Sadleir on the left-hand side of the house looking at the house from the direction of the railway gate. I saw you there with a party of men, and then I sent Miss Kelly to go on now and ask if she might go to the house.

The fifth question is: How long before the house was fired did Mrs. Skillion or Kate Kelly, Ned Kelly's sister, arrive on the ground? — It was Miss Kate Kelly. Mr. Sadleir, I never saw her; I saw Mrs. Skillion approaching and turned her from the house.

Question — Mr. Sadleir: My question is to elicit who was the woman approaching the building — that is the one I refer to? — I never had any doubt it was Kate Kelly.

Mr. Sadleir — My question is with regard to the woman that approached the building from the railway gates. — It does not matter if we both understand we mean the same person

Question by the Commission (to the witness): You sent on the sister to Mr. Sadleir, and I think what the Commission have to do is to ask how long before the fire was it she went to Mr. Sadleir? — I believe the man had already come back from the house. I think he had already returned from the house — the one that set fire to it.

Question: It was just at the time the house was set fire to? — I was coming round with this woman to find Mr. Sadleir. I saw the man running from the house after setting fire to it. It was only then I became aware the house was being fired; when I made an effort to get this woman to approach the house I did not know then the house was being fired, but I had heard that there was a cannon on the way.

This is question six: In the interval between her arrival (Ned Kelly's sister) and your approach to enter Mrs. Jones' house did you see me (Mr. Sadleir)? — Not at the time that I was called out to; that is, I did not see to take notice until the time I was called out to by Mr. Sadleir that I should not approach there without his permission, or some words to that effect.

Question seven: Please to describe where you went to search for me, and say whether this was after Mrs. Skillion's arrival or not? — That is a question I have already answered.

Question eight: How long were you detained altogether before your ministrations to Ned Kelly were completed — That is difficult to answer.

Question nine: Was it not possible that while you were so engaged, or even before your arrival on the ground, or after that, the police were acting under definite orders without your knowledge? — It was quite possible that they might be acting under definite orders. I have not made any remark that I know which would show they were not acting under definite orders. My remark, I think, was to the effect that the only uniformity I observed was in the intermittent firing at the house — that there was uniformity in that. They used to begin at one end of the cordon and fire all round till they reached the other. But what I generally felt impressed with was (as I might say, a post factum witness of the scene) that firing had commenced at the house when I believe it ought not to have been done — that is, when all the innocent people were there. I maintain that as it was the practice of those men to stick up people wherever they came to, it was not a fair thing to fire into the house while the innocent people were there. This is where, I think, discipline was wanting; and then continuing till the people burst out of the house, and then firing at them as they burst out. I am referring now as a post factum witness — one that came there and heard what had been going on.

Question ten is: Might not the outlaws have been called on to surrender without your hearing? — Quite possibly, but in reply to that I might say that I understand they were called upon — the idea they were called upon — I would look for occasions sufficiently long for them to see that they were not fired on. I would look for periods of time to be given them to come. Of course, I cannot say exactly what length of time there would be, or what time there was between one volley and the other. I can simply give my impressions in the evidence I give.

Question eleven is: Please to describe the particulars in which you observed the want of generalship, bearing in mind that the outlaws were in impenetrable armour, and the difficulty of knowing in what part of the building they were hiding? — I think I have already answered that question in my general remark upon the way the thing, just as I came there, impressed me, and it was continued while I was on the scene. I look upon the matter as being one which began in a blunder (I am simply stating my impressions), and that it was continued on until they were allowed to go beyond the bounds of the house they were confined to. Some described their condition — lying on the ground. Reardon described the condition of the women and children on the ground, and he was there until someone threatened to kill him by firing on him if he stopped; and then there was such an uproar on the part of the people confined in the place that at length they were allowed to come out and throw themselves on the ground. Now, I could not for the life of me make out how it was possible that the people would be confined to the house for so many hours, and the police would be surrounding it, and that they would not have known the condition of affairs in that house.

Question by Mr. Sadleir: What do you mean by the beginning? — I refer to the volleys that were fired on that house while the people were confined in it.

Question: Does that include the first attack? — Well, I dare say it will. There were more innocent people in that house than there were guilty, and if the police were to fire indiscriminately on us here what would we say?

Question by the Commission: When the first attack was made, you understand, we have it in evidence the police did not know that there were people in the house, and the first volley was fired from the house upon the police — you would not have such a strong opinion as to the first attack on the house? — Surely no one could have any misgiving about Mrs. Jones and her family being there.

Question: This was the first five minutes, when Mr. Hare rushed up and the order was given to cease firing and surround the house; you mean after they knew that the people were in it? — It was considerably before I came there; but I remarked already that I formed my opinions as, I might call myself, a post factum witness.

Question: You simply said there should not be indiscriminate firing upon the house when there were only two outlaws and a lot of innocent people in? — If there was one innocent life to be lost amongst them, I would say the guilty ought to be spared for the sake of the innocent.

Question: Do you think there was any chance of the outlaws escaping at all if there had not been a shot fired after you came? — I thought a guard might have been kept around the place, and the outlaws kept there without firing a shot, and in that condition it would have been impossible for them to have escaped.

Question by Mr. Sadleir: Not even in the darkness of the night? — Well, it would be hardly my place to say what would be another person's disposition in the matter, but I simply say my own.

Question: Are you making allowances for the darkness that men might crawl through the fence and might be mistaken for one of the guards? — If we had left them stay after daylight, would there not be a possibility of escape? — Then there would certainly have been the possibility.

Question by the Commission: We have it on evidence from Mr. Hare's official report that there was a very large number of prisoners confined at the house when they went to it at the first moment. Bracken, when he came down to tell about the Kellys, told them also that they had a very large number of people there. He said, "Mr. Hare, I have just escaped from Jones' Hotel, where the Kellys have a large number of prisoners confined."

There is one more question: What was the condition of the bodies of Dan Kelly and Hart when you touched them? — Were they stiff as if they had been any considerable time dead? — They were not stiff. I took hold of the hand of the one next to me, and it seemed limp, but from the pallid appearance and coldness I thought that it could hardly have been immediately before — only a short time dead; there would not have been such a settled look upon their countenances if they had not been some considerable time dead.

Question: Was the hand cold? — No, I do not feel able to say cold.

Question: Were the flames broken through? — They were. I could not judge of my own feeling in the matter. It would not be well for me to say I could judge of my own touch because I was hot and excited. I am told that a few minutes might cause the appearances that I saw. That is, if those men were in terror for a good while before and lay down, and if they were wounded and lost blood, and so on.

Question: You saw no marks of fresh blood? — No.

To Mr. Sadleir: Is there any other question you wish to put?

Mr. Sadleir: No, I wish to thank Dean Gibney for the trouble he has taken in coming here.

Question by the Commission (to the witness): With reference to seeing Mr. Sadleir at first, what time did you see him? — I saw him to recognise him for the first time when I was going with the woman Kelly in search of him. He was pointed out to me then standing with a party of men on the left-hand side.

Question: That was after the house was set fire to? — It was just as the man came running down. I saw him then again when I was going up to the house, when he called to me to stop in my course; and then I thought I would have gone to speak a word or two with him at that time, only I thought if these men were observing me from within they would say that I was one of the police and was coming with a message from them, and would have been more determined to take me down; that flashed across my mind, and after walking a pace or two towards where Mr. Sadleir was I stopped, and he then kindly gave me leave to go on. The next time I saw him was above at the house, after I had gone through, and he very kindly indeed, without a demur, thanked me for what I had done; for whether those men were burned alive or not, no one would have known if I had not gone in. Then the man Cherry was found; and I moved away from the scene after that, as I have already told you. I met Mr. Sadleir again when I went to attend to Cherry. He wanted me to stay for a moment, and asked me about the condition of the bodies inside; and I said I had to attend to this man and would explain after. In fact, one of my impressions at the moment was that this man was one of the party of the bodies that I met inside, and that he had life in him, and he was taken out, and I said to myself, "Is it possible I did not observe that, because I was certain they were dead?" Again I saw Mr. Sadleir when the whole thing was over, and he took occasion to thank me again; and I considered he was very complimentary to me. He called me by a name I never got before — "a hero!"

Melbourne, 1st July, 1880.

D. T. Seymour, Esq.,

Commissioner of Police, Brisbane.

Sir, — I have the honour to report that on Sunday, 27th June, at 7 p.m., I received a letter from Captain Standish (copy attached). I saw Captain Standish about 7.30 p.m., and informed him that I was willing to assist him, but, as I was under marching orders, I should like the Chief Secretary to wire to you, so as to hold me blameless if I should be doing wrong in going. I, with five troopers left here by special train at 10 p.m., en route for Beechworth. We arrived at Benalla at 1 p.m., and picked up Superintendent Hare and six men. From here our train was preceded by an engine, as a precaution. When, upon nearing Glenrowan Station, the advanced engine was observed to have come to a halt, and then we found that a man had rushed out of the bush, and informed the advanced enginedriver that the outlaws had torn up the rails about a mile further on. Superintendent Hare and I consulted, and we decided to draw the train. We went on up to the Glenrowan Station, so as to enable us to get out our horses to ride down to the torn-up rails. While in the act of getting out the horses, a constable named Bracken, who had been stationed at Glenrowan, rushed frantically down to us, and said: "I have just escaped from the outlaws, who are at Jones' public house; take care or they will be off." Superintendent Hare and I started at once towards the house, calling the men to follow us; but, owing to the confusion and noise in taking out the horses, I presume, some of them did not at once respond, as only Mr. Hare, myself, three or four white men, and, I think, about two of my boys, were in the first rush. We rushed straight for the house, and, upon getting within about 20 yards of the place, one shot, followed by a volley, was fired at us from the verandah. We returned the fire, and before I could load again Superintendent Hare called out to me: "O'Connor, I am wounded — shot in the arm; I must go back." I think the whole party were up by this time. I ordered the men to take cover, and I myself dropped down into a creek immediately in front of the front door, and about 20 yards from it; from here I kept a continual fire, until the outlaws were obliged to retire into the house; the others kept firing also.

I then heard the cry of a woman in the house, and cried out, "Cease firing," which cry was taken up by us all. I sang out, "Let the women out," and they immediately came, and passed to the rear. Superintendent Hare, after stating he was wounded, retired to the railway station, and in about 15 minutes went off in the engine to Benalla, leaving me as the only officer on the ground in charge.

I kept my position, and in fact, shot Joe Byrne before we were reinforced, or (of course we cannot say who shot Joe) before another officer arrived upon the ground, which happened at about 5.30 a.m., when Mr. Sadleir arrived with reinforcements from Benalla, thereby leaving me with only 12 men, viz., five boys and seven white men, from 2.30 until 5.30. During this interval I think I may say the heaviest of the fighting was. Of course it is unnecessary for me to give my opinion upon the conduct of Superintendent Hare, in running away to Benalla; I leave you to form your own opinion, when I tell you his wound is only through the wrist. Mr. Hare was only on the ground about three minutes. Ned Kelly, it appears, after going into the house, left by the back door, and was captured a few yards from the building. We then (Mr. Sadleir and myself) thought of rushing the house; but a senior-constable proposed to fire the building, which was done, and, at about 4 p.m., we took out of the house the charred remains of Dan Kelly and Steve Hart, and at the same time we recovered the body of Joe Byrne (about 4 p.m.), but not touched by the fire.

I will communicate further with you, as I see the credit which our party fully deserve the Chief Commissioner is reluctant to give to us.

Your obedient servant,
STANHOPE O'CONNOR,
S. Inspector.

Mr. D. T. Seymour's reply to Mr. Stanhope O'Connor:—

Brisbane,
15th July, 1880.
Sir, — I beg to acknowledge the receipt of your communication of the 1st July, giving an account of your proceedings during the encounter between the police and the outlaws at Glenrowan on the 27th June ultimo, and I regret exceedingly that, so far as I can judge from the very meagre information contained in your report, and the more fully detailed accounts given by newspaper correspondents, I am unable to find any cause for congratulation.

Your report, and that given by the correspondent of the "Argus," who, it appears, was on the ground, differ widely on some very material points, and it will be a source of great gratification if you are able, as I trust you will be, to show that yours is the correct version.

The portions of the proceedings which chiefly call for explanation are:—
1st — The apparent total absence of discipline or plan by which the affair was conducted from commencement to finish.
2nd — The indiscriminate firing which was permitted, whereby the lives of innocent persons were endangered, and, as it afterwards turned out, were sacrificed; and
3rd — The seemingly unnecessary burning of the premises in which the outlaws and others had taken shelter.

In your report you state that upon Constable Bracken's arrival with the information that the outlaws were in Jones' public house you "started off, at once towards the house, calling the men to follow," etc., but "owing to the confusion and noise in taking out the horses, some of them did not respond;" and you THINK about two of your boys were with you. How did you propose to capture the outlaws without your men; and under whose command were those who were left behind? It seems that each man was left to act as he thought fit — no definite plan of action having been decided upon, and the same want of management appears to have continued throughout.

With reference to the indiscriminate firing which is alleged to have taken place, your report is that "upon getting within about 20 yards of the place one shot, followed by a volley, was fired at us from the verandah; we returned the fire," etc., and a little further on you continue: "I kept up a continual fire until the outlaws were obliged to retire into the house. I then heard the cry of a woman in the house, and I cried out 'Cease firing.' I sang out: 'Let the women out,' which was done, and they immediately came, and passed to the rear."

The "Argus" report of this portion of the affair is very different; it runs thus: "The police and the gang blazed away at each other in the darkness furiously; it lasted about a quarter of an hour, and during that time there was nothing but a succession of flashes and reports, and the pinging of bullets in the air, and the SHRIEKS OF WOMEN WHO HAD BEEN MADE PRISONERS IN THE HOTEL*"; and again: "At about eight o'clock in the morning a heart-rending wail of grief ascended from the hotel. The voice was easily distinguished as that of Mrs. Jones, the landlady. Mrs. Jones was lamenting the fate of her son, who had been shot in the back, as she supposed, fatally. She* CAME OUT OF THE HOTEL CRYING BITTERLY, *and wandered into the bush on several occasions", etc. "She always* RETURNED, *however, to* THE HOTEL,*" etc. How do you reconcile this statement with your report? But, supposing the "Argus" version is incorrect, the matter is in no better light. The number of occupants, whether voluntary or compulsory, the strength and condition of the outlaws, the position of the passages and doors, and all information requisite to ensure the capture could have been obtained from Constable Bracken, who had himself been a prisoner, had a little more coolness and judgment been exercised on arrival at Glenrowan.*

When the premises were set on fire, it appears that an officer of the Victorian police was present in command; you had, therefore, nothing to do with that matter, but it would have given much satisfaction here had you objected to such a course, which hardly seems to have been requisite when so large a body of police was present.

In replying to this letter, which you will be good enough to do without delay, you will be careful to abstain from all reference to others, further than stating any orders you may have received.

All that I have to do with is the conduct of yourself and the troopers placed under your charge.

I have the honour to be, Sir,
Your obedient servant,
(Signed) D. T. SEYMOUR, *Commissioner of Police.*

In addition to the shooting of men, women and children, the police also shot several horses which belonged to district residents who had been held up at Glenrowan by the Kellys. It was, apparently, feared that the two youths — Dan Kelly and Steve Hart — would, in broad daylight, overcome the fifty armed policemen, and then, carrying heavy armour, escape on horseback.

A large crowd came on the scene from Benalla by the midday train. A party of three young men from a distance noticed a grey horse on the hill behind McDonald's Hotel with something like a lady's riding-skirt hanging from the saddle; they hastened to the spot and discovered that it was one of the Kelly's pack horses, and that it was a blanket which was hanging from the pack saddle. With a constable, who had just arrived on the scene, they removed the saddle and examined the pack. They found, among other things, a small oil drum containing blasting powder, and about 30 feet of fuse, and a complete kit of tools for shoeing horses. The Kellys were very practical men, and always shod their horses at home and on the track. The powder and fuse was intended for use on the railway line to prevent the train returning to Benalla against the wishes of the bushrangers. Even after the shooting of the horses of law-abiding citizens, the fifty police did not consider themselves competent to prevent the two youths from escaping on foot.

Now let us compare the record of Ned Kelly and the record of the police with the approval of the Government of the Colony of Victoria during the 'sixties, 'seventies, and up to the Police Purge of 1881.

NED KELLY'S RECORD

(1) At the age of 15 years he was charged with holding the bridle reins of a bushranger's horse. — Discharged.
(2) At 16 years old convicted with a sentence of six months re the McCormack affair, considered by the public as an outrageous Miscarriage of Justice.
(3) At 16 years old convicted and sentenced to three years; proclaimed by the public as a most outrageous Miscarriage of Justice.
(4) At 23 charged with drunkenness, riding across a footpath, and resisting the police. Fine and costs amounted to £3/1/-, which was paid. This was the only genuine conviction recorded against Ned Kelly before being driven to the bush.

POLICE AND GOVERNMENT RECORD

(1) 1028 Loaded Dice by Assistant Chief Commissioner C. A. Nicolson. Bring the Kellys up on any charge, no matter how paltry.
(2) Compounded a felony — horse-stealing by Aaron Sherritt.
(3) Compounded a felony — sheepstealing by John Sherritt — which apparently qualified the latter as bad enough or good enough to be accepted into the Police Force.
(4) Violation of the Liberty of the Subject — arresting without evidence of any charge, without the suspension of the Habeas Corpus Act, 22 Freemen.
(5) Illegal confiscation of Kelly Gang's property — the armour, green silk sash, &c.
(6) Illegally poisoning farmers' dogs.
(7) Allowing a bitterly biassed judge to try Ned Kelly for his life.
(8) Refusal by the biassed judge to state a case for the Full Court on objections raised by Ned Kelly's counsel to the illegal manner in which the trial was conducted and the admission as evidence of hearsay statements.
(9) The failure of the Royal Commission (six of whom were members of Parliament) to condemn the illegality of arresting 22 free men without evidence of any charge against them and without the suspension of the Habeas Corpus Act.

NED KELLY'S TRIAL AT BEECHWORTH

Martin Cherry died shortly after Rev. Dean Gibney had administered the last sacraments of the Catholic Church to him. His body was handed over to his sister by Supt. Sadleir, who wrote an official report, in which the following diabolical concoction appeared:—

"It was known at this time that Martin Cherry was lying wounded in a detached building, shot by Ned Kelly early in the day, as it has since been ascertained, because he would not hold aside one of the window blinds; and arrangements were made to rescue him before the flames could approach him. This was subsequently done."

The sworn contradiction to this misleading and slanderous official report sent by Supt. Sadleir to headquarters is contained in the following replies to questions put to Supt. Sadleir by the Royal Commissioners, before whom he gave evidence on oath on April 14, 1881. It was not convenient for the Coroner, Mr. Wyatt, to hold an inquest on the bodies of Martin Cherry and Joe Byrne, therefore Mr. Robert McBean, J.P., of Benalla, held a magisterial inquiry (not an inquest).

Question by the Commission: What was the magisterial finding on the case of Cherry?

Supt. Sadleir: Shot by the police in the execution of their duty.

Question: And in the case of Byrne?

Supt. Sadleir: That he was shot as an outlaw. (Although he ceased to be an outlaw on February 9, 1880).

(Although he ceased to be an outlaw before he arrived at Glenrowan on the day before he was shot, because the Outlawry Act had lapsed by the dissolution of the Parliament which passed it. Parliament dissolved on 9/2/1880. Joe Byrne was shot on 28/6/1880).

Question: Who was the magistrate?

Supt. Sadleir: Mr. McBean, J.P.

Question: Do you remember if a party of civilians offered, before the burning of the place, to rush it themselves?

Supt. Sadleir: One did — not to rush it. A man named Dixon [Mr. Tom Dixon, bootmaker, Benalla], a man I have already spoken of, said, "If you will allow me, I will go to the end building and bring out Cherry."

In answering a previous question, Supt. Sadleir said:—

"I got round the back of the building and found a man named Dixon, a private citizen of Benalla and, I think, three others lifting out Cherry."

Mr. Thomas Dixon volunteered before the house was set on fire to rescue Martin Cherry, who was lying mortally wounded by police bullets, but Supt. Sadleir would not give him permission to rescue this innocent victim of police bullets.

Supt. Sadleir seemed to be quite content to allow Cherry to be sacrificed, and if Very Rev. Dean Gibney had not gone into the burning hotel in spite of Supt. Sadleir, Martin Cherry would have been roasted alive.

After the fire had died down, the charred bodies of Dan Kelly and Steve Hart were plainly visible; they were removed to the railway platform, and Supt. Sadleir handed them over to Mrs. Skillion and Richard Hart.

To this dramatic close of the Kelly Gang activities now came a most pathetic incident: Mrs. Skillion kneeling between the two burnt bodies, in an outburst of passionate grief, delivered a telling invective on the police, many of whom seemed to have become very much ashamed of the discreditable part they played in the siege of Glenrowan.

There was no inquest or inquiry held on the remains, which the relatives removed to Kellys' homestead on the Eleven-Mile Creek; coffins for the burial were then obtained from Benalla.

There being no relatives of Joe Byrne present to claim his remains, they were taken by the police to Benalla and secretly buried in the cemetery there. Before the burial, however, the body was tied to a wall and photographed.

Captain Standish disapproved of the action of Supt. Sadleir in handing the bodies of Dan Kelly and Steve Hart to their relatives, and an effort was to be made to take the bodies from them. The relatives vigorously refused to give up the remains of their dead, and made preparations for a determined fight with the police.

Sixteen mounted policemen were despatched from Benalla to Glenrowan to secure these two bodies. They put up for the night at the Glenrowan police barracks, and were expected to go out to the Kellys' homestead next day and forcibly take possession of the remains of Dan Kelly and Steve Hart. Savagery directed by stupidity could not have gone further. The Kelly Gang ceased to be outlaws on 9/2/1880, when the Outlawry Act lapsed, but the police seemed to be ignorant of that fact.

It is true that a warrant had been issued for the arrest of Dan Kelly, provided he could be arrested while he was alive. But there was no warrant now to arrest the body of Steve Hart, and it is only fair to assume that as the authorities were not cannibals, they had no use for them.

A wake was held, and relatives and friends and sympathisers attended from far and near and gave vent to the intensity of their feelings at the conduct of the police at Glenrowan. The police authorities realised the danger of driving another party of civilians to the bush as bushrangers, and not desiring to prolong the disgrace into which the Victorian Police Force had fallen in their failure to come in contact with the Kelly Gang for over two years, it was decided to abandon the attempt to take the bodies of Dan Kelly and Steve Hart from their relatives, and the sixteen mounted policemen returned to Benalla much relieved and well pleased with the discretion thus manifested by the authorities. They did not want another fight.

A very large number of people attended the funeral of these two youths, who were buried in the Greta Cemetery. The evidence of the Very Rev. Dean Gibney put aside for ever the absurd concoctions which claim that Dan Kelly escaped from Glenrowan, and which formed the subject of a despicable book under his name.

Ned Kelly was removed from Glenrowan by train to Benalla. He was attended by Dr. John Nicholson, who found that he had been wounded in the instep, and also in the right hand and legs, and was very weak from loss of blood. On the following day (Tuesday) the captured bushranger was taken by train to Melbourne. Great secrecy was observed by the police in the arrangements made to remove Ned Kelly from the train to the Melbourne Gaol. A great crowd collected at Spencer-street railway station, but the police, fearing trouble, arranged to have him removed secretly from the train at North Melbourne. He was taken from the train to the Melbourne Gaol, while a great crowd of people were anxiously waiting the arrival of the train at Spencer-street. Ned Kelly was placed in the gaol hospital, and on account of the seriousness of his wounds he was unable to appear in court.

When his wounds had healed he was taken in chains under a very strong escort to Beechworth, where he was charged before Mr. Foster, P.M., with the murder, on October 26, 1878, of Constable Lonigan at Stringybark Creek. Ned Kelly was still suffering from the effect of his wounds, but to such an extent had official callousness developed that his sister, Mrs. Skillion, was not permitted to see him. She had been informed that Ned was in need of a change of underclothing; and promptly purchased what was required, but the Beechworth Gaol authorities would not allow the clothes to be given to Ned Kelly. Mrs. Skillion then offered to go with one of the gaol officials and make similar purchases again, and suggested that the officials should take the clothes from the shop, and that she would not do so much as touch the articles purchased. Even this offer was refused, and Ned Kelly, on trial for his life and suffering from the effects of his wounds, was denied a change of underclothing by the gaol authorities.

Mr. David Gaunson, who defended Ned Kelly at his trial, was permitted to have an interview with him in the Beechworth Gaol, in the presence of gaol officials. In the interview Ned Kelly said: "I can depend my life on my sister, Mrs. Skillion. I have been kept here like a wild beast. If they were afraid to let anyone come near me, they might have kept at a distance and watched; but it seems to me to be unjust, when I am on trial for my life, to refuse to allow those I put confidence in to come with in coo-ee of me. Why, they won't so much as let me have a change of clothes brought in!

"When I came into the gaol here they made me strip off all my clothes, except my pants, and I would not do that. All I want is a full and fair trial, and a chance to make my side heard. Until now the police have had all the say, and have had it all their own way. If I get a full and fair trial, I don't care how it goes, but I know this — the public will see that I was hunted and hounded from step to step; they (the public) will see that I am not the monster I have been made out. What I have done was under strong provocation."

During the trial of Ned Kelly at Beechworth (at the conclusion of Constable McIntyre's evidence), Mr. D. Gaunson again made application to Mr. Foster, P.M., that Ned Kelly's sister, Mrs. Skillion, be permitted to see him.

Mr. Foster afterwards told Mr. Gaunson that under no circumstances could the application be entertained. And yet the people of Victoria have been frequently told that in every Court of British Justice the prisoner is always assumed to be innocent of the charge for which he is being tried until he has been fairly and justly tried and convicted by an unpacked jury of his peers.

This is the same Mr. Foster, P.M., who illegally and unlawfully kept a number of Kelly sympathisers in the Beechworth Gaol from January 2, 1879, to April 22 of the same year, without any charge or complaint being laid against any of them, or any evidence heard to justify Foster's action.

The attitude of Mr. Foster on this occasion was a further demonstration of the fact that, in the so-called judicial mind, Ned Kelly had already been convicted, and his alleged trial was but a very formal affair.

Mr. Foster did not in any way comment on the very serious disparity between the evidence now given by Constable McIntyre at Beechworth and that given by him at Mansfield at the inquest on the bodies of Constables Scanlan and Lonigan on Monday, October 28, 1878. Mr. Foster committed Ned Kelly to stand his trial at Beechworth for the murder of Constable Lonigan.

The treatment meted out to Ned Kelly at Beechworth by the gaol and judicial authorities aroused a great deal of sympathy for him in the public mind, and the Government of the day, fearing that a Beechworth jury would not convict him, changed the venue of his trial from Beechworth to Melbourne.

HOW NED KELLY WAS TRIED AT MELBOURNE BY SIR REDMOND BARRY, WHO, AT BEECHWORTH, SENTENCED HIM TO 15 YEARS, THOUGH NOT CONVICTED, TRIED, CHARGED, OR ARRESTED

FRIDAY 15TH OCTOBER, 1880.

Mr. H. Molesworth applied for a postponement of Ned Kelly's trial until next month. In support of the application, he read the following affidavit made by Mr. David Gaunson:—

I, David Gaunson, of 17 Eldon Chambers, Bank Place, Melbourne, attorney for the above-named prisoner, Edward Kelly, make oath and say:

(1) That the friends and relatives of the prisoner have not been allowed the usual access to the prisoner as a person awaiting trial, and the prisoner has thereby been greatly embarrassed in preparing his defence.
(2) That the prisoner has been unable to provide the necessary funds for counsel, and I have therefore not delivered any brief.
(3) That the depositions are very voluminous, and in order to defend the prisoner I believe counsel will need an adjournment till the next sitting.
(4) That I am informed, and believe, prisoner's sister had arranged to borrow money for her brother's defence on land occupied by her, but on applying to the person who had promised her the loan, she found that the Government had confiscated the land.
(5) That on enquiry at the Lands Office Department, I found that this week the prisoner's mother had a selection under the amending Land Act, 1865, on which she had paid up all the rents under her seven years' lease. That she had borrowed money from the Land Credit Bank, Melbourne; that the bank sold her interest to prisoner's sister, but that the Lands Department, on the application of the police, had refused to grant the title to the land.
(6) That I therefore applied to the Minister of Lands, pointing out the injustice done in the Crown forfeiting the 14/- per acre paid on account of such land, and I have reason to believe that if this trial be postponed till next sitting that the title will be completed, and money raised on such land for the purpose of defending the prisoner.
(7) That the want of means has so embarrassed both the prisoner and myself in preparing a defence, that I can safely say that, in my judgement and belief, the prisoner will be unable to obtain his counsel and be seriously prejudiced in his defence if his application for a postponement be refused.

His Honor, Mr. Justice Barry, said no reasons founded on justice or principle had been given in support of the application being granted. Applications of this character were never refused except on substantial grounds, but in this case there was no reason for supposing that if the trial were postponed money for the defence of the prisoner would be raised in the meantime. He could not assume that the land had been confiscated improperly, for there was an Act of Parliament under which the proceedings would have to be guided, and as the grounds for the present application were vague, inconsistent and wholly unauthorised, he would refuse it. The Act of Parliament above referred to lapsed on the 9th February — eight and a half months before the above application was made.

Application refused.

Monday, October 18, 1880.

Mr. Bindon (counsel for Ned Kelly) said he had, on behalf of his friend Mr. Molesworth, an application to make to the court. It was, in fact, that the trial of the prisoner might be postponed until the next sittings, and he made a motion on the grounds contained in an affidavit sworn by Mr. David Gaunson, the prisoner's attorney, of which the following is a digest:—

"That an unsuccessful application having been made on the 15th instant to postpone the trial, an appeal was made to the Crown to supply funds for the defence, and Mr. Gaunson urged, in view of the length and importance of the case, counsel's fee should be fifty guineas."

"The sheriff replied, instructing Mr. Gaunson to undertake the defence on the usual conditions, viz., £7 /7 /- for attorney and £7 /7- for counsel, with 5/- for clerk's fee. The Crown Law officers would decide as to the amount of remuneration, if any, beyond that amount. The depositions in the two cases extend to eighty-five pages of brief paper, and in addition to fully acquainting himself with them, counsel would require to read the voluminous newspaper accounts of Euroa, Jerilderie and Glenrowan affairs, referred to in the depositions, and to study the law to see how far the Crown can get into them. An adjournment to next sittings was, therefore, applied for."

Mr. Smyth (for the Crown), after going into details, said: Although opposing the application, he was loth to do anything which would convey an impression that the prisoner had been improperly treated; and if his Honor thought a case had been made out that he ought not to oppose it, he would not do so. If his Honor could, therefore, adjourn the trial until Monday next, he, (Mr. Smyth) said he would not object to that course being pursued.

His Honor said that he would not be disengaged until the 28th instant. Mr. Smyth said that date would do, and the trial was accordingly postponed until Thursday, 28 instant.

DID NED KELLY GET A FAIR TRIAL FROM JUDGE SIR REDMOND BARRY?

Thursday, 28 October, 1880.

The Crown appeared to be thirsting for Ned Kelly's blood, and provided an exceptionally strong bar to secure a conviction.

Mr. A. C. Smyth, with Mr. Chomley, prosecuted on behalf of the Crown, and Mr. Bindon, instructed by Mr. D. Gaunson, for Ned Kelly.

They called Detective Ward and Constable P. Day to prove that a warrant had been issued for Ned Kelly prior to the battle of "Stringybark Creek."

Senior constable Kelly and Sergeant Steele were called to prove the capture of Ned Kelly at the "Siege of Glenrowan."

Constable McIntyre was the only witness who could give any direct evidence in connection with the charge of murdering Constable Lonigan.

The evidence of the following prisoners at Faithful's Creek — George Stevens, Wm. Fitzgerald, Henry Dudley, Robert McDougall, J. Gloster, Frank Beecroft and Robert Scott — could not prove that they knew, of their own knowledge, that Ned Kelly shot Lonigan at Stringybark Creek, and such evidence should not have been admitted at all.

The evidence of Constable Henry Richards, E. M. Living and J. W. Tarlton, all of Jerilderie, was intended to prove that they had reliable knowledge that Ned Kelly had shot Lonigan on the banks of Stringybark Creek, although their reliable knowledge was some remarks made by Ned Kelly when at Jerilderie. When Ned Kelly made any remarks which could be used against him these remarks were accepted by the Crown as gospel, but when he made a statement that was strongly in his favour the Crown treated such a statement as a tissue of lies.

Dr. S. Reynolds, of Mansfield, stated in evidence that there were four wounds on Lonigan's body. The fatal pellet entering the eye pierced the brain.

This closed the case for the Crown.

Mr. Bindon asked that the points in the evidence which he had objected to should be reserved, and a case stated for the Full Court.

His Honor: What points do you allude to?

Mr. Bindon: All the transactions that took place after the death of Lonigan which were detailed in evidence.

Judge Barry: I think that the whole was put as a part of the proceedings of the day (when Lonigan was shot).

Mr. Bindon: There was a period, after the death of Lonigan, when no further evidence was applicable.

Judge Barry: The way the evidence was put was that Lonigan was not killed by the prisoner in self-defence.

Mr. Bindon submitted that the only evidence available for the purpose of the prosecution was what had taken place at the killing of Lonigan.

Judge Barry: The point was a perfectly good one if any authority could be shown in support. But he thought the conduct of the prisoner during the whole afternoon after the killing of Lonigan was important to show what his motive was. He must, therefore, decline to state a case.

Addressing the jury, Mr. Smyth (for the Crown) said that, as the motive of the prisoner had been referred to, he thought that when they found one man shooting down another in cold blood, they need not stop to inquire into his motives. It was one of malignant hatred against the police, because the prisoner had been leading a wild, lawless life, and was at war with society. He had proved abundantly, by the witnesses produced for the Crown, who were practically not cross-examined, that the murder of Lonigan was committed in cold blood.

So far as he could gather, anything from the cross-examination, the line of defence was that the prisoner considered that in the origin if the Fitzpatrick "case," as it was called, he and his family were injured, and that the prisoner was therefore justified in going about the country with an armed band to revenge himself upon the police.

Another point in the defence was that because Sergeant Kennedy and his men did not surrender themselves to the prisoner's gang, this gang was justified in what they called defending themselves and murdering the police. He asked, would the jury allow this state of affairs to exist? Such a thing was not to be tolerated, and he had almost to apologise to the jury for discussing the matter.

The prisoner appeared to glory in his murdering of the police. Even admitting the prisoner's defence that the charge of attempting to murder Constable Fitzpatrick was an untruthful one, it was perfectly idle to say that this would justify the prisoner in subsequently killing Constable Lonigan because he was engaged upon the duty of searching for the Kelly Gang. (There was no Kelly Gang when Lonigan was shot.)

It would not be any defence to say that Lonigan was shot by some other member of the gang, because the whole gang was engaged in an illegal act. He thought it was not an unfair inference to draw that McIntyre was kept alive until his superior officer arrived only to be murdered afterwards, and thus not a living soul would have been left to tell the sad tale of how these unfortunate men met their deaths at the hands of this band of assassins. The prisoner wanted to pose before the country as a hero, but he was nothing less than a petty thief, as was shown by the fact that the gang rifled the pockets of the murdered men.

The murders committed were of a most cowardly character, and the prisoner had shown himself a coward throughout his career. The murders that he and his companions committed were of a most bloodthirsty nature. They never appeared in the open excepting they were fully armed and had great advantage over their victims.

Mr. Bindon, in addressing the jury for the defence, said it was his intention, in conducting the case, not to refer to or introduce a variety of matters which had nothing to do with the present trial; but, unfortunately, his intentions were rendered futile by the Crown, who brought forward a number of things foreign to the present case.

The question still remained how far this material was to be used in influencing the jury in arriving at a verdict. According to all principles of fairness and justice, these matters should not have been brought forward, because the only thing that the jury was concerned in was the shooting of Lonigan. With the shooting of Kennedy and the proceedings at Glenrowan and at Jerilderie the jury had nothing whatever to do at present, and he therefore requested them to keep these things from their minds.

In McIntyre's evidence a long account was given of what took place in the Wombat Ranges, but he would point out that he had appeared on the scene, not in uniform, but plain clothes, and armed to the teeth. An unfortunate fracas occurred, which resulted in the shooting of Lonigan. The point to which he wished to draw special attention was that the only account of the affair came from McIntyre, who was a prejudiced witness. He thought that McIntyre was not a witness who, under the peculiar circumstances, could give an accurate account of what occurred. McIntyre said he was as cool as possible, but he must have been in such a state of excitement that it could not be expected of him to distinguish correctly what actually did take place. Because the Kellys were found in the bush, it did not follow that they were secreting themselves; on the contrary, they were following their ordinary occupations in this solitary part of the country, when they fell in with this armed party of men. The Kellys did not know who these people were, and it was a most dangerous doctrine to rest on the evidence of one man, more especially when the charge was that one man shot another deliberately and in cold blood. The evidence of McIntyre should be received with very great suspicion; and with regard to the confessions of the prisoner made at various times, these were uttered either for the purpose of intimidation or to screen others who were associated with him, and therefore the evidence was of no use whatever in corroboration of McIntyre's version of the transaction. From that point of view, the conversation was merely illusory in its character. Even assuming McIntyre to be the most virtuous man in the world, it was necessary, under the peculiar circumstances, that the jury should receive his statements with the greatest caution. There were only McIntyre and the prisoner who could now say anything of the affair. The prisoner's mouth was shut, but if he could be sworn, then he would give a totally different version of the transaction. He asked them not to believe McIntyre's statement as regarded the death of Lonigan. Of course, it would be nonsense to say that Lonigan was not shot, but the point was by whom was he shot? The deaths of Kennedy and Scanlan were not to be allowed to influence the minds of the jury in arriving at a verdict on the first case. There was no ground for the Crown to say that the police had fallen amongst a lot of assassins. The whole career of the prisoner showed that he was not an assassin, a cold-blooded murderer, or a thief. On the contrary, he had proved himself to have the greatest possible respect for human life. The story of McIntyre was too good to be true. It showed the signs of deliberate and careful preparation, and of being afterwards carefully studied.

He would ask: Would the jury convict a man upon the evidence of a single witness, and that a prejudiced witness? If they had the smallest doubt, he trusted the jury would give a verdict in this case different from that which the Crown expected.

His Honor Judge Barry, in summing-up, said that if two or three men made preparations with malice aforethought to murder a man, even if two out of the three did not take part in the murder, all were principals in the first degree and equally guilty of the crime. They aided and abetted, and were as guilty as the man who committed the crime. The fact that the police party were in plain clothes had nothing whatever to do with the case. The murdered men might be regarded as ordinary persons travelling through the country, and they might ask themselves what right had any four men to stop them and ask them to surrender or put up their hands. These men were charged with the discharge of a very responsible and dangerous duty; they were executive officers of the law, in addition to being ordinary constables, and no person had a right to stop or question them.

The counsel for the defence had also told the jury to receive the evidence of McIntyre with very great caution; but he would go further and hope that the jury would receive and weigh all the evidence with caution. It was not necessary to have McIntyre's evidence corroborated, and he asked the jury to note the behaviour of McInyre in the witness box, and say whether his conduct was that of a man who wanted to deceive.

It was not necessary for him to go through the evidence, as it was so fresh in the memory of the jury. They were not to suppose that the prisoner was on his trial for the murder of Kennedy and Scanlan. The charge against him was the murder of Lonigan, and the object of admitting the whole of the evidence subsequent to the shooting of Lonigan was to give the jury every opportunity to judge the conduct of the prisoner and his intentions during that particular day. With regard to the other part of the case — the confessions made by the prisoner at various times — they had not alone to consider the confessions themselves, but also the circumstances under which they were made. They were not made under compulsion, but at a time when the prisoner was at liberty, and if he made these confessions in a spirit of vain glory, or with the desire of screening his companions, he had to accept the full responsibility. Counsel for the defence said that the prisoner's mouth was closed and that if it was not closed he could tell a different story to the one told by McIntyre.

But the fact was that the prisoner's mouth was not closed. That he could not give sworn testimony was true, but he could have made a statement which, if consistent with his conduct for the last eighteen months, would have been entitled to consideration; but the prisoner had not done so. As to whether the prisoner shot Lonigan or not, that was an immaterial point. The prisoner was engaged with others in an illegal act; he had pointed a gun at McIntyre's breast, and that circumstance was sufficient to establish his guilt. The jury would, however, have to regard the evidence as a whole, and accordingly say whether murder had been committed. It could not be manslaughter. The verdict of the jury must either be guilty of murder or an acquittal.

The jury retired from the court at ten minutes past five in the afternoon and, after half an hour's absence, returned with a verdict of guilty.

Upon the judge's associate asking the prisoner whether he had anything to say why sentence should not be passed upon him, Ned Kelly said:

Well, it is rather late for me to speak now. I tried to do so this morning, but I thought afterwards that I had better not. No one understands my case as I do, and I almost wish now that I had spoken; not that I fear death. On the evidence that has been given, no doubt, the jury or any other jury could not have given any other verdict. But it is on account of the witnesses, and with their evidence no different verdict could be given. No one knows anything about my case but myself. Mr. Bindon knows nothing about it at all, and Mr. Gaunson knows nothing, though they tried to do their best for me. I'm sorry I did not ask my counsel to sit down, and examine the witnesses myself. I could have made things look different, I'm sure. No one understands my case.

The crier of the court called for silence while his Honor passed the awful sentence of death upon the prisoner.

Judge Barry: Edward Kelly, the verdict is one which you must have fully expected.

Ned Kelly: Under the circumstances, I did expect this verdict.

Judge Barry: No circumstances that I can conceive could here control the verdict.

Ned Kelly: Perhaps if you had heard me examine the witnesses, you might understand, I could do it.

Judge Barry: I will even give you credit for the skill which you desire to show you possess.

Ned Kelly: I don't say this out of flashness. I do not recognise myself as a great man; but it is quite possible for me to clear myself of this charge if I liked to do so. If I desired to do it, I could have done it in spite of anything attempted against me.

Judge Barry: The facts against you are so numerous and so conclusive, not only as regards the offence which you are now charged with, but also for the long series of criminal acts which you have committed during the last eighteen months, that I do not think any rational person could have arrived at any other conclusion. The verdict of the jury was irresistible, and there could not be any doubt about it being a right verdict. I have no right or wish to inflict upon you any personal remarks. It is painful in the extreme to perform the duty which I have now to discharge, and I will confine myself strictly to it. I do not think that anything I could say would aggravate the pain you must now be suffering.

Ned Kelly: No; I declare before you and my God that my mind is as easy and clear as it possibly can be.

Judge Barry: It is blasphemous of you to say so.

Ned Kelly: I do not fear death, and I am the last man in the world to take a man's life away. I believe that two years ago, before this thing happened, if a man pointed a gun at me to shoot me, I should not have stopped him, so careful was I of taking life. I am not a murderer, but if there is innocent life at stake, then I say I must take some action. If I see innocent life taken, I should shoot if I was forced to do so, but I should first want to know whether this could not be prevented, but I should have to do it if it could not be stopped in any other way.

Judge Barry: Your statement involves wicked and criminal reflection of untruth upon the witnesses who have given evidence.

Ned Kelly: I dare say the day will come when we shall all have to go to a bigger court than this. Then we will see who is right and who is wrong. As regards anything about myself, all I care for is that my mother, who is now in prison, shall not have it to say that she reared a son who could not have altered this charge if I had liked to do so.

Judge Barry: An offence of the kind which you stand accused of is not of an ordinary character. There are many murders which have been discovered and committed in this colony under different circumstances, but none shows greater atrocity than those you committed. These crimes proceed from different motives. Some arise from a sordid desire to take from others the property which they acquired or inherited; some from jealousy; some from a bare desire to thieve, but this crime was an enormity out of all proportion. A party of men took up arms against society, organised as it was for mutual protection and regard for law.

Ned Kelly: Yes; that is the way the evidence brought it out.

Judge Barry: Unfortunately, in a new community, where society was not bound together as closely as it should be, there was a class which looked upon the perpetrators of these crimes as heroes. But these unfortunate, ill-educated, ill-prompted youths must be taught to consider the value of human life. It could hardly be believed that a man would sacrifice the lives of his fellow-creatures in this wild manner. The idea was enough to make one shudder in thinking of it. The end of your companions was comparatively a better termination than the miserable death that awaits you.

It is remarkable that although New South Wales had joined Victoria in offering a large reward for the detection of the gang, no person was found to discover it. There seemed to be a spell cast over the people of this particular district, which I can only attribute either to sympathy with crime or dread of the consequences of doing their duty. For months the country has been disturbed by you and your associates, and you have actually had the hardihood to confess to having stolen two hundred horses.

Ned Kelly: Who proves this?

Judge Barry: That is your own statement.

Ned Kelly: You have not heard me; if I had examined the witnesses, I could have brought it out differently.

Judge Barry: I am not accusing you. This statement had been

made several times by the witnesses; you confessed it to them, and you stand self-accused. It is also proved that you committed several attacks upon the banks, and you seem to have appropriated large sums of money — several thousands of pounds. It has also come within my knowledge that the country has expended about £50,000 in consequence of the acts of which you and your party have been guilty. Although we have had such examples as Clarke, Gardiner, Melville, Morgan and Scott, who have all met ignominious deaths, still the effect has, apparently, not been to hinder others from following in their footsteps. I think that this is much to be deplored, and some steps must be taken to have society protected. Your unfortunate and miserable associates have met with deaths which you might envy. I will forward to the Executive the notes of the evidence which I have taken and all circumstances connected with your case, but I cannot hold out any hope to you that the sentence which I am now about to pass will be remitted. I desire not to give you any further pain or to aggravate the distressing feelings which you must be enduring.

Judge Barry then passed the sentence of death, and concluded with the usual formula: "May the Lord have mercy on your soul."

Ned Kelly: Yes; I will meet you there!

On the 3rd November the Executive Council met and dealt with Ned Kelly's case. It was decided that the law should take its course, and the date for Ned Kelly's execution was fixed for Thursday, 11th November.

On Friday night, the 5th November, an immense public meeting was held in the Hippodrome. The interior was packed with 2,500 people, and another 6,000 persons were unable to gain admission. The meeting was very orderly, and was addressed by Mr. David Gaunson and his brother, Mr. Wm. Gaunson. The chair was taken by Mr. Hamilton, and a resolution was moved and seconded "That in the case of Ned Kelly, the prerogative of mercy should be exercised by the Governor-in-Council." This motion was carried unanimously.

A petition signed by 32,000 adults was presented to the Governor at the meeting of Executive Council on the 8th November. While the petition was being considered by the Governor-in-Council an immense crowd assembled outside the Treasury Buildings. The prayer of the petitioners was refused, and the date of Ned Kelly's execution was finally fixed for Thursday, 11th November, 1880.

At 10 o'clock on the morning of the 11th November, Colonel Rede, the sheriff, came forward in official dress and demanded the body of Ned Kelly. An immense crowd had collected outside the gaol

Ned walked calmly to execution, and when passing through the garden in the gaol yard he remarked on the extraordinary beauty of the flowers. He walked firmly after his spiritual advisers, Dean Doneghy and Dean O'Hea. He answered the priests, who recited the litany of the dying. The cap was drawn over his face, and, as the lever was drawn, Ned Kelly's last words were, "Such is life."

DEATH OF MR. JUSTICE BARRY

On the 23rd November, Judge Barry died from congestion of the lungs and a carbuncle in the neck. He suffered great pain, but death was unexpected. He survived Ned Kelly by only twelve days, when he was called before that bigger court, where he was sure to get unadulterated justice.

Judge Barry's unlawful, unjust, and maliciously threatened sentence of fifteen years on Ned Kelly at Beechworth in October, 1878, already referred to, was responsible for the deaths of ten persons. He was responsible for the shooting of the three policemen at the Stringybark Creek; he was consequently responsible for the shooting of Aaron Sherritt; he was further responsible for the shooting of Martin Cherry and Mrs. Jones' little son at Glenrowan; he was responsible for the deaths of the four bushrangers.

Ned Kelly's challenge, therefore, to meet Judge Barry where they both would get unadulterated justice was very significant, seeing that Judge Barry was so promptly called to answer that challenge.

On 25th November, Mrs. Ann Jones was charged with harbouring the Kellys and committed for trial.

BIAS OF THE PRESS.

"*The Age,*" November 12th, 1880:

"Under date 10th November, deceased (Ned Kelly) reiterated in a written statement the greater portion of his first statement. On the third page he says:—

'I was determined to capture Superintendent Hare, O'Connor and the blacks for the purpose of an exchange of prisoners, and while I had them as hostages I would be safe, as no police would follow me.'

"At the end of the last document prisoner (Ned Kelly) requests that his mother may be released from gaol, and his body handed over to his friends for burial in consecrated ground. [Neither request will be granted.]"

Because Mr. David Gaunson called public meetings for the express purpose of giving the public the actual facts relating to the case of Ned Kelly, and because he had the courage to address these public meetings and liberate the truth so carefully suppressed by the press of that day, the following comments appeared on page 5 of "The Age" of 13th November, 1880:—

"Though the leaders of the Assembly appear to be disinclined to take any measures to purge the House of the disgrace arising from one of its prominent officers exhibiting an active sympathy with a notorious criminal, the constituents of Mr. David Gaunson are not so compliant. A requisition is being signed in Ararat calling upon him to resign his seat. The press thorough the Colony is unanimous in its condemnation of his conduct.

'The Ballarat Star' writes:—

"It behoves the Assembly to take immediate steps to vindicate its own honor, which has been sadly besmirched owing to the behaviour of one of its principal officers. The retention of Mr. David Gaunson in the position of Chairman of Committees is an insult, not only to every member of the Legislative Assembly, but an affront to every law-abiding elector in the Colony. Whatever may have been the motives that prompted Mr. Gaunson to depart from the rules that regulate the profession of which he is a member, his conduct in the disreputable affair is equally reprehensible. He seems to have entirely forgotten — if, indeed, he ever realised the fact — that the position he occupies in the Legislative is one of honour, as well as of profit, and that decency of demeanour, both inside and outside the precincts of Parliament, is required on the part of the person who fills it.'

"The 'Geelong Times' and 'The Maryborough Standard' write in similar strain."

DEATH OF DAN KELLY & STEVE HART

21

DISTRIBUTION OF £8,000 BLOOD MONEY

IT was about one o'clock on Sunday afternoon when a telegram with After the capture of Ned Kelly and the destruction of his three mates at Glenrowan on June 28, 1880, the Victorian Government then gave some consideration to the paying of the reward of £8,000 offered in equal parts by the Victorian and New South Wales Governments for the capture or destruction of the Kelly Gang.

It was finally decided to appoint Mr. C. McMahon, Mr. Jas. Macbain, and Mr. Robert Murray Smith as a Board to take evidence on the services rendered by the various claimants, and allocate the reward as it (the Board) thought fit. The Board examined only five witnesses, viz.:

The Hon. Robert Ramsay, M.L.A., late Chief Secretary; Mr. Joseph Delgarno Melvin, an "Argus" reporter; Mr. George Vasey Allen, a reporter for the "Daily Telegraph"; Mr. John McWhirter, a reporter for the "Age"; Mr. Charles C. Rawlings, a farmer near Glenrowan.

After taking the evidence of these witnesses as to what took place at Glenrowan, the Board allotted the reward as follows:—

1 Supt. Hare £800 0 0
2 Thomas Curnow, State School teacher, Glenrowan 550 0 0
3 Senior-Constable Kelly 377 11 8
4 Sergeant Steel 290 13 9
5 Constable Bracken, Glenrowan 275 13 9
6 Supt. Sadleir 240 17 3
7 Stanhope O'Connor (in charge of the blacktrackers) 237 15 0
8 Jesse Dowsett, railway guard 175 13 9
9 Sergeant Whelan, Benalla 165 13 9
10 Constable Canny 137 11 8
11 Constable P. Gascoigne 137 11 8
12 Constable Phillips 137 11 8
13 Constable Barry 137 11 8
14 Constable Arthur 137 11 8
15 C. C. Rawlins, a witness before the Board .. .. .137 11 8
16 Constable Kirkham, Benalla 137 11 8
17 Senior-Constable Smyth 137 11 8

18 Constable P. Kelly 137 11 8
19 Constable Dixon 115 13 9
20 Constable Jas. Dwyer 115 13 9
21 Constable Wilson 115 13 9
22 Constable Milne 115 13 9
23 Constable Stillard 115 13 9
24 Constable Ryan 115 13 9
25 Constable Reilly 115 13 9
26 Constable Graham 115 13 9
27 Constable Hewitt 115 13 9
28 Constable Wallace 115 13 9
29 Constable Walsh 115 13 9
30 Constable Mountford 115 13 9
31 Constable Cawsey 115 13 9
32 Constable Healey 115 13 9
33 Constable Moore 115 13 9
34 Mr. McPhee, guard on pilot engine .. 104 4 6
35 Mr. Alder, driver, pilot engine 104 4 6
36 Mr. Burch, fireman, pilot engine 104 4 6
37 Detective-Constable Ward 100 0 0
38 Senior-Constable Johnston 97 15 9
39 Mr. Bowman, engine driver 84 4 6
40 Mr. Hallows 84 4 6
41 Mr. Bell, guard 84 4 6
42 Mr. Coleman, engine driver 68 3 4
43 Mr. Stewart, fireman 68 3 4
44 Senior-Constable Mullane 47 15 9
45 Constable Glenny 42 15 9
46 Constable McColl 42 15 9
47 Constable Meagor 42 15 9
48 Constable Armstrong (one of the four police at Sherritt's when the latter was shot by Byrne) 42 15 9
49 Constable Dowling (who was under the bed at Sherritt's) 42 15 9
50 Constable Duross (also under the bed at Sherritt's) 42 15 9
51 Constable Alexander (one of the four at Sherritt's when the latter was shot) 42 15 9
52 Constable McHugh 42 15 9
53 Constable Wickham 42 15 9
54 John Sherritt 42 15 9
55 Constable Dwyer 42 15 9
56 Constable Stone 42 15 9

57 Constable McDonald 42 15 9
58 Hero, blacktracker 50 0 0
59 Johnny, blacktracker 50 0 0
60 Jimmy, blacktracker 50 0 0
61 Jacky, blacktracker 50 0 0
62 Barney, blacktracker 50 0 0
63 Moses, blacktracker 50 0 0
64 Spider, blacktracker 50 0 0
65 Mr. Cheshire 25 0 0
66 Mr. Osborne 25 0 0
Total £8000 0 0

The following claims (24) for the reward were refused:—

Schedule "A." — Anton Weekes, Richard Rule, George Stephens, Anne Sherritt, Ellen Sherritt, Senior-Constable Patrick Walsh, Constable John Coghlan, Constable Robert Griffin, Constable Robert Bunker, Constable Thomas Walsh, ex-Constable Perkins, Constable J. W. Brown, Constable W. Parker, Constable J. Burton, Senior-Constable Shahan, Constable Hugh Stewart, Constable Skehan, Lawrence Kirwin (police spy), B. C. Williams (police spy), Constable Faulkiner, Constable McIntyre, Mr. Laing, S.M., Wangaratta; Mr. Saxe, P.M., Benalla; Mr. Stephen, S.M., Benalla.

The last five-mentioned claimants, although refused any part of the reward by the Board, were, under Schedule "C," recommended as worthy of special recognition for services rendered during the period of the search for the outlaws.

The Reward Board stated in its report:— "Some rewards have also been recommended for the individual service of certain claimants whose names will be found in Schedule 'D'; but beyond these the Board have not thought in within their province to distinguish further between members of a force, all of whom appear to have done their duty."

SCHEDULE "D" — SPECIAL REWARDS

Thomas Curnow, schoolmaster; Senior-Constable Kelly; Constable Bracken; Sergeant Steele; Mr. Jesse Dowsett, railway guard; and Senior-Constable Johnston (who set fire to Mrs. Jones' hotel, where Martin Cherry was lying mortally wounded).

It was not until the publication of the finding of the Royal Commission, which was subsequently appointed to inquire into the management and conduct of the police force during the search for the Kelly Gang of bushrangers, and also the best means of preventing another outbreak, that the nature of the scandal perpetrated by the Reward Board was fully realised.

The Reward Board gave Sergeant Steele £290/13/9 for the part he played in shooting innocent men, women and children who were trying to escape from Mrs. Jones' hotel at Glenrowan.

The Royal Commission, on the other hand, recommended that Sergeant Steele be reduced to the ranks for cowardice in not following the bushrangers from Wangaratta to the Warby Ranges, when the fresh tracks made by the Kellys were pointed out to him. The Reward Board gave Supt. Hare £800, although he left the field as soon as he received a wound on the left arm.

The Royal Commission, on the other hand, in a majority report, compared the cowardice of Supt. Hare in running away when wounded in the left arm, with the courage and leadership of Ned Kelly, who, although much more seriously wounded in the instep and arms, stood his ground until 7 o'clock in the morning, when, bravely attempting to rejoin his mates, he was overpowered by numbers. The Royal Commission recommended that Supt. Hare should, therefore, be retired from the police force on pension.

The Reward Board gave the constables who went under the bed at Aaron Sherritt's, when the latter was shot by Joe Byrne, £42/15/9 each.

The Royal Commission recommended that three of these four policemen be dismissed from the police force for gross cowardice and disobedience.

The fourth had already anticipated this finding, and resigned before the Commission drew up its report.

The Reward Board gave Supt. Sadlier £240/17/3.

The Royal Commission recommended that he be reduced in rank.

The Reward Board gave Mr. Stanhope O'Connor £237/15/-.

The Royal Commission recommended that Mr. Stanhope O'Connor be not again employed in the Victorian Police Force, although the Chief Secretary had intended to make Mr. O'Connor an inspector of police in the North-East district.

Although the action of the police force at Glenrowan, both officers and men, was considered an indelible disgrace to the police force of Victoria, no fewer than forty-five of them participated in the reward.

THE ROYAL COMMISSION

After the tragedy of Glenrowan, the public press of Victoria was more emphatic than ever in its condemnation of the heads of the police force. As the result of this criticism, the Chief Secretary was requested by Captain Standish to institute a full and complete inquiry into the proceedings and management of the police force from the tragedy at Stringybark Creek in October, 1878, to the destruction of the Kelly Gang at Glenrowan.

Mr. C. H. Nicolson wrote to the Chief Secretary as follows:—

"I have the honour respectfully to request that, before proceeding to acknowledge the services of those engaged in the destruction of the Kelly Gang of outlaws, a searching inquiry be held into the whole circumstances and transactions of the police administration in the North-Eastern district since the Kelly outbreak in October, 1878, and particularly into the circumstances of my recent withdrawal from that district."

Mr. Stanhope O'Connor also wrote to the Chief Secretary requesting an inquiry.

After considering these three requests, the Government of the day acceded to their wishes and appointed a Royal Commission on March 7, 1881, under letters patent:—

(1) To inquire into the circumstances proceeding and attending the Kelly outbreak.

(2) As to the efficiency of the police to deal with such possible occurrences.

(3) To inquire into the action of the police authorities during the period the Kelly Gang were at large.

(4) The efficiency of the means employed for their capture; and

(5) Generally to inquire into and report upon the present state and organisation of the police force.

The Government appointed a Royal Commission of eight persons, six of whom were members of Parliament:—Hon. Francis Longmore, M.P., Chairman; W. Anderson, Esq., M.P.; E. J. Dixon, Esq., J.P.; G. R. Fincham, Esq., M.P.; Jas. Gibb, Esq., M.P.; Hon. J. H. Graves, M.P.; G. W. Hall, Esq., M.P.; G.C. Levy, Esq., C.M.G.

The first meeting of the Commission was held on Tuesday, March 15, 1881, and sat at regular intervals, and visited many centres in the North-East. The evidence given before this Royal Commission was so contradictory and so conflicting that it was very clearly seen that perjury among some of the police force had developed into a fine art.

"That immediately prior to the Kelly outbreak, and for some time previously, the administration of the police in the North-Eastern district was not satisfactory, either as regards the number and distribution of the constabulary, or the manner in which they were armed and mounted; and that a grave error was committed in abolishing the police station at Glenmore, and in reducing the strength of the stations at Stanley, Yackandandah, Tallangatta, Eldorado and Beechworth.

"That the conduct of Captain Standish, as Chief Commissioner of Police, as disclosed by the evidence brought before the Commissioners, was not characterised either by good judgment or by that zeal for the interests of the public service which should have distinguished an officer in Captain Standish's position. The Commission attribute much of the bad feeling which existed amongst the officers to the want of impartiality, temper, tact and judgment evinced by the Chief Commissioner in his dealings with his subordinates; and they cannot refrain from remarking that many of the charges made by Captain Standish in his evidence before them were disproved by the evidence of other witnesses.

"That Mr. Nicolson, Assistant Commissioner, has shown himself in many respects a capable and zealous officer throughout his career in the force, but he laboured under great difficulties through undue interference on the part of Captain Standish and the jealousy occasioned by that officer's previous favouritism exhibited towards Supt. Hare. The want of unanimity existing between these officers was the means of preventing any concerted action in important matters, and the interests of the colony greatly suffered thereby. In view of these facts, the Commission do not think that the force would be benefited by reinstating Mr. Nicolson in the office of Acting Chief Commissioner of Police. Further, we recommend that, in consequence of his age and impaired constitution, which suffered through hardships endured in the late Kelly pursuit, Mr. Nicolson be allowed to retire on his superannuation allowance.

"That the charge made by Supt. Hare in his report of July 2, 1880, that Mr. Nicolson, Assistant Commissioner, 'gave me (Hare) no verbal information whatever when at Benalla,' is disproved by the evidence.

"That Superintendent Hare's services in the police force have been praiseworthy and creditable, but nothing special has been shown in his actions that would warrant the Commission in recommending his retention in the force, more especially when the fact is so patent that the 'strained relations' between himself and Mr. Nicolson have had such a damaging influence on the effectiveness of the service. This feeling is not likely to be mitigated after what has transpired in the evidence taken before the Commission; and we would therefore recommend that Mr. Hare be allowed to retire from the force as though he had attained the age of 55 years, and, owing to the wound that he received at Glenrowan, that he receive an additional allowance of £100 per annum, under Clause 29 of the Police Statute, No. 476.

"That the evidence discloses that Supt. Sadleir was guilty of several errors of judgment while assisting in the pursuit of the Kelly Gang; that his conduct of operations against the outlaws at Glenrowan was not judicious or calculated to raise the police force in the estimation of the public; that the Commission are further of opinion that the treatment of Senior-Constables Kelly and Johnston by Supt. Sadleir was harsh and unmerited; and the Commission recommend that Supt. Sadleir be placed at the bottom of the list of superintendents when the changes necessitated in the force by the recommendations of the Commission have been carried out.

"That a most favourable opportunity of capturing the outlaws at a very early period of their career in crime, namely, on November 4, 1878, was lost, owing to the indolence and incompetence of Inspector Brook-Smith. Your Commission consider that Inspector Brook-Smith committed a serious blunder in not having started in pursuit of the outlaws immediately upon receiving information of the gang having been seen passing under the bridge at Wangaratta, and also in not having properly followed up the tracks of the outlaws in the Warby Ranges, a proceeding which would have warranted your Commission in recommending his dismissal from the force. Your Commissioners, however, having in view his former efficiency, recommend that Inspector Brook-Smith be called on to retire on a pension of £100 per annum.

"That, in the opinion of the Commission, Detective Ward, while he rendered active and efficient service during the pursuit of the gang, was guilty of misleading his superior officers upon several occasions, more especially in connection with Mr. Nicolson's cave party, Supt. Hare's hut party, and the telegram forwarded to Senior-Constable Mullane by Mr. Nicolson when the latter was superseded on June 2, 1880. The Commission therefore recommend that Detective Ward be censured and reduced one grade.

"That in the opinion of your Commissioners, the conduct of Sergeant Steele was highly censurable in neglecting to take action when, on November 4, 1878, he received reliable information that the outlaws had been observed on the previous morning passing under the one-mile bridge at Wangaratta. Although despatched on special duty, there seems no reason why, having under his command at the time a large body of troopers, he should not have gone immediately in pursuit. The tracks were plainly discernible; the men observed were undoubtedly the outlaws, and had they been followed they must have been overtaken in the Warby Ranges, inasmuch as their horses and themselves were exhausted in their journey to and from the Murray. Sergeant Steele had full power to act upon his own discretion, and there can be little doubt that, had he exhibited judgment and promptitude on that occasion, he would have been the means of capturing the gang, and preventing the loss of life and the enormous expenditure of money incurred subsequently in the extermination of the gang. Your Commissioners therefore recommend that Sergeant Steele be reduced to the ranks.

"That the constables who formed the hut party on the night of Aaron Sherritt's murder, viz., Henry Armstrong, William Duross, Thomas Patrick Dowling and Robert Alexander, were guilty of disobedience of orders and gross cowardice, and that the three latter — Constable Armstrong having resigned — be dismissed from the service.

"That the entries made by Supt. Sadleir in the record sheets of Senior-Constables Kelly and Johnston be cancelled, and the Commission recommend these members of the force to the favourable consideration of the Government for promotion.

"That the Commission approve of the action taken by Constable Bracken when imprisoned by the Kelly Gang in Mrs. Jones' hotel at Glenrowan, and recommend him for promotion in the service.

"That in consequence of the reprehensible conduct of Mr. Wallace, the State school teacher, during the Kelly pursuit, and his alleged sympathy with the outlaws, together with the unsatisfactory character of his evidence before the Commission, your Commissioners think it very undesirable that Mr. Wallace should be retained in any department of the public service. We therefore recommend his immediate dismissal from the Education Department.

"That the conduct of Mr. Thos. Curnow, State school teacher, in warning the special train from Benalla to Beechworth on the morning of June 28, 1880, whereby a terrible disaster, involving probably the loss of many lives, was averted, deserves the highest praise, and the Commission strongly recommend that his services receive special recognition on the part of the Government.

The Commission desire to record their approval of the conduct of Mr. C. H. Rawlings during the attack upon the outlaws, and consider that his services deserve some consideration at the hands of the Government.

"The Commision desire also to express their approval of the assistance rendered to the police at Glenrowan by the members of the Press present.

"That your Commissioners desire to record their marked appreciation of the courtesy and promptitude displayed by the Queensland Government in forwarding a contingent of native trackers to Victoria to aid in the pursuit of the outlaws. We take this opportunity of expressing our approval of the services of the blacktrackers as a body, and deeply regret that any misunderstanding amongst the officers in command of operations in the North-Eastern District led to unpleasant complications.

"The Queensland contingent did good service, and your Commissioners trust the Victorian Government will not fail to accord them proper recognition.

DR. DIXON'S MINORITY REPORT

Mr. E. J. Dixon, J.P., one of the Royal Commissioners, was not satisfied with the attitude taken up by the majority of the Commission in recommending the removal of Supt. Hare from the police force. He then wrote a minority report, in which he claimed that Supt. Hare should be allowed to return to duty. His advocacy of Supt. Hare's claim for reinstatement resembled a paraphrase of the official report put in by Supt. Hare after the capture of Ned Kelly at Glenrowan. In that report Supt. Hare lauded himself to the skies to such an extent that its correctness was openly and earnestly challenged by other officers of the police force. Mr. Dixon's minority report so angered Messrs. Francis Longmore, George Wilson Hall, George Randall Fincham, and William Anderson, that they, as the majority of the Commission, replied as follows:—

"Mr. Dixon's protest should be found a mere paraphrase of portions of Supt. Hare's official report, which has been the source of so much mischief, and which we have no hesitation in declaring to be in its essential features a mere tissue of egotism and misrepresentation. There seems every reason to believe that Supt. Hare was throughout in direct collusion with Captain Standish in the petty and dishonourable persecution to which Mr. Nicolson was subjected for many years while endeavouring to honestly discharge his duties to the best of his ability.

"Captain Standish described Nicolson's report as 'twaddle'; Hare describes it as 'infernal bosh.'

"Hare's letter in reply to Nicolson:— 'I would suggest to Mr. Nicolson the advisability of his devoting his attention to answering the serious charges preferred by witnesses examined before the Commission against himself, instead of attempting to find fault with my conduct. — Francis Hare, 26/9/81.'

"Comparisons may be odious, but it cannot fail to strike one as singular that, while Supt. Hare felt himself obliged to leave his post and return to Benalla, under the impression that the wound in his wrist would prove fatal, the leader of the outlaws, with a bullet wound lodged in his foot and otherwise wounded in the extremities, was enabled to hold his ground, encumbered, too, by iron armour, until seven o'clock, when, in the effort to rejoin his companions, he fell overpowered by numbers.

"Supt. Hare's bill against the Government for surgical attendance amounted to £607, about £480 of which was paid to his relative, Dr. Charles Ryan; while this officer was being petted and coddled on all sides, and a special surgeon dispatched almost daily some thirty miles by train to attend him, the Government questioned the payment of £4/4/- for the treatment of one of the blacktrackers who had received a wound in the head at Glenrowan."

(Signed):

GEORGE WILSON HALL.
FRANCIS LONGMORE.
GEORGE RANDALL FINCHAM.
WILLIAM ANDERSON.

Hon. J. H. Graves did not sign the report because he had to give evidence as a witness before the Commission.

Kelly sympathisers were arrested and thrown into gaol for over three months because they looked at the police or watched them. Now, what would have happened to Messrs. Longmore, Hall, Fincham and Anderson if they had spoken as above immediately prior to the arrest of the Kelly sympathisers? They, too, should have been arrested as sympathisers? They, too, should have been arrested as sympathisers and thrown into gaol.

It is surprising, therefore, that the Royal Commission did not refer in its report to the illegal arrest of twenty free men as Kelly sympathisers, and the outrage perpetrated by Supt. Hare in keeping these men, unlawfully, in gaol from January 2, 1879, to April 22 of the same year.

It is also very surprising that the Royal Commission did not censure the conduct of Sergeant Steele at Glenrowan. Apparently the attempted murder of Mrs. Reardon, her baby and her son by Sergeant Steele were not as serious in the judicial minds of these four politicians as Steele's neglect to follow the tracks of the Kellys from Wangaratta to Warby Ranges. It is very clear that the anti-Kelly prejudice was so firmly rooted in the minds of the so-called ruling class of that day that while they connived at police rapacity, they mildly censured police cowardice and perjury.

There was evidently one law for the police and another for high-spirited civilians.

Now, if these four Commissioners were so very angry with the heads of the police force — Captain Standish and Supt. Hare — merely because Commissioner E. J. Dixon spoke or wrote on their behalf, what would they not have done had they received but one-half of the provocation or persecution and injustice to which the Kellys had been subjected by the bench and the police?

Even after fifty years the bias of the Government does not seem to have appreciably diminished. Mr. David Gaunson was hounded down, in 1880, for speaking on behalf of Ned Kelly, and on 12th April, 1929, the Government, through its departmental heads, brought its brutality to a fitting climax by failing to make provision to prevent the desecration of his grave in a manner that would cause a nation of savages to feel ashamed. In connection with this horror, the author wrote to the Hon. the Chief Secretary (Dr. Argyle) as follows:—

68 McCracken Street,
Essendon, W.5,
16th April, 1929.

To the Honorable,
The Chief Secretary,
Melbourne, C.1.

The Desecration of the Grave of Ned Kelly.

Dear Sir, — It was with intense feelings of horror that I read of the hunnish desecration of Ned Kelly's grave, and I hasten to congratulate you on the commendable action you propose to take to, in some way, counteract the outrage committed on the remains of one whose penitential dispositions before death earned for him the forgiveness of his sins, and the right to receive the last rites of his Church.

It would be well, in this Christian community, for our Governmental heads to recognise Christian principles, and regard Ned Kelly as he now appears before his Creator, and cease condemning him on the refuted testimony of the various Judas Iscariots, whose perjury sold him for so many pieces of silver.

"The Complete Inner History of the Kelly Gang and Their Pursuers" has been eagerly bought up, and is now in the second edition, and read by the people of Australia, who are now, for the first time, in a position to form a correct judgment on the virtues and vices of both sides — the Kellys on the one side, and the Judiciary and Police on the other.

Ned Kelly's heroism in defending his mother's integrity, his sister's honour, and his brother's innocence, has claimed for him a place in the hearts of fair-minded people of Australia.

Would it not, therefore, be a gracious act on your part to hand over the remains of Ned Kelly, when removed from the "head-hunters," to his only surviving brother, Mr. Jim Kelly, of Greta, for interment in consecrated grounds?

Yours faithfully,

J. J. KENNEALLY.

[The Chief Secretary, The Hon. Dr. S. S. Argyle, M.L.A., replied on 19/4/1929 that he had no power to authorise the adoption of this suggestion.]

THE POLICE PURGE

The forced retirement of Captain Standish (retired on age limit), Supt. C. H. Nicolson, Supt. F. A. Hare, Inspector Brook-Smith, Constable Duross, Constable Dowling, and Constable Alexander was recommended in the report of the Kelly Gang Royal Commission. Constable Armstrong got his resignation in before the report was issued.

Review by Jim Kelly

Eleven Mile Creek, Glenrowan West, December, 1930.

Dear Mr. Kenneally, — I have read your book, "The Complete Inner History of the Kelly Gang and Their Pursuers," with a great deal of satisfaction, and I must congratulate you on having rendered a great service in the cause of TRUTH AND JUSTICE.

I purposely delayed reviewing your book in order to give the enemy an opportunity to challenge any part, section, or sentence of it; but as no such challenger has appeared on the horizon, I take it that your book is freely admitted to be unchallengable.

You are the only author who has the courage to do justice to the Kelly Gang; you have liberated the truth, so long suppressed, regarding the policy and administration of the police; through your book the people of Australia are now in full possession of the truth. You must have gone to no end of trouble, and displayed great patience, judgment, and tact in collecting inside official police and judicial documents and information, in order to let the world at large see for themselves how the various members of my family had been hounded down by the heads, as well as by the rank and file, of the police force. Some members of the Judiciary, too, were so strongly prejudiced against the Kellys that the law was, not infrequently, strangled and violated in order to give vent to Judicial bias. This is shown by you very clearly in the cases of two police magistrates — W. H. Foster and Alfred Wyatt — and Judge Barry.

In the case of Barry, the challenge of my brother Ned to meet him (Barry) before a higher court seemed to have preyed on a guilty conscience, to such an extent that Barry died a few days after Ned Kelly.

My brother Ned holds a very unique position among the great men of the world. Great men are proclaimed great almost exclusively by their friends, supporters, sympathisers, and admirers; but you have proved that my brother, Ned Kelly, was proclaimed the greatest man in the world by his bitterest enemy.

I am proud of my brothers, Ned and Dan, and now that your book is fast displacing the various dishonest publications, the overwhelming majority of Australians are ardent admirers of Ned's unsurpassed courage, manly manhood, and high moral character...

Wishing that your book will be found in every home in Australia.

I am, Yours sincerely,

JAMES KELLY.

AAlso Available from ETT Imprint

THE KELLY GANG
The Outlaws of the Wombat Ranges

George Wilson Hall

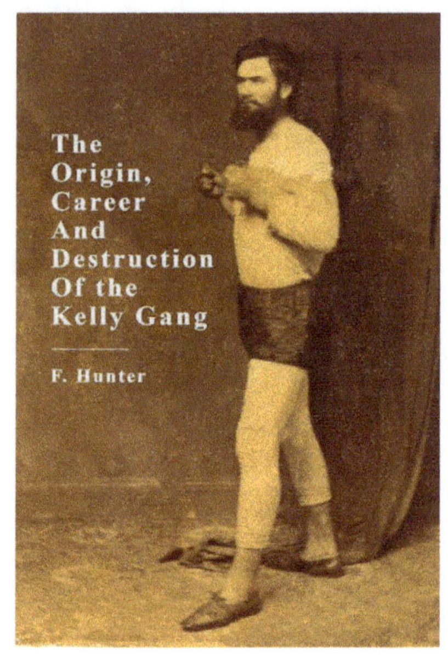

The True Story of the Kelly Gang of Bushrangers

C. H. Chomley

IMPRINT CLASSICS

www.ingramcontent.com/pod-product-compliance
Ingram Content Group Australia Pty Ltd
76 Discovery Rd, Dandenong South VIC 3175, AU
AUHW011107250625
412966AU00002B/2

9 781923 205659